A Banker's Journey

CHARLES COLTMAN III

outskirts
press

A Banker's Journey
All Rights Reserved.
Copyright © 2023 Charles L Coltman III
v3.0

The opinions expressed in this manuscript are solely the opinions of the author and do not represent the opinions or thoughts of the publisher. The author has represented and warranted full ownership and/or legal right to publish all the materials in this book.

This book may not be reproduced, transmitted, or stored in whole or in part by any means, including graphic, electronic, or mechanical without the express written consent of the publisher except in the case of brief quotations embodied in critical articles and reviews.

Outskirts Press, Inc.
http://www.outskirtspress.com

Paperback ISBN: 978-1-9772-5695-9
Hardback ISBN: 978-1-9772-5696-6

Cover Illustration by Larry Whitler © 2023 Outskirts Press, Inc. All rights reserved - used with permission.

Copyright Registration Number TXu 2-314-309

Outskirts Press and the "OP" logo are trademarks belonging to Outskirts Press, Inc.

PRINTED IN THE UNITED STATES OF AMERICA

Table of Contents

1	An Unusual Start	1
2	Vietnam…..and US Army Intelligence	7
3	Trainee	16
4	The Philippines….and Marcos' Opposition	26
5	Australia	37
6	New Territories	52
7	Iran	78
8	Regional Interlude	96
9	Latin America Debt Crisis	105
10	Fighting New York….and the Federal Reserve	117
11	New Markets….New Tactics	135
12	Chief Credit Officer	150
13	Culture Change	180
14	Acquire, Merge or Be Acquired	211
15	The Worst Acquisition in Banking History	229
16	National City and Regulatory Overreach	257

Chapter 1

AN UNUSUAL START

I HAVE OFTEN wondered if my Dad would have shuddered at the thought I might become a banker. He died while I was in Vietnam in 1966 when he was only 52 so never saw the banker I became. In fact, as a product of the far left and an original member of Americans for Democratic Action, he never considered anything for my future but working for the government which he considered the most worthy of careers.

More recent generations of the Coltman Family were ministers and physicians, with my great grandfather moving to China in the late 1880s, later becoming the leading physician serving the pro-western faction of the court in Peking just outside of the Forbidden City. My grandfather started a small trading business between Kalgan and Ulan Bator in Mongolia until he was shot and killed in 1921. My great uncle worked for Standard Oil (Mobil Exxon) but in general there was very little discussion at home about capitalism as I grew up.

Dad wasn't against capitalism, just ambivalent about it having anything to do with my life. After World War II he moved the family to

China to work for the United Nations in the capital city of Nanking. In 1948 we had to flee from the communist revolution, moving to Thailand where we spent the next nine years. In those days, Bangkok was a pretty isolated place and we had no exposure to things American except the weekly Time magazine I read avidly.

I remember in the early 50s there was a lead article on Communist China. My Dad and I used to discuss political events often, especially when we got the latest Time. I commented how sad it must make him feel that his adopted country had become communist. He responded that, on the contrary, he was glad, observing that if the Chinese people ever fully adopted capitalism they would dominate the United States economically which he never wanted to see. He was a prescient man. His grandfather was equally prescient. In 1908, Dr. Robert Coltman met with President Theodore Roosevelt and warned him about what he described as the increasing militarism of Japan which Coltman believed intended to expand in Asia.

Growing up in a foreign country, especially one so very different than the United States like Thailand, brings with it a political awareness to which most young Americans rarely get exposed. Twice in my early childhood I experienced coup d'états, which involved substantial fighting and bombing and leaving a strong impression. The second one, in 1951, started during the ceremony at which the US ambassador to Thailand presented a dredge, the *Manhattan,* to Thailand when a group of Thai Marines kidnapped the Prime Minister, which my dad witnessed. A newsman in his early life, he started to follow the rebel marines until one of them stuck a rifle in his gut.

At the time, my family were the only westerners living on the Thomburi side of the river controlled by the rebel Thai Navy. We lived in a large compound shared with the resident head of the British MI 6, a man named Eric Morris. Surprisingly, while we often lost electricity and sometimes water during the coup, the telephones never stopped working the whole time so my dad became a reliable source to the CIA on what was going on on the 'enemy' side of the river.

We were about 250 yards from the river's edge and quite near the only bridge over the Chao Phraya river at the time. Right next to the bridge, the Thai Navy placed their largest warship, the cruiser *Ayuthia* which regularly fired shells into Bangkok. The army and police took a dim view of this and ordered the Air Force to bomb the ship using small trainers they had in their arsenal. Those trainers did not have bomb bays so bombs were tied to the wings using ropes. Suffice to say, accuracy was extremely poor and one compound five down from us was hit.

On the third day, a navy truck with a mounted anti-aircraft gun appeared outside our compound. My Dad and Eric Morris were concerned that if they started firing at the planes our compound might become a target. Accordingly, they took three bottles of 4 Roses whiskey and negotiated with the gunnery sergeant in charge not to fire but to sit out the coup. He did.

My father's territory included all of Asia and when returning from various trips we would discuss what was going on, especially the internal politics. As part of his job he would get newspapers from these countries, albeit only the English language ones, which, without any English radio, TV and few. books, I would read the major stories. Osmosis is a good teaching tool and even by the age of 13 I was a student of Asia. Unlike other American kids in Bangkok, I spent most of my time on the streets with Thai kids, eventually becoming fluent in the Thai language but not its written word. When my sister and I finally returned to the United States for Quaker boarding school, it was quite a cultural shock.

Over the next few years I was acclimatized into American culture. My father had spent 90% of his formative years in a foreign culture and my mother did not want that to happen to my sister and me. Westtown School near West Chester, PA was a safe environment and I enjoyed it immensely. Early in my senior year I applied to Yale with the help of one of my fathers friends. They turned me down but I was fortunate to be accepted at Tufts University. Already I was heading toward a potential diplomatic career. That would have been perfect for my Dad; government service with an international flavor. The Fletcher School of Law and Diplomacy at Tufts was as good as it got and I was hoping to attend graduate school there.

At Tufts I majored in international relations with a minor in history. I took history courses that covered Asia, Europe, Middle East and Latin America. I avoided taking any business courses at all, although I did take basic economics and one course on the Soviet economy, the latter helping me understand why planned economies don't actually work very well. By senior year I was ready to take the Foreign Service exam and get on with my life.

I failed it! And I learned one of the more important lessons of life. Don't assume! Do your homework! I thought I was so well prepared. I studied international politics all over the world. I knew their cultures. I knew their history. I understood how governments work and the various ideologies that had guided nations since the world wars. I failed because I didn't know the United States. I didn't know US history, art, music and culture. In retrospect, all I had to do was read up on what the Foreign Service exam required and taken a totally different design of courses at Tufts. After all, the diplomatic corps is intended to sell the United States to the rest of the world and to do so you have to know the United States and that was my biggest weakness.

The early 60s was a time of idealism but also tragedy. John Kennedy inspired so many of us with his call of service to country, and then struck down at the peak of his life. I had attended his last political rally at Boston Garden on the day of the 1960 election. I also attended a talk he gave to summer interns on the White House lawn two years later. On the Sunday night after he was killed, three friends and I drove all night to witness the burial march led by Haile Selassie and General Charles DeGaulle followed by the horse with boots turned backwards, the caisson and the Kennedy family.

Although it did not pay well, the Peace Corps was still appealing to someone like me who wanted to get back to Asia. I knew that with my language an assignment in Thailand was likely and could possibly lead to another way into the diplomatic community. I took the exam and passed easily so at least there was one option for me after graduation.

There was another path I could take, however, which I began to pursue as soon as learning I had failed the Foreign Service exam. There is the normal civil service exam that everyone takes but there is also an elite civil service exam given to college graduates and those with masters degrees. Like the Foreign Service exam it took about three hours and, if you passed, you went on to interviews with top civil servants in the US government. I did pass with a pretty high grade and had an unusual interviewer spend a couple of hours with me. He was from the CIA and at the end of our discussion made it clear that I was going to pass and wanted to know if I would accept an assignment with them.

My father was believed by many people to work for the CIA in Thailand and it hurt his ability to function so I declined, thinking that once a CIA man you will always be one which was too limiting. Over my banking years, however, there were many moments with CIA people and I learned to deeply respect their competency.

I was anxious to begin my career. Knowing that three years in the Peace Corps would do little to enhance my résumé I decided to take the elite civil service position. My parents helped me find an apartment in DC while I waited to start my job at the Navy Department on July 1, 1964. On June 30, President Johnson announced a federal hiring freeze. I had no job.

The civil service told me they were trying to get an exemption for their management training program and to hold tight. In time, my mother found a volunteer position for the Democratic Party to increase registrations of Democrats. While enjoying the effort, I was was much more interested in the congressional campaign being run in another part of our very large room. By making myself useful, I eventually became the candidate's (Royce Hanson) personal assistant and driver, taking him all over Montgomery county and the northwestern parts of Maryland.

For the first time in my life, I learned what hard work was. When I was not on the road with Royce, I had to learn his positions on issues and be able to memorize sound bites I could use with the press covering his campaign. I worked 16 to 18 hours a day six days a week, and 8 hours on Sunday because, thankfully, Royce and family attended church. We were included in any events held by the other Democratic Party candidates, Joe Tydings for Senate and Carleton Sickles for Congressman at Large. I was also privileged to drive Hubert Humphrey, one of my father's heroes, to a rally.

This was heady stuff for a 21 year old but it all came crashing down on Election Day. I was given the job of taking calls from the precincts reporting results. After the first five reports, I had to tell Royce he had lost. He was the only Democrat who lost in Montgomery County, MD that year. A month later I received my draft notice; the Vietnam war was heating up.

Chapter 2

VIETNAM…..AND US ARMY INTELLIGENCE

A DRAFTEE HAD to serve two years, a volunteer three. Officer candidate school was also an option but graduates had to serve for four years. I chose to volunteer for army intelligence, specifically for six months training in offensive collection after basic training, similar to the courses that the CIA taught. There were only 12 people in the course, nine of whom were experienced noncommissioned officers. The other two college graduates were like me. In early 1965 the US Army's primary intelligence collection effort was mostly in Germany, targeting the communist bloc. With my Thai language capability I was certain that's where I would be sent. Silly me! Two months in I got my orders to Germany.

Some courses were useful in my career at the bank, such as Elicitation, Recruitment, and Analyzing Human Emotions; others less so, lock picking, clandestine radio, and hostile interrogation. Landing on Hollywood Beach Florida from a submarine was a lot of fun. Halfway through the course I got new orders to Bangkok. Perfect!! Three weeks before the end I got new orders: 5th Special Forces Group, Nha Trang, Vietnam. Not so perfect.

Everyone knew about the Special Forces, a unit created by President Kennedy. The common myth was they only lived in the jungle. And ate snakes. I couldn't. We also all knew they thrived on danger, being at the center of every conflict. That wasn't exactly what I had signed up for. When my plane landed at Tan Son Nhut airbase the first person that entered the plane was a master sergeant wearing a green beret. He called out two names, one of which was mine and asked us to step to the front of the plane. We disembarked and walked straight to a camouflaged C123 and took off for Nha Trang. I remember thinking I was roadkill. The next morning the 5th Special Forces Group commanding officer and full Colonel apologized to me. He said his people needed a 97E (photo interpreter) not a 97C (me). He hoped I wasn't too disappointed. I wasn't.

I was reassigned to a unit based in Saigon working with Vietnamese counterparts recruiting agents to identify and locate the enemy. I was based at Ban Me Thuot in the central highlands and sent Montagnard agents into mountain areas and across the border in Cambodia. Our unit located and identified the first North Vietnamese division based in Cambodia, a fact heavily publicized in April 1966, only to be denied a week later because at that time it was not politic to recognize North Vietnamese regulars were occupying Cambodia. That was a valuable lesson for my future banking career. Never trust what governments say.

Shortly thereafter I agreed to extend my tour in Vietnam until the rest of my enlistment but when Dad died unexpectedly my mother asked me to try to reverse that, to which the US Army agreed. In late August 1966, I returned to the US to take up an assignment with the Counterintelligence Analysis Branch (CIAB) of Army Intelligence, also starting MA studies at American University in Washington DC.

My initial assignment at CIAB was to read captured North Vietnamese documents to attempt to identify their intelligence structure that had been in South Vietnam for many years. One morning a thick captured document crossed my desk which was a report on the intelligence group I had work with, headquartered in Saigon. The report identified every external office we had, including location and staffing with descriptions. The section on Ban Me Thuot was about me, based on the weapon I carried. The last section of each report described vulnerabilities. They had correctly noted that virtually every night I traveled to the officers club located in an old Mountain retreat of emperor Bao Dai. The report noted that I would normally take different routes from my home to the club (as taught in class) but reported on every Wednesday I took the same route. I don't remember if that was true but if it was they were pretty good operatives themselves.

I had a fantastic advisor at American University, a Dr. Kenneth Landon. Dr. Landon's wife Margaret had written *Anna and the King of Siam* years before so we had lots to talk about. One of his first assignments was for the class to write a paper on whether the United States should ever have gotten involved in Vietnam in the first place. I was proud of my service but as a student of Asia also knew it did not have to be that way. I was familiar with a book, *The Unfinished Revolution in China*, written in 1948 by my Dad's boyhood friend Israel Epstein, a communist who was on the Long March with Mao Tse Tung in the 30s. His book argued that the communist revolution in China would inevitably be successful, a point of view that my father, while not a communist, also believed. My dad believed that corruption inevitably destroys a government's legitimacy.

I saw a parallel in Vietnam, pointing out in my paper that one of Ho Chi Minh's heroes was George Washington. I argued we should have stayed out, never air-lifted French troops back into Hanoi and Saigon after the Japanese surrender. Dr Landon related he was asked to write

VIETNAM.....AND US ARMY INTELLIGENCE

a State Department paper about the future of Indochina in late 1944, a copy of which he shared with the class. On the top right corner was a hand-written note: "The French must never be allowed back into Indochina." The initials were FDR.

In early 1967 I was given a special project to examine the rise in insurgency in Thailand and prepare a 15 minute briefing for the Assistant Chief of Staff for Intelligence (ACSI). The project fit with my masters program as my thesis being written at the time was on the Communist Party of Thailand. For some reason this briefing turned into a pretty big deal. I was required to give the briefing to three different groups as preparation before I gave it to the ACSI, a Major General McCristian. The briefing went well and I thought I had done a good job.

When it was over, McChristian said he very much appreciated the briefing but wondered why it was being given in the first place. His aide, a full Colonel, explained that about four months earlier the general had written a note on a CIA report on Thai insurgency that he would like to hear a little more about it. The general said he had a vague recollection about that but a five minute conversation with me would have been sufficient.

This was a good lesson. My report, when you consider my time and all the time of the many people who had to read it and comment, the preparation briefings, etc. probably cost at least $300,000. Had the Colonel just asked a simple question "How would you like that, general?" a whole lot of time and effort would have been saved. People in power with titles intimidate their subordinates, who are often afraid to simply ask for clarification. Unfortunately, for the first 10 years in my banking career, I forgot this lesson.

However, having wasted a lot of time and money in its preparation, the Army decided to use it again. First, I gave it to the Army Policy

Council headed by Secretary of the Army Stanley Rezor. Next the CIA was pressured to hear it. Because I gave the CIA credit for most of the research, they arranged for a similar briefing for a staff member of the President's National Security Council. On the personal level, I was given an Army Commendation Medal for the work and also a job offer as a GS 11 civilian employee, to start following one semester at American University. Most important, however, was that I learned to be comfortable around people of authority which served me well as an international banker.

CIAB was organized into four teams, the largest of which covered Europe and another Latin America. I worked on the Asian team. There was another team under a GS 12 named Emmanuel Roth who answered questions from other parts of the US Army on domestic matters; Manny's team was only identified on organization charts by his name and when I asked him why he just said the brass didn't like him talking about what he did. He told me since the Watts riots he had taken some calls about the Black Panthers but more recently the Anti-Vietnam War movement was his focus.

In the summer of 1967, White House staffers were concerned that the United States was in the early stages of our own insurgency and CIAB was ordered to examine the possibility. Since the White House questions focused on the anti-Vietnam War movement normally Manny would have been given the task, but with my Vietnam experience and paper on the Thai insurgency I had the assignment.

There were almost no similarities between the environments in Thailand, Vietnam, China and even 1917 Russia with the United States, notwithstanding a strong antiwar movement that was clearly gaining traction. I had studied all these movements but knew I was a babe in the woods compared to the professionals of the US Army's Special Warfare Center based in Fort Bragg, North Carolina.

My bosses arranged for some of their top people to meet with me but also had been told not to give them any advance information, so I started the meeting by simply posing the question, "Is there an insurgency developing in the United States that could become a threat?" Virtually everyone was skeptical but over the next two days we examined all the possibilities. The group concluded that there were two common elements to every successful insurgency, external financial support and a committed intelligentsia prepared to sacrifice comfortable lives for an ideology. We saw no evidence of external financial support to the antiwar movement nor did we see any common ideology; the anti-Vietnam War leaders were **against** something not **for** something.

Another indicator of future insurgency was an active, aggressive student leadership who, after a year or two, disappeared, moving underground to form cells. Our group came up with a list of more than 20 such student leaders around the country who had not been heard from recently. Were they going underground? That was really the only possible indicator we came up with; the group remained quite skeptical that there was any insurgency threat to the United States. Unfortunately, the White House was not satisfied with our assessment even when those student leaders were later found to have left for Canada, become professors or even joined communes for a simpler life. This experience was especially valuable to me when I later evaluated country risk in the Philippines, Angola, South Africa and Iran.

In mid July 1967 race riots broke out in Newark, New Jersey and there was concern that the US Army might be brought in should the New Jersey National Guard prove incapable. CIAB was put on alert but proved unneeded. A week later, however, unrest spread to Detroit, Michigan. After a few days, the US Army was put on alert and airborne units moved into the city. I was on duty at about 4 AM when CIAB received a phone call from a colonel in the 82nd Airborne. In a deep southern accent, he explained that he had captured a subversive and wanted to know what to do with him. I had absolutely no idea so resorted to the obvious, asking a question so I could have time to think. I asked him how does he know this person was a subversive and he replied that the man belonged to 'one of those subversive organizations'. "Which one", I asked. "The NAACP", he replied. I explained that this man was no subversive and could probably help the Colonel communicate with local residents.

I am sure this incident alone did not start the U.S. Army on the slippery slope of spying on civilians but it was certainly a factor. The US Army was totally unprepared for this mission, using ESSO maps to make their way around the city. After the riots abated, CIAB was tasked with the mission to identify all political groups within the country, from extreme right (Ku Klux Klan, John Birch Society) to the extreme left (Black Panthers, Communist Party). We used open sources for the most part but also some classified FBI reports. Our final compendium was about four inches thick and published with a bright yellow cover.

Not completely satisfied, army commanders wanted us to identify which cities were likely to require federal troops and what events might cause that to happen. This was a much more difficult exercise, requiring more analytics a bit similar to the insurgency analysis I had done earlier. Size of the city and high percentages of African-Americans living in poverty were obvious factors but so were militant local leadership and an undisciplined and harsh police force. We broke the cities into four categories: Large cities that would riot and need federal troops, Large cities that would not riot, Large cities that would but not need troops, and Medium size cities that would riot and might be more than local law enforcement could handle.

I don't remember too many of the details but Washington DC, Chicago, Baltimore, Kansas City and Los Angeles were in category one. Two cities I remember were placed in category two but for totally different reasons, Milwaukee and Philadelphia. Milwaukee was home to a radical Catholic priest, Father Groppi, who had been successful in mobilizing local leadership in support of change. Philadelphia, on the other hand, was home to a brutal police force led by Frank Rizzo who we believed was harsh enough to prevent riots from breaking out. Both assessments were correct. Two of the names I remember in category four were Wilmington Delaware and Cambridge Maryland. I also remember our forecast of what would be the worst possible event. Within three hours after the assassination of Martin Luther King, federal troops were crossing Memorial Bridge in Washington DC from Fort Myer Virginia.

One of the tough early decisions I had to make at Philadelphia National Bank was whether the 1975 Soweto riots in South Africa were a precursor to a revolution or insurgency. This study helped me make a decision that we could safely stay. All in all, my early years with the government prepared me well for the decisions I would eventually have to make as an international banker.

None of the three studies I describe involved the US army directly spying on American civilians but it was the beginning of army intelligence focusing on domestic matters. From there, it was easy to direct attention to the antiwar movement, using army intelligence agents to penetrate various antiwar groups. During the major demonstrations at the Pentagon in October 1967 army operatives were not only inside defending the building but also outside posing as demonstrators. An even more ridiculous extension of army involvement in domestic politics was sending agents to observe Ralph Abernathy's Poor Peoples Campaign in Washington DC. I prepared daily briefings using reports from the many Counterintelligence agents assigned to the task. Many were appalled at what they were being asked to do, one actually reporting on how many people wanted tuna salad or egg salad sandwiches. Their cynicism was justified.

A year after joining Philadelphia National Bank, I received a phone call on a Saturday morning. The caller identified himself as a senior staffer.of Senator Ervin of North Carolina. The Senator was about to conduct hearings on U.S. Army spying on civilians and wanted me to testify as a former member of the CIAB. By this time I had already learned bank management was highly critical of any adverse publicity so I politely declined, at which point the caller threatened me with a subpoena. Knowing this was a time for discretion, I assured him that I would certainly comply with any subpoena but suggested while he was probably talking to the wrong person; a Mr. Emmanuel Roth had been involved in the domestic group of CIAB since its inception and would have a far greater understanding of what the group did than I would. I did not feel too much guilt about what I had done because I knew that Manny was a liberal and quite unhappy about what had been taking place under his watch.

The next 18 months were filled with lots of routine and frankly quite uninteresting tasks. I finished my MA course work with a 4.0 average and passed my comprehensive exams but was unable to get the actual MA degree without a language and I did not want to take the time to learn how to read and write Thai. My two year anniversary came and I fully expected to be promoted to GS 12. I wasn't. Complaining, I was told that while two years might be a minimum for promotion, four or five years were more normal: I probably wouldn't be able to reach GS 16 until I was in my 40s.

I prepared my résumé and sent it to almost 100 companies, all of which had business in Thailand or other Southeast Asian countries. I expected to get 15 to 20 replies. I got none. A headhunter my mother recommended suggested I apply to a bank. "They take anybody", he said.

Chapter 3

TRAINEE

THE PHILADELPHIA NATIONAL Bank (PNB) was the second oldest continuously operating bank in the United States, behind the Bank of New York. It's strength was commercial banking, with the oldest, biggest and most prestigious companies in the region and into the Midwest as their customers. Senior management mostly came from old Philadelphia families and their sons had ready access to PNB's credit training programs.

Most officers lived in the western suburbs along the train tracks of the Paoli local, known far and wide as the Main Line. There were two other acceptable places for officers to live, Chestnut Hill and Huntingdon Valley. If you were getting the impression PNB was a product of the Philadelphia elite, you are correct. There were three other large banks headquartered in the city (First Pennsylvania, Girard Trust and Fidelity) but PNB is where the best and the brightest wanted to work. But I did not know that at the time.

PNB had one of the best credit training programs outside of New York City but I did not know that either. The bank hired most of the trainees out of college but at least a third of them had MBA degrees.

After a few weeks of familiarization, domestic trainees started into formal credit training six months long. The first six weeks taught accounting from a banker's perspective. After that, accounting was interspersed with lectures from different parts of the bank and on specialized topics that gave trainees an opportunity to consider what assignments they might want as well as giving the various departments an opportunity to assess individual trainees. After that each trainee would spend about six months in different departments assisting the officers. Each trainee had three such tours before finally being selected into a permanent assignment. Six months later most would be promoted to banking officer, approximately three years after having joined the bank. All along the way, of course, people dropped out if deemed unworthy.

That was the normal progression in the bank. The International Division, into which I had been hired, was different. International trainees were selected for their more specialized skills, such as forsign language or residency/travel. Most had little, if any, business or accounting knowledge. Because of that deficiency, international trainees were hired knowing that they would spend 6 to 12 months (four months of which included international operations training) before being sent to the credit training program. The objective was to give them time to be assessed as to whether they could handle the credit work.

Upon completion of credit training, an international trainee would return directly to international for further development. About 2 1/2 years after being hired the trainee would prepare for his or her first trip abroad. The first trip would be at least a month where they would plan most of their own activities. The only proviso was that at least nine days would be spent training in one or more of our foreign bank customers selected by senior officers and graded by them. Upon returning home, senior management would decide whether they would be kept and promoted. Since promotions were only made four times a year, making international banking officer took between three and 3 1/2 years. Every trainee's goal, mine included, was to do it in three years.

The international division had four areas. Area I was Asia, Middle East and Africa; it was the smallest area and the one in which I was hired. Area II was Latin America which was the largest. Area III was Europe and held the most prestige because, since our customer base were foreign banks, the biggest and best foreign banks in the world were based there. Area IV consisted of US companies with strong international activities, like large importers and exporters. The people working an Area IV tended to be from the domestic side of the bank.

A key part of any bank is the operations group. Since international transactions were so specialized, we had our own operations people. They handled things like international payments, letters of credit, and export/import collections. Foreign exchange was another separate team in the international division. PNB International Division's business was to lend money to foreign banks and, in exchange, obtain as many international transactions as possible from those banks in order to gather demand deposits from them on which we would earn income. Those transactions also generated fees paid for in cash. Operations handled those transactions and it was important that we banking officers had good relations with them. Although there were a few officers among operations management, most of the 120 operations employees were skilled clerical.

When I first joined the bank, I knew absolutely nothing about any of this. It might as well have been Greek. The only graduate business course I had was one about working in teams and how to get a team to do what you wanted. That was it. The fundamental course for any potential banker, of course, is Accounting, and I had none. My first day on the job, I signed up for Accouting I at Philadelphia Community College. Some of my competitors were accounting majors. Those who weren't took the course at Wharton.

One early incident showed how far behind I was. A few weeks into my employment, a banking officer from area four was being visited by a large exporter of sugar to the Philippines and asked me to bring him the company balance sheet. I had been assigned to a more experienced trainee named Bob Chase to get me acclimated. I went to Bob and asked him "What is a balance sheet?". Bob shuddered but helped me get it. The officer then proceeded to ask me some questions about it which was an embarrassing experience.

Area I only had four officers when I joined, with the one trainee, Bob Chase. I was hired to support the man handling Southeast Asia, based in New York City. In those days banks were not allowed to branch outside their immediate territory but were allowed to open offices in other cities, only for doing international business. These were called Edge Act banks. Ours was very small and did very little at the time. The Area Head, Tony Newton did not know very much about Southeast Asia but he knew more than the man in New York who knew almost nothing but had been posing as a Southeast Asia "expert". Had I met him during the interview process, I probably would not have accepted the job; fortunately, I did not see him very much and did most of my work for the other officers.

My first big assignment was to help the area head plan for his next trip which was to Australia and New Zealand. I was to prepare a Travelogue, the contents of which included economic and political backgrounds on the countries, current financial information on the banks he was visiting and details of the international transactions that passed between us and the other banks. Finally, for each bank visited, I was to suggest topics of discussion. Although there was an established format to follow, the amount of detail was left up to each preparer. Since standard practice in government work was overkill, overkill I did!

TRAINEE   19

We had to consider both the individual risk of lending to a particular bank and also the risk that the country would have sufficient dollar reserves to pay back any dollar loans we might make to the banks. Country risk involved both economic risk and political risk. For Australia and New Zealand there was virtually no political risk or, for that matter, economic risk but that did not stop me from providing a vast amount material on both subjects. I also got a great deal of information on transaction activity flowing between us, pointing out any operational problems since the previous time we had visited. We would be asking those banks to send us more transactions while they would resist doing so since their primary relationships were the big New York banks. As part of their arguments against us, our customers would play out every mistake we had made. We would deflect that by pointing out where they had made the mistake. What games we played!

Although I was given more time on this first travelogue, the expectation was that it would take me a couple of weeks. In fact it took four weeks because I wanted it to be the most thorough document he had ever seen. It was. I handed Tony Newton two folders the combined height of about 5 inches and probably over 10 pounds. Once I started using travelogues myself, I had a pretty good idea what he had done with my work before he took off on this trip, discarding most of it. It was certainly too much information but he never complained to me directly.

So for the next six months I prepared a travelogues for other officers (much shorter this time), spread statements from Bank annual reports into our own format, responding to inquiries from customers, both foreign and domestic. I also researched operational problems as they were brought to our attention. The latter task meant spending a lot of time in operations which I enjoyed. It was an area of which I was ignorant but knew I would have to master the details before progressing. One travelogue I enjoyed doing was for a Birtan Aka, a Turkish woman whose markets were India, Pakistan and Iran. When I joined the bank, Birtan had already made a couple of trips and was the first female international traveling officer for any American bank. Later she opened our office in Tehran, becoming also the first female foreign representative for an American bank.

Area I made the least money and had the weakest people, both officers and trainees, although my area head was well regarded by senior management. The division had three young officers a few years older than me being groomed for greater things, including Bob Palmer, Deputy division head. There were also some really bright officers just below the area heads, a couple of years younger than me, all of whom have been able to avoid military service in Vietnam. Back then I saw the Army and Vietnam as career impediments; today I treasure I served. The Latin American group had really strong trainees, such as Peter Burns, Mark ledger and Peter Longstreth, son of a well-known political figure in the city.

I am not really sure where my competitiveness came from. Perhaps some came from the various references made about my lack of business education when I first arrived. But I don't think so. The 1964 congressional campaign certainly drove me to seek excellence, which carried over while in the US Army, first in Vietnam and later as a civilian employee. Whatever it was, it was there. And I saw all of the other trainees as competitors who already had a lead on me. Although I knew that some of them would make officer status before me, I wanted to beat their time doing so.

The first step was to be selected for operations training. At most, only two trainees were sent for that training at the same time because of the burden it imposed on operations staff. There was a class distinction within operations' officer class. Most operations officers felt inferior to those division officers traveling abroad. Most of the trainees reflected those attitudes and sometimes suffered subtle harassment as a result. My dad had taught me always to respect what he called the "little people ". He never used that description in a derogatory way; he talked about them being worthy of respect despite never having. gone to college. He always pointed out that they often had more skills than others deemed superior. As a kid the only time he was really harsh with me was when my behavior showed I was acting otherwise. Trainees often acted as liaison between officers and operations, so I set out to make friends on my own. It was a strategy I maintained throughout my career, not always successfully or often enough.

After a few months I was complimented on how efficiently I was able to get support from operations and was therefore not really surprised when told that the head of operations, John Ryan, recommended me for training after only four months. Time differences between my customers in Asia and ourselves meant that some of our operation staff worked staggered hours, so I started coming in earlier and staying later. I usually alternated between one or the other locations in order to take advantage of greater training time. On the alternating days I would make sure to be seen working on the banking floor even though I didn't have to because operations training was full time. In my final evaluation Ryan reported I regularly worked overtime, which surprised my superiors because they had also seen a lot of me. A basic principle of early success is not only to work harder than anyone else but also to be seen doing so!

A major reshuffle in the international division took place later that first summer. The officer handling Southeast Asia was fired. The division head, Frederick Heldring became Vice-Chairman in the office of the chairman. A very bright and energetic young officer, Bob Palmer replaced him. Tony Newton was moved to the large corporate division in domestic. We were shocked when our AVP, Alan Ballard, who handled Japan was not appointed as the new Area head. Instead, a first level officer handling Brazil was moved in as co-head with Alan. His name was Roland Bullard, an incredibly bright and very aggressive man two years younger than me. Roland got Birtan Aka and me. Alam got all the rest. My thinking at the time was that Roland had no chance but I learned pretty fast never to underestimate him. I had done some work for Alan and did not find him in the aggressive international division mold. A year later Roland was the new area head.

The first thing Roland did as co-head was to bring over a young training named Bob Sampson whom he had hired to work on Brazil earlier. When Roland announced it, he said it was to "give Chuck a little competition". Roland's management style was to create competition between his direct reports, which he thought gave incentive. When I eventually took over Area I, I started doing the same thing. Fortunately, over time I realized that it could be more destructive than creative. In retrospect it took me too long to figure this out. I am not sure Roland ever changed his style very much and perhaps that hurt him. But there is no question that Bob Sampson's presence put an even sharper burr under my saddle so in that respect Roland's tactics worked with me.

The first assignment Roland gave me was to write a travelogue for his trip to the Philippines and Thailand. Meaning to make a really strong first impression, I worked hard on it, spending many nights at home doing the research. Fortunately, these were countries I knew well and my intelligence background allowed me to provide insights on the politics few others could, and Roland recognized it. Young readers have no idea of how difficult communications was in those days. No Internet. No text. No fax. International telephone calls from both countries had to be booked hours in advance and lines were often dropped. The same is true for the only other instant communication method, the telex. With the time difference, I would have a telex from Roland each morning. However, it did not get delivered to my desk until 9 AM at the earliest and I would not have enough time to answer him before he went to bed that night. Accordingly, I started going in by 7 AM, rummaging through the incoming telexes for the division to find his. That allowed me to answer him which he could pick up after he came back to the hotel from dinner. He liked that.

My wife Joann and I were still living in the city, the slums or Society Hill, depending on which of us you spoke to. One night we were lying in bed watching a movie about deadly smog enveloping an American city. There were lots of people running around screaming. The scene then changed but the screams continued. We quickly realized the screams were coming from outside our apartment at street level. I reached over and pulled out my revolver and rushed to the door. Joann urged me to stay put but I felt safe with my weapon. As I opened the door I saw a car parked across the street. A man was grabbing a woman's hair, slamming her head into the hood. I shouted, "stop! Stop! I have a gun and I'll shoot", waving it in the air. Fortunately, he did not have one and ran off toward South Street. I almost shot him. The woman was obviously hurt and I called her to come over to me, only about 10 yards away. She kept hesitating and I wondered why, until Joann appeared at the door, pointing out I was in my underwear. I sold that revolver shortly thereafter.

That was enough for us. We were moving to the suburbs. I didn't want to live on the mainline both for expense reasons and cultural ones. Somehow going to the hardware store in green pants with elephants on them didn't appeal. Obviously I am a reverse snob. Joann set up some appointments at a town called Swarthmore which she heard was very nice and had great schools. None the houses we looked at were acceptable. Disappointed, we headed home. Suddenly, Joann shouted, "Stop! That's the one I want." Trying to explain to Joann that the house was not for sale didn't work so I headed up to the door and, somewhat sheepishly, explained my wife wanted to buy their house. Much to my surprise the owners told us they planned to put it on the market the following month. We bought 410 Park Ave. for $32,000 with a

$24,000 mortgage. And that's how Joann and I raised our family in Swarthmore Pennsylvania.

Credit classes were given three times a year so you knew what you had to shoot for. I started working at the bank in early February. Using 12 months as the barometer, my two choices for starting credit was either early January or the middle of May, either under 11 months or as many as 15. The problem was that I wouldn't complete Accounting II until the end of January, which was a prerequisite for starting the class. I had been told that getting anything below an A in accounting was worthless; you either got it or you didn't. I already had the A in Accounting I That was the most important for the credit class so I made friends with the head of the credit department and he agreed that if I had A's in all the tests before the January class he would break the rule. But first I had to be recommended for credit training by the international division since only three of our people could be in the class at the same time. I was going to have to try to move ahead of at least two others. One of them was not performing very well which made things easier.

I made the January credit class. Despite my lack of accounting, numbers seemed to speak to me. Changes in the balance sheet from year to year spoke volumes on how a company was doing and where it was having problems. Towards the end of the credit class we took our final exam in accounting and I came in second, losing only to a man with an MBA in accounting. Although final rankings were never published, Roland told me that I had come in first in the credit class, in part because of challenging questions I posed to the various presenters. Lack of awe to positions of authority and title learned at my time at the Pentagon certainly helped.

Chapter 4

THE PHILIPPINES....AND MARCOS' OPPOSITION

UPON RETURNING TO Area 1, I started to prepare for my first trip. I was going to be spending a month in the Philippines, followed by a week with Roland in Thailand where we were considering making an investment in a new finance company with the principals of the Thai Oil Refinery. On his previous trip, Roland had arranged for three days of training with three different Philippine banks, our best customers. One of our domestic customers was the largest importer of sugar from the Philippines so I arranged to visit the largest sugar plant in the country, Victorias Milling. I also planned side trips to the two southern cities of Cebu and Bacolod, which filled about three quarters of my schedule.

I was also planning to visit local subsidiaries of domestic companies. The worsening economic situation in the Philippines had already resulted in my briefing Vice-Chairman and PNB director Wing Pepper of Scott Paper. He told me to visit their subsidiary where there was concern about the high cost of borrowing pesos. The parent company had no problem putting in dollars but under Philippine exchange rules at the time any such parent to subsidiary loans had to be for a minimum of five years, with the attendant exchange risk for the parent. Because of their increasing foreign exchange problems, the Central Bank was loath to ease those terms. Instead, they had raised local borrowing rates to encourage more dollar inflow. Foreign banks, however, were given a break; they could now deposit dollars into a local bank without maturity and for any purpose, as outlined in a new regulation called Circular 343. Scott Paper's assistant Treasurer, Axel von Borsig, asked me investigate whether there was any applicability to his needs.

My flight out on Philippine Airlines brought an incredible piece of luck. The Philippines had been experiencing problems and were in early negotiations with the International Monetary Fund (IMF) for a loan. On my flight, in first class, were Cesar Virata, Minister of Finance, and Gregorio Licaros, Governor of the Central Bank of the Philippines. Halfway through the first leg of the trip, I parted the curtain into first class and approached them, with the intent of asking some economic questions. They were very amenable, especially Cesar Virata. He was a quiet, self-effacing man with a reputation for honesty and integrity, rare commodities among Philippine government officials. We were flying on a Boeing 707 which normally made the hop from Honolulu to Manila easily. However, the aircraft was facing strong headwinds and was forced to make a fuel stop in Guam. We were able to get off the plane to stretch our legs and I saw Virata standing by himself. I went up to him and we talked for at least half an hour. He must have decided my background interesting because we shared a lot of opinions. Over the years, our relationship continued and it did me wonders at the bank. He was a good man, although I never understood how he could work for a man like President Marcos. My sense was he thought the country needed him at that particular time. Unlike almost everyone else, however, he never made much money at it.

One of the things I had talked about with Virata and Licaros was Circular

343. Could a foreign subsidiary use it? No. Could a bank Circular 343 deposit be used as collateral? Yes. Could that deposit collateralize a local bank's peso loan to someone else, such as a foreign subsidiary? Unsure! They must have discussed it on the flight because when speaking with Virata in Guam he thought it could be done. PNB eventually worked out a $5 million deposit to Far East Bank which used it to collateralize the peso equivalent to Scott Paper Philippines at a 1.5% spread, saving them 6% per annum. We took the bank risk; Scott guaranteed their subsidiary. Later PNB used this transaction for a color ad in Business Week for our international division. Axel got his picture in it; I didn't!

I was greeted in Manila by representatives of the Central Bank, and an earthquake. Over the years I learned that when the central bank met you at the airport they had financial problems. If they didn't, things were good. The earthquake happened when I was standing in the middle of my room on the 14th floor of the Manila Hilton. It really scared the hell out of me. My first call was that Monday morning when I made my first mistake. There were two business districts in Manila, The original very old one (Escolta) and the very modern one (Makati). I assumed the headquarters would be in the modern building. Most bank headquarters were, but all the Chinese-owned banks kept their headquarters in the more active old commercial area. I went to the wrong place. It was embarrassing but a good lesson. Do your homework! Don't assume!!

My last call of the first day was with the head of International for a smaller bank, Security Bank and Trust. His name was Joselito Yap. We ended up talking for more than two hours, eventually over a drink or two. My left wing tendencies at the time, combined with some of the classified information I had, made me highly skeptical about Pres. Ferdinand Marcos. Gradually it became clear that Yap and I shared that opinion. Meeting a second time later on, I asked him if he could arrange visits for me with some of the political opposition.

The first one was at night. I was given a description of the car that would pick me up. I saw it drive-up but no one got out. A hand waved me over. After I was seated, I was handed a hood to put over my head and told that it was being done so that I could not provide directions to where they were going. It was totally unnecessary because I would have been lost after two turns in that huge city. But they didn't know that. At the destination there were three people who spoke with me. I could tell they were real extremists. Most of the dialogue was directed from them to me as if they were giving me a lecture. They only answered a few of my own questions. By the time I left, it was pretty clear that I had met with part of the communist underground, perhaps representatives of the New Peoples Army, a lot more than I had asked for.

The second meeting Yap arranged resulted in probably the best political conversation I have ever had. It was with a Philippine Senator, one of the leaders of the opposition and likely presidential candidate, named Benigno Aquino. Originally he had agreed to give me 15 minutes. Our two-hour conversation covered everything imaginable. He was an incredibly dynamic man with a clear vision for his country. He decried the endemic corruption which robbed the economy and its people. His dislike of Marcos was intense and he hinted that he did not believe Marcos would step down as president when his term ended. This was quite a shock to me; the only other place I saw that opinion was in a secret CIA assessment of Marcos. We talked about the Philippines approaching the IMF for a loan. Despite his view of Marcos, he thought it was something American banks should support. Aquino must have liked my challenging questions and I certainly was a true believer by the time I left, especially after he told me to call him 'Ninoy', not Senator.

I learned a lot during my training sessions with the Philippine banks. I discovered there was often a wide disparity of views between the international division head and his direct reports, who handled the details.

The division head was only concerned with maintaining his good relations with the major New York banks which sent him so much business and lent him huge amounts of money. The lower-level people had to deal with their domestic customers whose transactions the New York banks often messed up. Errors were common in a big bank but far less likely to happen at PNB. So I sold service quality, suggesting that they pick two of their customers most concerned with errors and send those transactions to us. They explained that directing business was determined by the international division head, but I urged them to do it anyway. When I monitored the activity upon my return to Philadelphia, I found that some of them actually did and I emphasized to our operations people how important those specific transactions were.

This experience was a huge lesson. Most international bankers, including PNB at the time, defined success of a trip by how senior the people they were able to visit and speak with. Being entertained by the President, for example, was ideal. Ego of the American calling officer was also a factor because meeting with a President made them feel important. To some extent that was valid because the president could direct his people to give business. However, what really counted was what the people in the trenches were thinking and, more importantly, were actually doing. It was they that the customers yelled at for problems (or rewarded with dinners and gifts) when things went right. The president or division head could direct where to send business but it was the lower-level people who actually had to perform the function and suffer any consequences. Selling to the low-level instead of the senior-level became the fundamental characteristic of my marketing strategy then and for the rest of my career.

Perhaps the best single evidence that it worked was many years later when I visited the Philippines to attend the retirement of long time division head Jaime Ros of the Far East Bank and Trust. By this time

I was a vice-chairman. Jaime took me and my team out for drinks, as he was wont to do. With one arm around my shoulder and the other around his best bar-girl friend, he turned to me and said: "Chuck, we have always had a wonderful personal relationship over the years. My only regret is that we were never able to develop too much business between our banks." What he didn't know was that half of his US dollar business was going to our New York edge act Bank, Philadelphia International Bank (PIB). Chemical Bank of New York owned a third of his bank. Even as I became more senior and was forced to meet with various bank presidents, I would often reserve a few minutes to spend with the AVPs running different operations groups.

Roland was pretty impassive about my first training trip when I returned. Later I learned that he had told people it was probably the most successful trip he had ever heard of. Roland was not someone likely to praise, only to criticize. Again, this was a characteristic of his that I followed much too often over my career. I never really learned to offer praise until the latter stages of my career. This was a major flaw, which I deeply regret.

One direct result of the trip was a long-term loan to the Central Bank of the Philippines and another to finance a nuclear power plant being built by Westinghouse, a National Division customer, guaranteed by the Philippine National Bank. The contacts I had made at high government levels made it possible to get those term loans approved. The bank's normal philosophy, with the exception of Latin America, was to only lend to banks on a short-term basis financing trade transactions. I always believed in that approach and tried to follow it throughout my banking career. Roland was used to Latin America where term loans to banks were routine. Roland asked me to invite Gregorio Licaros, the central bank governor, to Philadelphia in order to 'announce' our participation. We got a lot of fanfare with it but I suspect Licaros was quite disappointed at the low amount we were lending. I also don't think it was my winning personality that got him to come. Cesar Virata was a graduate of Wharton and I suspected that might be the real reason.

Also after this trip, Roland asked me to take a proposal for a $5 million loan to the Thai Oil Refinery. He had developed a close personal relationship with principal of the company, Chow Chowquanyun. I didn't like it. The company was too dependent on gasoline prices that were fixed by the Thai government. When politicians decided to subsidize gasoline prices the refinery would have absorbed losses. Although Chow would guarantee the loan, he would not provide any financial statements. Roland wanted to do this loan in the worst possible way. Fortunately, he was traveling when I presented the loan to committee. My less than total enthusiasm may have been apparent because the loan was turned down. In retrospect, Roland's judgment of Mr. Chow's character was right but so was my credit discipline. Nevertheless, we subsequently made a 20% investment in a new finance company with Mr. Chow, assigning a bright domestic banker, Michael Heavener, as general manager. With my Thai language and background, I was a little jealous.

PNB's International Division was growing. We had opened a representative office in Brazil and were looking at Venezuela, Argentina, and Mexico City. Roland wanted the same for Area 1. He directed Alan Ballard and I to take a trip to Australia to investigate the possibilities. Joann was well into her pregnancy by this time and I asked that the trip be delayed until after the child's birth. I did a lot of research before the trip and thought it feasible despite the high cost of opening an office.

Many of our large corporate customers had subsidiaries or affiliates in Australia or New Zealand. The Reserve Bank had a regulation that required foreign entities to borrow 75% of their long-term money from overseas. Foreign banks seemed to have a guaranteed market. Accordingly, our proposal's projections showed that 75% of our revenues would come from that source. Furthermore, another Edge Act bank of ours, Philadelphia International Investment Corporation (PIIC) had just made a 20 percent investment in a small merchant bank in Sydney, which would help defray costs.

Charles Lilly Coltman IV's arrival was six weeks early. Joann had a very hard delivery but was incredibly brave. We had both been to natural childbirth classes and she was intent on following through. However, it was a posterior breech presentation and extremely difficult. Soon after Charlie's birth, I headed off to Australia with Alan Ballard. Nothing that we learned changed our original conclusions. When we got back, I was asked to write a formal proposal, which I did. It was a bit of a surprise when I was also asked to actually make the formal presentation to senior management. It seemed to me that Alan should be doing a lot more if he was the guy expected to perform over there. I knew that I would never depend on someone else so much.

So I was very surprised in August 1972 when Roland approached me and asked me to be the new representative for Australia. I never knew whether I was the person that Roland wanted all along or if for some reason Alan did not want the job. Roland always kept everything close to his vest. Roland also told me that I would continue to handle the Philippines from Australia.

We planned to leave on October 1 1972 on a direct flight to Australia. In late August, a bomb went off at an opposition rally in a plaza in Manila Philippines so I knew that I would have to take an early trip to that country. On September 23, Ferdinand Marcos, now in the latter stages of his second term, used the bombing, which might have been a 'false flag' operation, as pretext to take complete power, declaring martial law in the country. Ninoy Aquino was immediately arrested and detained in Camp Crame, a military base near Manila. Roland asked me to go to Manila on my way to Australia. Manila was not exactly 'on the way' and I was also concerned about subjecting my family to an unstable situation. I grimaced, but I knew Roland was right.

My trip's timing made me the first foreign banker from headquarters to visit the Philippines after the declaration of martial law. There was a great deal of concern in both business and government circles about how these events would impact the creditworthiness of the country. As a result, we were met like royalty, with a entourage from the central bank taking us to our hotel in one of their newest limousines. In addition, no matter what level my appointments were with my bank customers, I ended up meeting with Presidents and Chairmen, all of them seeking to gauge my reaction and to emphasize that nothing had really changed. Nevertheless, under questioning. the smartest of them confirmed my belief that martial law would continue for a long time. One of them, Willie Tecson of Consolidated Bank, agreed to arrange a meeting for me with Aquino at Camp Crame. I made two phone calls back to Roland during that week. Both times I was cut off when I broached political subjects, the first time when I mentioned Ninoy Aquino's name and the second when I suggested that Pres. Marcos was never going to give up power.

I had chosen to stay at the luxurious Manila Hotel not only because post martial law prices were so low but also because of its location, near parks and lots of government buildings where I thought it would be safer. Joann had no compunction on taking Charlie out in his stroller. She was also taken for some great shopping by several of the wives and we were entertained royally at night.

I had two particularly memorable experiences on that trip. Several years before I joined the bank, PIIC, had made a $1 million investment in Manila Electric, why I don't know. The company was owned by the Lopez family; it's patriarch, Ferdinand Lopez, ex-Vice President of the country and a Marcos opponent, was its Chairman. PIIC had made an appointment with a finance person in the company whom I had met previously on my training trip. When I arrived at their building I was sent instead to the offices of the holding company, Meralco Securities. There I was ushered into the vice chairman's office to meet with Eugenio Lopez, Jr., ('Henny') Ferdinand Lopez's nephew.

He was young and very bright. We talked for well over an hour and I must admit that some of my past knowledge from the intelligence community showed itself more than it should have. He obviously enjoyed it because he invited Joann and I to dinner at his home in Forbes Park, the elitist of the elite communities, for that Thursday night. Joann and I were picked up by limousine at the hotel and taken to one of the most beautiful houses I have ever seen at 17 Flame Tree Road. I remember it vividly to this day, perhaps because of the sliding roof over the 50 meter swimming pool. Henny's wife, Chita, was the most beautiful woman I've ever seen. The only other guest was the general manager of ABS-CBN, another Meralco Company, the primary television broadcaster in the country with a strong anti-Marcos bent. Bert must have been one of Henny's closest confidantes because no subject was off-limits. We had a fabulous dinner with one servant standing behind each person. After dinner, Henny moved us to a sitting area next to a window. We were all huddled up which seemed odd at the time. Each time a servant approached, everyone became silent and by hand signal we were urged not to speak. And when they did speak it was in a whisper.

After a pause in the conversation, Henny announced that he was probably going to be arrested very soon. I asked why and he said he would be accused of trying to assassinate the president. I was shocked but suggested that such an accusation would be difficult without any proof. He paused, and said that there might actually be some evidence. Apparently, a foreign national spent some time with him at a property outside Manila. That person had an unsavory past and had been arrested a few days before. Henny never admitted anything but he was plainly very scared. He was arrested in November and detained for many years. Later, he escaped from his maximum security prison along with the son of another anti-Marcos politician, Sergio Osmena, Jr.

The other incident that took place the next day, Friday and our last day. My planned visit with Benigno Aquino at Camp Crame prison was scheduled for 9 AM. About 8:15, I got a call from a person who claimed to be a colonel in the military intelligence service. He informed me my appointment was canceled. I protested and told him I was going to go out to the prison anyway. He told me to stay where I was for the next 10 minutes. It was a little less than that when I got another phone call, this time from Wilfredo Tecson who originally arranged the visit. He told me it was canceled and if I were to make a fuss it would not be helpful to him. Given our strong relationship with him and his bank, I demurred. In retrospect, it seems likely that I was followed the night before to Henny Lopez's house and that visit killed my chance to see Aquino.

Chapter 5

AUSTRALIA

WE ARRIVED IN Sydney via Hongkong on Sunday morning, very cranky. We were both very tired, Having been up until the wee hours on Friday night enjoying Hong Kong, we had left at midnight. It didn't help that Roland had not agreed to buy a seat for young Charlie. Granted he was only a year and a half but it still made travel difficult. He was tired so we laid him on the aircraft floor in front of us and he slept like the baby he was. Of course, when we got to the Wentworth Hotel he was bright-eyed and bushy-tailed.

The first few weeks were busy getting organized. Joann jumped into the task of finding a house. She chose one in Mosman that had been vacant for some time and was pretty dowdy but it had an absolutely gorgeous view of Sydney Harbor just above a path leading down to Chinaman's Beach. It was a fantastic place to live especially with a young son. The price was over our budget but Roland agreed which I really appreciated. It was a great house, perfect for young Charlie with one exception. He loved jumping from one level in the backyard to another. One Saturday morning he was playing his games and I heard a bloodcurdling scream from Joann. Charlie had jumped onto a piece of glass and his ankle was bleeding so badly that it looked like he had cut an artery. We bound the wound and rushed to the hospital. It took about 15 stitches to close the wound; at one point the doctor stretched the ankle and I could see the tendon contract and expand. But Charlie was very brave.

I had to organize my limited office space at our joint venture merchant bank, Australian Finance and Investment Company (AFIC). The MD, Peter Watts, was pretty pompous and thought himself well above my station. He assigned me a secretary but I quickly realized that everything I did would get to him and so proceeded to hire my own. Her name was Nerryl Roper and she became a good friend to both Joann and me. She is now an established artist in Sydney.

Early on, we had the opportunity to learn some Australian language and customs. We held our first dinner party one Saturday night. We started with cocktails and hors d'oeuvres. Then a large first course followed by heavy roast beef. Dessert was a Pavlova, after which I pushed away from the table and said, '...I am full'. The comment. was followed by some tittering from the women and chuckles from the men. Asking why, I was told in Australia that phrase meant that I was drunk. So I decided to substitute words and said, "OK, I'll use an American expression. I am stuffed." This time everyone roared with laughter. That phrase was worse; it had serious sexual references. So much for the language.

The first cocktail party we attended was a lesson for both of us, especially Joann. It was just before the election and Joann walked up to a group of men discussing politics. They ignored her. At the first opportunity, however, she asked if they thought the Labor Party was going to win.. The men seemed shocked. They suggested that she might want to go talk to their wives who could give her some pointers on childcare in Australia.

Women's rights were not all that established in Australia. This was reinforced later when, at the first dinner party we attended given by one of our customers, the husband tinkled a small bell in front of him at the end of the first course. We had not seen a server but assumed she must be in the kitchen. There was none. His wife, less than 10 feet away at the other end of the table, dutifully got up to remove plates.

Both economic and political conditions in Australia were changing from the time we made the initial proposal late that summer. The Conservatives had been running Australia for 30 years. Its leaders had lost their fire, becoming increasingly unpopular despite an inflow of foreign exchange investment into the mining industry from Japan, which resulted in revaluation of the Australian dollar to 1.19/1US$ and hurt our projections. A snap election had been called and in early October 1972 Gough Whitlam became the first Labor prime Minister in 30 years.

He was an aggressive, charismatic leader but surrounded by ministers who had never governed and whose philosophies originated in the Socialist 1930s. The first thing he did was to revalue the currency once again to 1.29/1US$, further hurting our projections and depreciating my US dollar based salary. When dollars continued to flow into the country, he issued an edict that ruined our plans.

Virtually the entire basis of our decision to open Australia was based on the fact that foreign companies could only borrow term money from abroad. Accordingly, we would not have to compete with local banks but only the foreign banks and we knew we could get our share of that business. What Labor did was to eliminate that requirement and, further, imposed a 25% reserve requirement on all borrowings from abroad thereby increasing the cost of foreign borrowings by one third over local borrowing costs,. The local banks were ecstatic; foreign representative offices were out of business. I called Philadelphia in a panic but no one seemed to fully appreciate the impact. When I eventually got their attention, both Roland and Bob Palmer seemed resigned to riding it out. All I could see for my immediate future was three years of wasted time with nothing positive to show for it.

I was familiar with the regulations governing foreign banks. I knew that we could start up a finance company but any funding from Philadelphia would result in the reserve requirement imposition. Also, since companies now only wanted to borrow in Australian dollars, we would also have to take the exchange risk. Neither was possible. PNB had what we thought were great relations with Australia's banks. I went to each of them to see whether they would lend Australian dollars with our guarantee. After hemming and hawing, they said they would but only at a 1 1/2 percent spread over prime lending rate. That was ridiculous. With such a cost of funds we would never be able to earn enough income to satisfy our profitability requirements. That wasn't going to work.

Outside of the traditional banking system, there were many Australian investment banks and finance companies. Most of them were started with the objective of leading US $ term loan syndications. Traditional commercial banks rarely cooperated with one another, which made that strategy possible, to some extent. They was also a burgeoning money market in which borrowers took money for 90 or 180 days. Those assets were funded by much shorter interbank borrowings. Shortly after I arrived in country, our local PIIC investment, Australian Finance and Investment Corporation (AFIC) had purchased a low-end portfolio of pure finance company assets. This was obviously not something we wanted to do but one of AFIC's executives, Ed Blackadder, had a lot of experience in that business. Without too much to do, I spent time in Ed's office watching how he funded his longer-term portfolio.

The Australian money market was substantially different than the then well-established Eurodollar market in London which I was used to. The overwhelming majority of Eurodollar deposits were either 90 days or 180 days. Overnight money or other short maturities were rarely used. Australia was exactly the opposite. Roughly 85% of all such deposits were on what was known as 24 hour call. This meant that if the lender asked for his money back it would be returned 24 hours later. Despite the apparent short duration, 24 hour call money usually stayed for a pretty long time, sometimes for years. If rates in the market rose, the borrower would raise the rate given the depositor and the money would stay. So what appeared a very unstable funding base actually was pretty good. However, any funding on this basis incurred substantial interest rate risk because the funded assets have substantially longer maturities then did the deposits from a rate perspective. By way of example, suppose you had a one year asset yielding you 6% funded by 24 /hour call money beginning at 4% yielding a nice 2% spread. Then suppose rates move upward. Your spread starts to evaporate and could even go negative. I will give a much more real example below.

I went through an intensive learning exercise over the next few weeks. What I couldn't figure out was how PNB could borrow in that market. Our finance company subsidiary option would have very low capital because we would not want to take the exchange risk. Low capital meant high-risk to money market lenders even if they had actually heard of a regional bank like PNB, which most had not. I remember when I was working on Roland's term loan to the Thai oil refinery, they had wanted to borrow in baht and we experimented with the idea of getting a local bank to fund the transaction against our standby letter of credit as collateral. The beauty of that instrument for the funds provider is that if the conditions in the loan document are not met, the beneficiary could immediately draw on the stand-by letter of credit. There would be no lawsuits, just going to the bank, certify that they had not been paid, and get their money.

While not common, stand-by letters of credit were well known in Australia. Still, a major education program would be necessary. I tested the idea with many of the larger market lenders and found that the bigger ones, being more sophisticated, were amenable to the idea but the majority of lenders were not. At Ed Blackadder's suggestion, I visited five of the top 10 money market brokers who arranged placements between borrowers and lenders for a small fee. They didn't really understand the concept at first but were very interested, seeing that I could broaden their market. I was encouraged. I had struck up one friendship with another American banker, David Benn of Chemical Bank. Over a few days he and I discussed the idea of forming finance company subsidiaries of the bank funded by the US standby letters of credit. We both thought it could work.

I was now excited. Although I had given some hints about where I was headed to Roland, he had quite logically not paid much attention and no one else at the bank was available to discuss it. I wrote it all up in a six-page memo and arranged a conference call with him and Bob Palmer, at nine dollars a minute. I can't remember how many times I was asked, "Is it legal?", but it was a lot. Both of them realized that this was the only shot we had to make our representative office profitable so they agreed to take it to Fred Heldring. The one requirement was, because we would have to fund with 24 hour call money, I needed the bank to agree I always have **pre-signed** letters of credit on hand at all times, requiring only my counter-signature to become valid. The trust I was asking them to have in me was really quite remarkable when I think about it now.

Fred was a very cautious man. Unlike me, he had a very healthy respect for authority. He asked me to meet with the Treasurer of Australia and get his specific written agreement that it could be done. I was convinced that this was just Heldring's way of turning me down in a nicer way. However, it was a normal courtesy for new foreign bank representatives to visit with the Treasurer's office in Canberra to pay respects. With the political changeover I hadn't yet done so. I knew that, if I fully explained what I was about ahead.of time, they would find ways to turn me down or possibly change the regulation before we even had a chance to meet. So I used the normal introduction process as pretext for an appointment.

The new Treasurer, Frank Crean, decided to see me himself. I can only infer it was because he had not met many US bankers and, as an old-fashioned socialist, thought it might be fun. I came to the meeting armed with copies of all the relevant regulations. Quoting from them, I explained what we intended to do. I did not ask permission as Fred Heldring might have done. The way I put it was, "Am I correct that there is nothing in the regulations that would prevent PNB from doing this? The senior civil servant in the room shook his head, "No". I asked for a letter documenting the fact which he agreed to do. Mr. Crean then told me that although there was nothing in the regulations that could stop me, he did not want us to go ahead, saying further that he intended to close this loophole immediately. I think I described Mr. Crean's reaction to Mr. Heldring as being '… not supportive'.

I was given the go-ahead but warned that we needed to get Federal Reserve Bank approval first, which was expected to take at least a month. I knew we couldn't wait that long. David Benn was meeting in Canberra the following week, which would put the idea of regulation changes to prevent it on the front burner now two banks were going to do it. So I did something that I have never told anyone. I incorporated PNB International Finance Company of Australia, Ltd (PIFCO) using $1000 of my own money. Once we got Federal Reserve approval, I would pass ownership to the bank. No one ever noticed the difference in dates between incorporation and Fed approval, not even during the Federal Reserve examination of PIFCO. Given the way we did it, the Federal Reserve would probably have been okay since ownership was in my name. However, my career would have been damaged. PIFCO and First Chicago Australia, Ltd were the only such operations set up before the Reserve Bank of Australia closed the loophole.

While I was going through the effort to get things started, I became quite frustrated with the lack of support from Philadelphia. No single individual was assigned to respond to my questions. These frustrations only grew over the next six months as I tried to generate new business and some revenue to offset my expenses. The first thing I did was to hire someone familiar with the money market to help fund our operation. The two of us and my secretary were all I had for all three years of my tour.

To get things started, I bought $10 million worth of high-quality corporate paper from the market, funding these assets with a mixture of 24 hour call money and a few longer maturities. Before we could purchase that paper, however, we had to approve the issuer's credit risk which could only be done in Philadelphia. That required support, and it was almost impossible to get. On a previous trip to Australia, I had made a corporate loan to fund computer leases for older IBM 360s to a company called Computer Resources. Now that I had an Australian dollar lending capacity we were able to book a number of smaller transactions which I finally did get approved. My book was building. Calls on local subsidiaries of US customers brought more assets. Eventually, we had a book of about 50 million, all funded by very short maturity deposits supported by standby letters of credit from our parent.

In the beginning we were earning about 1.2% on the overall portfolio, which included both commercial paper and our corporate loans. The only way this was possible, of course, was by funding the portfolio very short, meaning at least 50% with 24 hour call money which was the maximum proportion approved by headquarters. Bob Palmer was rightfully concerned about liquidity risk and wanted to make sure that we didn't have too many maturities of deposits coming due at the same time. What he also made clear specifically was that he was also concerned with interest rate risk, worrying that should rates rise rapidly the spread of our overall portfolio might shrink or even go negative. Roland reinforced that point regularly. He effectively instilled in me the fear of interest rate increases, especially likely under the new Socialist policies.

Not long after the Labor government took over, they were forced to revalue the Australian dollar once again, to 1.29/1US$, with two more subsequent increases to 1.49/1US$. The results was further profit pressures on the office and even more importantly from my perspective, a big loss in personal purchasing power since my salary was not adjusted. Resistance from Philadelphia to any adjustment made me furious, just adding to issues from lack of support for the office at headquarters. Our relationship became increasingly tense.

Joann became pregnant again not long after our arrival in Australia. The baby was due in December just before Christmas. That was fine with me; it meant another tax deduction in 1973. Christmas came and went. New year was approaching. We had a big party New Year's Eve and Joann and I danced a lot. Clayton was born on January 5, 1974.

During my two investigative trips, I had visited a meat exporter, named Smorgan Consolidated Industries. They were customers of the ANZ Bank in Melbourne which had a relationship with one of our own large meat importers. ANZ's International division head, John Holberton, had turned down my request for more of their letters of credit so I decided to try my luck with the Smorgons directly. Thus began a decade-long relationship with what was the best private company with which I worked, among the best in the world.

The Smorgans were a Jewish family whose patriarch was a butcher immigrant from Russia early in the 20th century. During World War II, so many young males from Australia entered the army, regular things they did in the outback did not get done. As a result the rabbit population was unchecked and millions of them caused major damage to the wheat fields, on which much of the Australian economy depended. The Smorgans saw the opportunity and started to process jackrabbits for export to a starving Europe. With that start, they moved into range-fed beef, which they processed and froze for shipment all over the world. By the time I met them, they were the second largest such company in Australia.

My first visit was exploratory, for both of us. The company was now under second-generation rule, the visionary Victor and his first cousin, the disciplined and organized Sam. The two worked in the same 40'x40' office, facing each other (was that because each could react to the other's visitor without being seen?). Just below the ceiling of the room were row after row of small blackboards with numbers on them. Every so often, from outside the room, one board would be replaced with a new set of numbers. Victor explained that this allowed them to monitor every aspect of expense and revenue, daily.

On my first trip, I talked only with Victor, covering a wide range of subjects. I felt under interrogation; Victor had never met with an American bank without ANZ with him. He was challenging, to say the least. He asked about our credit process, which I described. I asked Victor for his financial statements. He sort of smiled, asked me, "Whatever for? What value could they be?" After swearing they must remain top secret, he handed me two pages, one with numbers and the other an audit disclaimer. They showed almost no equity. There were six asset categories. The current ratio was .3. He asked if we would lend on those numbers. I said 'No'. He then asked what ratios would we want to see. I told him. On my next trip, he proudly showed his new two-page set of numbers. The ratios were what I had given him, a current ratio of 2-1 and a quick ratio of 1-1.

Victor Smorgon was a sponge for information. I told him American banking was different than in Australia, especially how we rarely required blanket liens, and how if one were given to one institution it would prevent another institution from lending. Since most private companies had only one bank that was not a problem in Australia. I discussed the advantages of using bankers acceptances to finance his exports, an instrument which often carried lower rates than normal loans. The advantage for us was it by-passed ANZ's blanket lien on Smorgon assets. As a result, he instructed the ANZ to direct more business to us.

Victor enjoyed hour long discussions, as did I. After a couple more trips, I was invited to attend the daily Smorgon luncheon. Sitting at a large round table, every Smorgon family member working in the business had a seat at the table, no matter their age or position. Discussion was open and challenging. The younger family members were in their late teens. Just before graduating from high school, a male Smorgan would be asked if he wanted to work in the company or do something else. If the latter, he would go off to college. If the former, he worked for two years rotating around various parts of the company and always in the most menial of tasks. If he did well he was put in a more permanent position for a couple more years, then sent off to university to study whatever skills the company would need in the future. If he didn't do well, he would become a lawyer or doctor etc.

As I said before, Victor was a visionary. We spent hours talking about his intent to diversify. His first venture was to take on the cardboard manufacturing virtual monopoly called Australian Paper Manufacturers(APM). Smorgon was a heavy user of their product. APM controlled more than 80% of the industry and made sure prices were set. Anti-trust legislation in Australia had never become law. We argued about why he should try to go after such a huge company. "It is simple," he said. "The bigger the company, the larger the bureaucracy. The bigger the bureaucracy, the more inefficient the company. Their managers will be more concerned with protecting their turf than running the most profitable operation. We will never take more than 15% of the total market and we will let them set prices because doing so will be very profitable for us." And that's exactly what the Smorgons did.

Over the years, they successfully went after other Australian monopolies. The glass company Australian Consolidated Industries was next . Then they went after the biggest one of all, BHP. BHP was the largest company in Australia, controlling virtually the entire steel industry. The Smorgons were successful each time. Years later I asked Victor why he kept taking on new challenges. He told me he had no choice. If he didn't, his young people will eventually rebel. He was right, but they did anyway, replacing him as leader. Victor's time had passed.

Victor Smorgan taught me a lot about family companies, a skill I would use later in my career. He was the first person outside the bank to have faith in me. At my most frustrating point in Australia, when the lack of support from Philadelphia was at its worst, he offered to fund a company with $1,000,000 in capital which I could use however I wanted. When Philadelphia finally came through and I turned Victor down, he said something that I have often quoted since, with a little poetic license. Bankers are wannabe entrepreneurs without guts.

After nine months of increasing frustration, Roland agreed to meet me in the Philippines. On April 3, 1973, Roland had written me that he was giving me a performance rating of 4.0 (out of 5) and a salary increase of 6.5%. The bank was also increasing my cost of living allowance by 15% which would cover about half of the exchange rate movement since I arrived. Big deal!

While flying up from Sydney I wrote out my resignation. I had had enough. The lack of support was just too frustrating. I also had expected to be promoted the previous December.. Roland arrived first. I called him in his room in the hotel and he asked me to come up. I knocked and he opened the door, handing me a piece of paper which read: I. I was promoted to Assistant Vice President, 2. My salary was increased and 3. From now on we would have a realistic cost of living adjustment. I said thank you. I described what I believe was Roland's one weakness previously. Other than that, Roland was perhaps the smartest and best leader I've ever worked for.

Roland then told me about a new hire, one Richard Clarke, designated to provide back-up for me. He was originally hired as a domestic banker and had done very well in the credit class. He had corporate lending credibility, at least for the international division. That's what I needed. Rick was a lifesaver, responding very quickly to all of my communications of which, I admit, there were many. He got things done. Simply put, without him I would have failed.

With Rick Clarke, things moved much more quickly. But given the nature of our money market operation long-term success would depend on having some level of local lending authority. Solving that was a long term effort. Although I did not know at the time, it started on my first trip to Australia when I met the chief operating officer of the Rural Bank of New South Wales, Ken Dennewald. He had asked me to set up a short term line of credit for one of his major meat exporters. The Rural bank was small and had extended the maximum amount of credit they could to this customer. They were afraid that the customer would go to a larger back, and rightly so. We got it done but it was very difficult. Their bank had all the assets encumbered. However, bankers acceptance financing which carved out financed assets to the acceptance lender helped solve the problem.

Over the course of discussions, Ken and I talked a lot about credit philosophy and I was very impressed with him. He was the only Australian banker I had met who really understood cash flow lending.; most just looked at collateral, and fixed assets at that. On his next visit to the United States, I asked him to visit Philadelphia, arranging for him to spend a great amount of time with our top corporate lenders, including attending a domestic loan committee, Our people were suitably impressed. Eventually, when Ken retired, we hired him as chairman of our Australian company, giving him direct lending authority. Ultimately, that is what made our subsidiary successful.

Not too long into the life of our subsidiary, I made a decision that was quite risky. Interest rates in Australia under the new Labor government had been rising. Early in 1974 they began to rise quite rapidly. I was concerned how that was going to effect the profitability of PIFCO since at least 50% of our assets were being funded by 24 hour call money. As rates rose, our margins would be squeezed. Accordingly, I decided to borrow over AU$50 million for 180 days, while at the same time, buying short term commercial paper of corporate and investment banks previously approved. I recall the cost of those borrowings was about 12%; over the course of the next 180 days the short term paper yield rose to 24%. As a result, the margin on the entire PIFCO portfolio exceeded 6%. We were hugely profitable while most other companies like ourselves had big losses and some even failed.

When I returned for home leave to Philadelphia, I was expecting to be praised for my quick action and decision-making. Not so. My first meeting was with Roland and Bob Palmer. They were not smiling. Bob took the lead. He asked me why I had violated the funding guidelines he and Philadelphia had set. I told him I had not. He pointed out that I was restricted from funding our portfolio with more than 50% of 24 hour call money. (That was called 'short funding'.) I repeated that I had not violated those conditions, noting that what I had done was 'long funded' the portfolio.

Bob was still not happy. He pointed out that there was really no difference. While I may have not violated the letter of the guidelines I had certainly violated their spirit, by taking rate risk, He was correct but I had thought the most important aspect of the guidelines was to avoid liquidity risk and rate risk at the same time, not just the rate risk that I exposed the bank to. When we left Bob's office, Roland asked me whether I understood the point Bob was making. I told him I did. Then Roland congratulated me on my quick thinking and decision-making. Nevertheless, I remain convinced that this incident was one of a couple of reasons why the bank later decided not to name me head of International after my time as head of Area I.

On a personal level, the tour in Australia was an absolute delight. Beautiful beaches, gorgeous views, wonderful picnics and great friends. Life simply could not be better. Professionally, however, it put a strain on me. Once interest rates had started to drop again, we had reverted funding heavily with 24 hour call money. That was fine but it was dependent on being able to access cash quickly. As noted earlier, we did that by having pre-signed standby letters of credit in our safe, which only required my countersignature. So I couldn't leave Sydney for more than 48 hours. Hence, no vacations, which gets a little old after 2 1/2 years.

There was another reason I was getting antsy. I paid a lot of attention to who was getting promoted and I sensed that others who were more visible at headquarters might be getting ahead of me. I didn't like that. Ken Dennewald, a mentor, used to say when one gets a new position, start thinking about your next position, and how that could fill in gaps in your skill set. Great advice I have given to others often over the years, I knew it was time to get back to headquarters and be more visible. Roland was OK with that because he also wanted to move and wanted me to take over part of his growing group. Rick Clarke was happy to take my place in Australia.

Chapter 6

New Territories

Area I (Asia, Middle East and Africa) had changed for the better under Roland's leadership. Area II was the engine (assets and profits) and Area III was the golden child (prestige and image). Area I had finally passed Area III in profitability, thanks to a wave of Japanese bank borrowing following the first oil price hike of 1974. The bank was comfortable lending into Latin America but not very comfortable in any other markets except Japan. We had been doing bank lending into the Philippines under my watch which continued. However, getting increased country limits there was not easy.

With my return, Roland divided the area into two, with Alan Ballard having North Asia and me the rest (Australia, Southeast Asia, and Africa and the Middle East). It sounded like a lot but really wasn't much. During my stay in Australia, Roland had started to lend in South Africa and Iran. He also made a $1 million loan into Zaire and we had some trade financing in Angola which the Portuguese still controlled. He had only recently hired two Arabic speaking trainees, very important given the increasing power of the Arab world following the oil price increase. So far, not much had happened but the prospects were positive.

Area II had already opened two more offices in Latin America in the previous year. Roland did not like them getting ahead of us; neither did the rest of us. He asked me to prepare a proposal to open an office in the Philippines. The problem was that we didn't have anybody that could immediately take the position. Nevertheless, we started doing research. I made the presentation and we were approved to move forward. Roland had been in negotiations with our investment Edge Act (PIIC) to move the Managing Director of our joint venture in Thailand (Multi-Credit Corporation) to our Area. He was Michael Heavener, who eventually ran Wells Fargo International until 2011. The problem was Michael couldn't take the position for another three months while he wound up his tour in Bangkok. The plan was for Mike to move directly from Bangkok to Manila. That was fine, except he had absolutely no training in international banking operations which would be vital to our efforts there. I knew I would have to train him myself which we planned for early in the new year.

In the meantime, I decided to take a visit to the rest of my new territories, none of which I had ever visited before. I went alone to Zaire to check on the term loan, then South Africa. From there I flew to Kuwait to meet our Magdi el Tanamli, a Kuwaiti, then to Saudi Arabia with our Ellie el Hadj, an Iraqi , finally ending up in Tehran with Birtan Aka who had been in Area I since before I joined the bank. Both Magdi and Ellie had US MBAs.

Zaire was an absolute mess. The central bank wanted me to lend more money which I declined. I had real doubts that we would ever get back the million Roland had put in earlier. I was fortunate to get a room at the the Kinshasa Intercontinental Hotel. It was the best because it was the only hotel a foreigner would be willing to stay in. Originally I thought I might go to Luanda in Angola to check on the government bank we were lending to. However, there was a civil war going on and one faction had hired American and European mercenaries to fight on their behalf. It wasn't going well for that group and I had earlier read reports many were fleeing into Zaire, which proved to be true. Most seemed to be moving into the Intercontinental. It was pretty scary seeing so many armed men sitting in the lobby, weapons laid casually across their laps. Many were drunk and very angry. They didn't like to lose but even more importantly didn't expect to be paid.

A newswoman named Robin Wright was interviewing them about their experiences which she agreed to share with me. I realized that when I got back to Philadelphia I would have to do something about the $1.5 million of trade finance we had in Angola. Robin did not have any employer; she was a stringer trying to find stories the networks might pick up. She had a local cameraman with her but I sensed she was concerned he might not be sufficient to ward off the advances those mercenaries were making toward her. Accordingly, she and I pretended to be working together. I don't know what happened after I left but she had not planned to stay more than one more day.

Fifteen months later,, Robin would be even more help to me in South Africa and much later became a top foreign correspondent for the LA Times, often appearing on TV covering Middle East issues. Robin is now an icon, one whose views should be considered in whatever crisis the world finds itself whenever the moment in time.

South Africa was a real education. I had read about apartheid and thought I understood it. It was so much worse than I had imagined. Nothing that I have ever seen in the United States could compare. The visible pain of the African made me cringe. There were many different African tribes but the Zulus and the Xhosas were dominant. There were two white tribes as well, the English and the Africaaners. While the Boer war was won by the British, the peace was won by the Boers (Africaaners). The Afrikaaners controlled politics; the English most of commerce, with the exception of the mining industry. English dominated in Cape Town, Africaaners in Pretoria, Stellenbosch, and much of the interior. Johannesburg was equally divided. The white groups did not particularly like each other. There were English banks and Africaaner banks. We worked with both. I surmised that the two white groups would work together only if they were under threat from an African uprising.

There were more elements of risk for PNB than in any other country I'd been to date. Risk of local upheaval was obvious. The country also had balance of payments problems, which could hurt us. The Reserve Bank wanted term loans, which of course we had no intention of doing. The banks were friendly but saw us as a minor player. Finally, there was US domestic political risk. Doing business in South Africa was not popular. I decided that the best way to proceed was to be extremely direct with both the government and the banks with which we did business. No topic was off-limits and I was highly critical of apartheid. I would very publicly support the Sullivan Principles, which set standards of behavior for US companies operating in the country. The Reverend Leon Sullivan was a Philadelphia civil rights icon. No one really liked me saying what I did but ultimately I believe they ended up respecting me, which served me well over the years we were still doing business in South Africa. The governor of the Reserve Bank, Chris Stals, eventually used me as a barometer of US political opinion about his country. He was a good man in a very tough job.

As reprehensible as apartheid was, I determined that it was not a threat to political stability at that time. I was reminded of the assessment we made on the risk of race riots in the city of Philadelphia back when I was based in the Pentagon years before. Our Intelligence assessment was that the extremely autocratic regime of Frank Rizzo was sufficient to keep the city under control in most situations. The difference here, of course, was that in Philadelphia whites dominated a black minority; in South Africa whites were a clear minority. On the other hand, the

Africaaner secret police (BOSS) made Rizzo look like a bleeding heart liberal in comparison. Most African leaders were already in prison, Nelson Mandela the best example, but younger firebrands like Steve Biko were gaining traction. Desmond Tutu was still able to speak in public, as were township leaders like Nelson Motlana but these weren't seen as a real threat to the regime.

One thing that especially concerned me were the black townships. Whites could only visit with a permit and BOSS refused my request. These were huge areas (Soweto was bigger than Johannesburg) where only Africans lived; there was little electricity and almost no running water in the townships. The Africans lived there but were bussed into the cities to work for the white minority. There was almost no white control in those communities and I wondered what kept the people pacified. Fear, most likely. I decided we could safely increase our country limit.

I arrived in Kuwait on Saturday and was met by Magdi el Tanamli. We had an orange juice at the hotel and I crashed for the night. Kuwait was modern but very Arabic. I didn't see much opportunity for us in the country. Magdi was quite arrogant and clearly did not have a high opinion of me. He kept reminding me that Roland hired him and he answered to Roland. Not a good start!

From there I flew to Jeddah, Saudi Arabia where Ellie met me at the airport. What a contrast! Jeddah made Southeast Asia look like Europe. There was only one mediocre hotel. We had reservations; Ellie showed me the telex confirmation because he said you had to have proof. It wasn't good enough. There were simply no rooms and even our attempt at a bribe didn't work. Someone else must have bribed them a lot more to get our promised room. They sent us to another hotel down the street. There was room. It had two single beds, no pillows and one light blanket. No other furniture. There was a bathroom down the hall.

No water; the toilet had not been cleaned in weeks. It did not flush. Not good. We left our bags in the room but took our toothbrushes and razors.. We figured we would go to a restaurant, eat, and then shave, brush our teeth and go to the bathroom. The shower was out. We only had three days to live this way and figured we could work it out somehow.

We had a nice dinner at a seaside restaurant. I really enjoyed the food. Ellie had a little bit of the "Roland is my boss" but he was a lot nicer about it than Magdi. We took a cab back to the hotel. As we were driving around a circle, I saw a sign down the street that said "hotel". We turned around immediately. It looked fabulous. However, we found out that there were no rooms and that it was actually fully rented out to Americans working in the oil fields up north. The doorman acknowledged that the rooms were mostly vacant but said that the renters could arrive at any moment. We did a deal. At the ridiculous price of $200 a night, we took over an apartment. We made a commitment to the desk clerk that we could be out of the place in five minutes and we would always keep it spotless. We had a great stay, with hot water no less. We were never bothered. The first call the next day turned out to be the most memorable of my entire career.

During the three days I was in Jeddah, we visited with this group a total of six times, morning and evening. It was not a bank but a money changer. Elie explained that the banks were not inclined to do much business with a small bank in Philadelphia. They liked the big New York banks. But Elie thought the money changer might have need of a US Bank. He also explained that it would be two or three years before we would be able to get the account; They had to know we were "serious" and doing that required time. I was game; there was nothing much else to do in Jeddah.

Imagine one large room, 20 foot across by 50 feet. At the furthest end, there was a single desk where the principal sat. In front of him were two cushions for guests. On either side of the room were six desks, behind each was a single individual. Behind each were piles of money. One desk sold British pounds. Another deutsche marks. Another French francs. Another Japanese yen. By far the biggest pile was US dollars. And the last desk had gold bars behind it. I had been warned by Ellie not to stare at the money. That wasn't easy. I don't really know how much was in each pile but the US dollar desk had only 100s and 50s. Easily there was $500,000 behind that desk. The gold bars were small, about 2" x 4". But there were a lot of them. While Ellie and I sat talking to the principal, Sheikh Suleiman al Rajhi, business was conducted at each of the desks almost constantly. Every once in a while the sheik would call a customer up to talk to him and our conversations ceased. Business first, solicitation second. We spent hours talking about very little but every once in a while a very sharp question would come. The sheikh was doing his due diligence.

A couple of years later our chairman, Morris Dorrance, visited Saudi Arabia just to meet the sheikh and we got the account. It was very profitable over the years. We helped get two of his many sons into Wharton and both trained with our operations groups, in Philadelphia and New York. During Dorrance's visit, we visited the Sheikh's house in Riyadh. It was huge, with a large central area where the sheikh stayed. There were three wings off the main house for his three wives. Morrie observed that he found it hard enough to keep one woman happy. Sheikh Suleiman explained his secret. He said each wing was exactly the same as the others, including the furniture. He always bought three of everything. Each got the same clothes allowance, He made no exceptions. After 9/11, and after I retired, I heard Sheik Suleiman was accused of financing Al Qaeda. I doubt it was true, although I could see how the group could have been involved in funds flows.

Birtan Aka met me in Tehran. She was already an officer when I joined the bank so I was more worried about her accepting me as boss than anyone else. She was fine. She had done some real good work building relationships with the banks, especially Iranians bank that was partially owned by Citibank. One big issue was whether we would do business with people who described themselves as 'friends of the Shah'. Although Birtan pointed out her office would be a lot more profitable if we did, she was perfectly honest that there was a lot of corruption associated with these people. In the end, we agreed that we would not, a policy that we sustained throughout our time in Iran. Our country limit for Iran was $40 million and Birtan wanted to raise it to $100 million. We settled on $75 million. It seemed like a decent risk given the steady oil income but the spreads were very narrow, only about 3/8 of 1% on short term loans to the banks. We did not want to make term loans if we could avoid it and still obtain transaction flows.

On my return to Philadelphia, I immediately began to deal with the Angolan situation. It was my second experience with a country crisis; the Philippines in 1972 was political but Angola was both economic and political. The problem was we had $1.5 million in 180 day loans to the government bank which had just been renewed. Angola was the third largest exporter of coffee in the world at the time and also produced oil from offshore wells. However, the civil war for independence was threatening the offshore rigs and, based on what I heard from the mercenaries fleeing into Zaire, the Portuguese planters were starting to leave for Brazil or Mozambique in the wake of the unrest. This looked to be the last coffee harvest and the country was probably going to run out of foreign exchange within months.

The coffee trade in the United States was mostly handled out of New York by well-established trading companies. As a result US importers rarely opened letters of credit to facilitate the trade. Had they done so all the paper would have gone through the importers' own banks, of which we were not one. Fortunately, since transactions were on a collection basis, the paperwork originated at the Angolan bank. The bad news was that those Angolan banks always used New York banks to collect the proceeds, not PNB. I also had serious doubts PNB would be a payment priority for them to repay our loans if they were running out of dollars.

Somehow we needed to get the Bank of Angola to send collection documents to us so US dollars would flow through that bank's account on our books. The normal fee for an export collection was $50, paid by the Angolan Bank. We printed up a fancy brochure (much harder to do in those days than today!) which we called the **Global Coffee Collection Desk** for our New York operations center, (Philadelphia International Bank - PIB). Collections would be free. We printed it in three languages, French (Ivory Coast), Portuguese (Angola and Brazil) and English. It wasn't real, and we only sent it to Angola. We held our breath but heard nothing for three weeks and the harvest was only a month away. Then we got a telex from the bank asking us to call them to discuss our 'coffee desk'. The Portuguese were still in control of the bank and, fortunately, Roland had been our Representative in Brazil and spoke Portuguese. As I recall, he was able to explain to the Angolans we could do it for free because the funds flows benefitted us. They did, but not in the way the Angolans thought.

As the harvest began, hundreds of collections began to arrive at PIB. At first I remitted the proceeds normally, but after a while I stopped and the demand deposit account balance built. The Angolan bank sent inquiries which we ignored. When the balances in their account exceeded the amount they owed us, I informed them we would henceforth only remit proceeds in excess of their debt to us. They were livid, legitimately so. But there was nothing they could do. It was too late to stop the flow of collections. There was also the banking claim of 'anticipatory breach' and the right of 'set off' which when used together gave us legal cover. Once our loans were repaid and coffee flows ceased, the Bank of Angola closed their account with us, pointedly noting that they would never work with us again. But we were paid, and their level of anger suggested to me that they never intended to pay us back. By this time. Angola was in total chaos and the Portuguese were fleeing the country. As it turned out, the files must have been lost because in the late 90s we got the account again.

This was my first experience trying to collect money from a country in crisis using funds flows from exports. It wouldn't be my last. Shortly after I took over the Division in 1983, Poland experienced similar problems. Our loans for trade were coming due and not being paid. There weren't any export collections to use. However, one of PNB's best customers was SUNOCO which made large payments to the Polish government bank every other month. However, the payments were being made through a New York bank. We met with the company and they agreed to make the next payment through us. The payment was for $1.5 million and we were owed about $1.2. When the cash came in, we 'set off'.

When Poland eventually had to restructure their loans, the New York banks negotiating terms tried to get PNB to give the money back. We refused on the grounds that trade financing always had priority in payment; unfortunately, they claimed our documentation was not good enough. We could not prove our loans were for trade and our 'clean advances' were re-scheduled. This was another two lessons for me. Never trust a New York bank! They will always interpret things for their own benefit. Second, make sure of your documentation. This experience helped prepare me for the Latin American debt crisis restructurings in the early 1980s.

In late 1975, I went back to Australia and later to the Philippines where Mike Heavener joined me. We located office space and hired office staff, a lovely secretary named Chit Suria, who later worked herself up to serving as Representative. Mike expected to move to Manila in the new year. Mike knew nothing about correspondent banking and even less about international operations. But he was a quick study and I planned on trying to teach him a month's training over one weekend and five nights.

I had set up a series of introductory calls on the banks, two at each. The first was the obligatory call to introduce Mike to the International Division heads and Presidents, if he deigned to meet us; the second was the more important in my opinion, the Export Bills Manager. It was he who would control how much business we were sent and was rarely called on by other US bankers who saw their success based on senior level contacts. It was pure happenstance that our first call on Monday was at the Pacific Banking Corporation. That call would turn out to be the second of the four events that made my career at PNB.

We spent the weekend at the Manila Intercontinental pool going over trade documents and payment flows. Then we moved on to sales pitches for each product we sold. Mike was not happy when I told him that for calls on the junior people he would lead and make the sales pitch. At breakfast on Monday he asked if I would step in if he got stuck. I said 'No', the only way to learn is to struggle. I did suggest he might ask a question at that point to give himself time to think during the reply. That's what happened and what Mike did at our first call that day with Max Madridejos of Pacific Banking Corporation. At one point after an uncomfortable silence, Mike asked, "What is the most difficult problem you have in collecting export proceeds in the United States." A great question, and Max's answer led to the most successful and profitable product in PNB history. It was still used by Wells Fargo ten years ago and maybe still is.

Max explained that Japanese imports in the Philippines were settled in dollars at the New York agencies of Japanese banks. Philippine banks calculated 10 days of interest in the exchange rate they used for these bills of exchange. If the bill was collected in less than 10 business days they would make a profit; longer than 10 days they had a loss. But somehow it was always 10 days, and Pacific Bank was convinced the Japanese agencies were holding the proceeds until the 10th day to maximize their own profit Since the Japanese banks provided large trade finance lines of credit to them, the Philippine banks were in no position to complain. When they did, it was usually by a phone call or telex to their relationship manager in Tokyo or New York. Nothing ever happened.

This was news to me. Mike and I had already been discussing setting up a daily courier service (we had just set one up in Australia) to carry 'cash letters' (a product collecting $ checks invented by Fred Heldring years before which earned PNB the name as the "Cash Letter Bank' internationally). We had been losing market share to New York banks' couriers via FedEx and we needed to counter. If our courier (DHL) could carry checks, collecting them directly from each bank, why couldn't it also carry export bills. Could we speed up the process in some way, sharing the gain with our customer?

Our cash letter service made money by generating float in the accounts on our books from foreign banks. The average check size was in the hundreds of dollars. I asked Max what kind of volume they were talking about. He indicated that Pacific would have several thousand transactions each year with an average dollar amount of $40,000 to $50,000. That was huge to me and I could imagine a high level of float if we could only keep the balances for a couple of days. Furthermore, this was after the first oil price increase and inflation was rising. The value of these free balances would be rising over time as interest rates rose.

For the next few days, we visited all of the other Philippine banks.

While some of the time was spent training Mike, we also asked each of them whether they had similar problems with New York agencies of Japanese banks. They said yes, and complained bitterly. Most gave the same answer on volumes as Pacific. During the week we took the possibilities even further. We asked about processing at the New York banks. In our sales process, we would often bring that up and usually people acknowledged that there was usually a queue for handling drawings under letters of credit or collections at New York banks. Why? They had a virtual monopoly on trade transactions and were, accordingly, more concerned about costs than productivity and customer service. Managers were rewarded by keeping lean; if customers had to wait a few more days so be it. Customer complaints usually went to relationship managers who had little authority over bank operations people and could be ignored for the most part. Small operation centers like our PIB concentrated on accuracy and speed but we were only just nipping at the edges. The big New York banks dominated.

By the end of the week, we knew that there was an opportunity. What we did not know was whether there was a way that PIB could actually speed up the collection process. What I was envisioning were "the actions of a collection agency". The key would be whether we could identify the right person in each Japanese agency or New York bank that handled the specific type of transactions we were attempting to speed up. If we could, we could be calling them directly so action could be taken. One phone call they may ignore, possibly even two. But if we were prepared to call two or three times a day I was convinced that they would eventually start paying our items faster just to avoid the phone calls! But how would we get the documents, once sent to us, into the right hands? A dilemma!

By the end of the week we went back to Pacific Bank. We proposed that they send us all their collections drawn on the New York Agencies and New York banks so we could test our speed against theirs. Max rejected us categorically. He said he would never risk losing a New York or Japanese bank relationship over a few days speed. Besides, his Division Head was friends with the New York bankers he met and entertained several times a year. And he had no evidence we would be faster anyway. We compromised. He agreed to select a single New York agency of a Japanese bank. Over the next two weeks he would complain regularly about being paid so slowly. On our part, we would set up a system involving direct presentation to the right department in that agency and follow up by telephone in order to speed up payments. What I didn't tell him was that I had to convince Chip Levengood, the head of PIB, to participate in the experiment. We would start in three weeks.

Chip was skeptical. As head of PIB, his primary product was dollar clearing, or settlement of Eurodollar and foreign exchange transactions in New York City. The customer base for that activity was European banks. Nevertheless, because he wasn't doing too much for my group, he agreed to the experiment. We discovered quickly that at 2 AM each morning, the operations groups of the New York banks met at a single location to exchange documents. That solved one problem. We learned each PIB clerk kept phone numbers of their counterparts at the New York banks in case they needed them. Their lists included New York agencies of Japanese banks. While there was no central file, we quickly made one up. That solved the second question. We were ready. Pacific Bank chose Daiwa Bank for the experiment.

It was a home run. After one month we had reduced collection-time from the normal 10 days down to five, even after holding up our credit to their account one day to pay for the service. Some of the advantage was from using the courier not our new process. But it wasn't that obvious to the customer and we certainly emphasized the importance of our aggressive telephone calls which gained a day or two. Even before the experiment was over, Pacific Bank started to send us business drawn on other New York Agencies of Japanese banks. The Reimbursement Collection Service (RCS) was born.

Ultimately, after the debt problems in Area II, RCS turned Area 1 into the most profitable unit in the Division, the best from a return on risk perspective. It was the foundation of our business. With the profits from RCS we did not have to stretch our credit standards for income. Everything we did for the next four years was based on RCS. Area II (Latin America) had 'assets' and spread income from high risk lending, Area III (Europe) had prestige but we had profits from risk-free services. RCS became the third leg for PNB International behind credit and dollar clearing.

Roland Bullard had already established our hiring process for the area which I continued. We hired people with specific language and political science education. We were not of sufficient reputation in business schools to attract the best talent. Those people went to New York. Our primary source was the School of International Service (SAIS of Johns Hopkins University. Roland had already hired the two Arab speaking trainees and also Carroll Wetzel who spoke Chinese. We trained them ourselves with the emphasis on country risk, political and economic. I had figured out that, over time, the Japanese banks would learn how we were using the RCS product against them. My assumption was that we would be a good weapon for the Japanese to use against the New York banks, which were also very slow in paying them. We needed a Japanese speaker and one of my best hires came from the Fletcher School of Tufts, John Waterman, a Japanese speaker. While he was in training, I put John in charge of monitoring our RCS experiment.

By this time we had several of the Philippine banks using the product. All of a sudden, we started to receive irate communications from them, reporting that we had failed to credit them for over a week. We couldn't understand what happened. I sent John up to New York to find out. We learned PIB had assigned one clerk to handle the incoming collection documents. The mail room had been told to put all of the documents from the Philippine courier on one particular desk. The clerk then handled it from that point. That clerk had resigned days before and the pile of documents was more than a foot high on that desk. Nobody had done anything with them. We had a potential disaster on our hands. I sent my entire staff up to New York and we processed them all in 24 hours. All of the team, including me, also took a turn with the collections department to make the phone calls pushing for quick payment. We recovered, but barely. John Waterman was my new hero.

Elie el Hadj was a most creative person. He was tasked with developing our business in the Middle East, along with Magdi el Tanamli. Cash was pouring into the Middle East from higher oil prices but we had no history in the region and their banks were only interested in developing relationships with the big New York banks. Wherever Elie went, he was asked for only one thing: Training. We did not have the resources to do that but the New York banks did. Mostly, New York trained the Arab bankers in operations. For us to succeed, we needed something more.

Almost from the first day I arrived to run the team, Elie asked for permission to set up a joint training program with his alma mater, Wharton. Roland had already turned him down. To keep him quiet, I told him to see what he could do. After a few months he came back to say that Wharton had agreed to arrange a two weeks session for minimal cost. By this time, and after my first trip to the Middle East, the idea had also become interesting to me. If we did something like this, there would be little question that Arab bank senior management would pick their best and brightest for such a program. Over time, these individuals would become leaders of their international divisions. But two weeks in Wharton was not enough. . Inexperienced Arab bankers needed both the macro economic education and operations training, but also practical experience in overall banking. Ellie and I designed a banking curriculum and appealed to many different parts of our bank to support us. After much internal discussion we convinced them to do so, in part because we explained that we would make at least $30,000 on the course. Next we had to convince Wharton to expand their offering.

We met with the head of the business school and pointed out that Wharton had virtually no presence in the Middle East and our students were likely to become banking leaders in the future. We used the example of Cesar Virata, a Wharton graduate who was now Minister of finance of the Philippines. Wharton had many Philippine students as a result. Wharton agreed, expanding their part of the program to six weeks with many of their top professors participating.

The icing on the cake was that they agreed to provide each graduate with a Wharton certificate, which would give our program prestige and something for each banker to add to his resume and hang on his wall. Elie wanted to keep the program limited to Arab bankers but I felt the class would be too small but also the interaction between the Arab bankers and other bankers from around the world would be a value to both parties. We decided to open it to all. We planned the first course to start in September and began marketing it around the world in January. Our success was mostly with other Asian countries but we did have a few attendees from Europe which helped make the course more successful. We called the course the Advanced Management Program for Overseas Bankers, or AMPOB.

AMPOB ran for many years. Over time, we reduced the amount of time from six months to four weeks but it was still a tremendous success. Many graduates eventually did became head of their international division and even Presidents. Those contacts became invaluable to our growth and prestige as an international bank. Wharton became the dominant US business school in the Middle East, with increasing full-time students from the area. The relationships established between students from the different countries were lifelong. Many of the classes held reunions in various parts of the world. It was another home-run, and I had Elie el Hadj to thank for it.

The first AMPOB class was especially memorable. TheIr only complaint was the accommodations. One of the students was from South Africa, Ian Rainey. His complaint was that there was nothing nearby where he could play soccer, which gave me an idea. We wanted to have a celebration on the last weekend before graduation. Why not have a soccer game between PNB and AMPOB? We had one outstanding player (Chris Wilmot) who had played professional soccer in England and some decent players in the international division, as well as some from other groups. We were slaughtered! Afterwards Joann and the other wives organized a fantastic cookout. It was a good bonding experience which we continued each year thereafter. Eventually, we started to win the games when my two sons Clayton and Charlie joined our team. We ignored the suggestion that we had ringers.

Ian Rainey helped make the first AMPOB class a success. He was charming and pulled the diverse class together. He was a consummate salesman. I liked him enough to call him in South Africa and offer him a job. He was a great addition. Not only did he have a lot of sales success in Asia, he was also an excellent representative in Manila. When I had a brief tour in the domestic side, I took him with me and his English accent was a constructive asset in our regional market.

As the reader will see, I attribute my success at the bank to four key decisions I made, and also for five people who really helped me along the way. One of those is Ian Rainey. I have referred to my excessive intensity before and unfortunately it will come up again. After one such time, Ian asked to speak with me. I remember being surprised he had his coat on when he came in.

He was calm and seemed a bit nervous. He started out by telling me that the largest rivers have the most tributaries, and I should think of the river as my career and the tributaries as people prepared to work hard for a leader with vision and drive. He said I had both those traits but that the way I treated employees pushed too many of them away. He gave examples of how I would walk right past people without even acknowledging them. He said the fact that I had a lot on my mind and was thinking was no excuse. He said people wanted to be with me because I brought creativity and success. But they did not want to stay with me very long because I often angered them as well. He ended by telling me that if I didn't change my approach I would not go very much further in the bank. He then got up and left.

I was furious. No subordinate had ever dared talk to me that way. I stewed for a while but gradually started to think about what he said. I did understand it. I also realized how much courage it took for him to do what he did. I don't remember exactly when but shortly afterwards I went to Ian and thanked him. He was relieved and told me he had had his resignation in his coat pocket to hand me if I had fired him on the spot. I never forgot this experience and credit Ian for what he did.

Area I was growing. We had added Harry Hayman earlier from First National Bank of Maryland as well as Steve Nichols from the domestic side, an extremely smart and highly creative banker with a reputation for having some sharp edges. A couple of years later, I hired Vic Dewan, a Wharton graduate from India. If I had any prejudices it was Indians (my father had been hurt immeasurably by the Indian head of the FAO) so I was reluctant to even interview him. He became a fabulous employee and is ending his career as President of the Philadelphia Zoo.

About the same time we added Susan Brinn, a Chinese speaker, and Jill Ensmann right out of college.

I was an early supporter of women in the international division but it wasn't for any altruistic reasons. I had watched Birtan Aka be successful for a number of years. She had originally been hired because she spoke Turkish. But we weren't doing any business in Turkey, so she used English in her visits to India and Iran. If she could be successful using English, why couldn't American women do the same thing?

Early in my Area 1 history I used to say that I would never hire women to do business in only three countries: Japan, Australia or Saudi Arabia. The one country I maintained that view on was Saudi Arabia. Our first branch manager in Tokyo was a Japanese woman. Helen Leung ran Peking. Jill Enzmann ran Australia and London. Barbara Stockler started as a junior clerk and became one of the most effective administrative people we had. Elizabeth Vale was another example. And I know I am forgetting many others.

When I took over the division in late 1981, Rick Clarke was in charge of Latin America but his two deputies were women, Heather Cordero and Mariana Wilson, much to the chagrin of the many males who dominated the Latin American group in the previous five years. Julia Mattingly ran Singapore for a few years. Another woman was representative in both Panama and Brazil.

In the mid 80s, I was also an early manager to accept the concept of part time work for women. Mariana Wilson had resigned because she was going to have her first child. I pleaded with her to stay. She agreed to come back after three months and work only four days a week. Six months later it was three days and she finally resigned, despite my appealing for her just to work two days a week in a job share. I wasn't being a hero here for women's rights. Mariana was simply fantastic and she was my pick to run the division, at that point, after I left. She did not stay but many years later she re-joined us in our investment bank.

On 16 June 1976, I woke up to the news that one of my fears might be coming true, namely that the stability of South Africa could fall apart. Riots had begun in Soweto, people were killed and fire was burning down many of the beer houses in that community. I had been the one who pushed so hard to increase our exposure in South Africa, had assured senior management, that while there may be periodic incidents, there would be no uprising. Some on the loan committee had been skeptical. I needed to find out what was going on.

Within two days I was on a flight to Johannesburg. Upon arrival, I again asked for permission from the secret police (BOSS) to visit Soweto and was turned down. Most of the Afrikaners I spoke to were not worried but the British bankers had a more pessimistic view. I did speak to Chris Stals of the Reserve Bank who admitted there was some capital flight, but assured me it was limited and they could control it if they had to.

On the second night I was there I ran into Robin Wright who was covering the riots, again as a stringer but with access to CBS News. She had her camera person with her and equipment that allowed her to broadcast live directly from South Africa which she did from the hotel roof pool area against the background of fires burning in the distance. Before I watched her make the broadcast, she had told me she had permission from BOSS to go into Soweto the next day. I asked her if she would let me go with her and she said she only had permission for herself and her cameraman. She didn't want to take any chances. I said I could help her with questions she might direct to government officials. She had not focused on the possibility of capital flight at that point but she immediately understood the implication. She agreed to smuggle me in with her the next day.

The actual entry into Soweto was uneventful. She had arranged to set up base at the YMCA, which gave good cover for people she wanted to talk to bringing their kids to play. She let me attend all of the interviews and I even was able to ask a couple of questions. The only person I recall being willing to be quoted and interviewed was a local leader, Nelson Motlana. It was from him that I got the definite impression what was going on was spontaneous and had no organization behind it. When I got back to Philadelphia, I arranged for our contributions committee to donate enough money to Soweto YMCA to build a basketball court. It was still there five years ago. With that, and similar comments from others, I was comfortable to even increase our exposure in South Africa.

We continued to do business in South Africa for many more years, into the mid-1980s. Then I got a phone call from CEO Morrie Dorrance. He told me to meet him in his office the next day and plan on at least an hour and a half. He took me to the federal courthouse in Philadelphia where we met an African-American judge, Leon Higginbotham. He had written several books on South Africa and was thoroughly knowledgeable of its history and politics. At Morrie's urging I explained to him the kind of business we did, with whom and the various positions I took, especially our support of the Sullivan principles. He smiled at me, and said "yes, that's all very nice. I am sure you are helping move the needle a little in South Africa. But this is not about South Africa. This is about Philadelphia and you, as representative of the Philadelphia National Bank, must stop doing business in South Africa". Morrie said very little on the way back to the bank and as we parted he said it was my decision on whether we would stay or leave. Although I am pretty sure that had I made a different decision, eventually we would have left sooner rather than later. But after thinking it over at length, I decided that it was best if we withdrew.

1977 and 1978 were steady growth years, based on higher spreads on lending to Japanese banks financing the higher cost of importing oil and the success of RCS in Japan and the rest of Asia. Demand deposits were growing and their value rising from higher interest rates. John Waterman was successful travelling to Japan, as was Carrol Wetzel to Taiwan and Mike Heavener working in the Philippines. We eventually lost Carrol to a New York investment bank, but Susan Brinn filled the void,

In late 1977, Steve Nichols replaced Birtan in Iran. Birtan had done a good job in a tough environment. There was a lot of pressure to make medium term loans to the country and its banks which was against our corporate strategy. She resisted most of them. There were also many "friends of the Shah" who were still looking for personal loans. Given the massive corruption in that country we continued to resist those as well. When I visited Steve early in his tour we pushed hard for bank short term loans. One way to do that was to call on major capital exporters in the United States and ask them to request their dealer's Iranian banks send their letters of credit to us so that we could do the acceptance financing. We were not particularly successful but there was one company that did. Steve and I met with their dealer and we established a nice relationship, so much so that the family opened an account with us. That was to become a critical event a few years later which is why the company is not identified here.

To say that I was intense and aggressive would be an understatement. Area I was still not the most profitable area of the International Division. We certainly had the least prestige. I was looking over my shoulder at the other areas all the time. They were also led by two young highly competent bankers, Mark Ledger and Peter Longstreth. As I described before, Division Head Roland Bullard liked to encourage aggressive competition between his direct reports when he was head of Asia. That had not changed now that he was running the division. The prize, of course, was who would replace him.

Roland had a strong emphasis on controlling costs, to which I paid too much attention. Opening representative offices was extremely expensive and hurts the bottom line for a couple of years before the office generates incremental income. Finally, I came to my senses. We had a tremendously successful product in RCS. We were growing well but we needed permanent presence in each market to make it grow substantially faster.

In late 1977, Roland got his wish and was transferred to run the National Division, trading places with that Division Head, Tom Liggett. Tom was one of the nicest people on the corporate side but knew nothing about International and never really earned the professional respect of the three young turks running the three Areas. He had a really tough job.

Hong Kong and Singapore had many new foreign bank branches opening up, the majority of which were Japanese. I sent all of the Asian team back to their markets and arranged that we all meet in Hong Kong at the end of the trips. John Waterman was to test whether the Japanese banks, big users of RCS from Japan, would also use it for their branches in Hong Kong and Singapore as a way to compete with local banks. The others would reconfirm the popularity of the product and our ability to increase relationships and volume. We met in a conference room, about eight of us. The question was, "Should we open three new representative offices immediately: Tokyo, Hong Kong and Singapore.'

This was probably the first time (unfortunately, for I should have done so often!) that I sought input from my team before making a major decision. I put this decision down as one of the key ones I made in my career. We were going to increase expenses by $1 million a year. That's a lot! I started around the table giving every individual their say. I remember Ian Rainey and John Waterman being the most supportive. Harry Hayman was supportive but cautious.. In the end, I announced

NEW TERRITORIES 75

that we would go ahead. Japan would be first, then Hong Kong and Singapore. A few years later we would add Taiwan and Bangkok, with Peking and Jakarta following on. Getting approval was easier than I expected as Tom Liggett was supportive.

This decision proved a good one. The number of relationships and transaction volume we generated were a little higher than the original plans but the profitability of the decision was many times projections. Why? The combination of the second oil price increase in 1979 and the inflationary policies of Jimmy Carter moved interest rates to historic levels. Our product was based on creating float, or demand deposit balances, in the accounts of our bank customers. Their value was huge and it made Area I, post the Latin American debt crisis, the most profitable part of the division, by far.

Not long afterwards, the question of succession in the international division was coming to a head. Everyone knew Tom Liggett wasn't going to stay. The three area heads were looking at each other and wondering which of us would succeed him. Senior management, however, was not prepared to choose between us. The bank had recently hired a new head of wholesale banking, Bob Siff, from Citibank. He was also very ambitious, and I believe had set his sight on becoming CEO at some point. In my opinion he saw Bob Palmer as his primary rival, who now headed retail. One way Siff went after Bob was to criticize the international division, especially its country risk analysis which Bob had developed years before. He started to attend our credit committees and made all of us furious with his comments. Some were justified but others were not. Specifically, he criticized our lack of organization and information discipline. So it probably should have been no surprise when the three Area Heads were told that none of us would get the job; the bank would hire a new division head from outside the bank. His name was Joop van Vollenhoven, a Dutchman from an obscure international bank but a Citibank pedigree. We were not impressed with his resume.

Roland pulled me aside, knowing how disappointed I must be, and asked me to join him at Large Corporate. I was complimented of course. However, we had just made the decision to open the new offices and I didn't want to hand implementation over to someone else. Furthermore, I had been working under Roland now for eight years and thought I had learned most of what I could from him. He was not happy and I have wondered if he ever fully forgave me for what he could have seen as a personal slight.

I did not know it at the time but senior management was also worried about my reaction, so Joop made me the first Area head with which he spoke. Joop was worried about my reaction as well. He said he would understand if I wanted to leave the division and offered to help get me placed in a good position. I told him that I did not want that. I said that while I disagreed with senior management's decision, they must have had a reason why they did what they did. I said he obviously had skills senior management wanted us to learn and I was prepared to accept that. But I also told him that by the end of 1979 I wanted to move into the domestic bank where I could learn domestic credit.

During 1978, Area I went from one success to another. We were opening new accounts right and left based on the RCS product and our new offices. Rates were rising rapidly following the second oil price hike and Jimmy Carter's inflationary economic policies. Float from the product became more and more valuable so our offices were profitable almost immediately. Japanese banks were financing oil imports at ever increasing spreads. PIFCO in Australia was growing well. Ken Dennewald was now the Chairman, with local lending authority. In the Middle East, Magdi had left to start an investment bank in Kuwait but Ellie had taken over and was also opening new accounts for banks, which had little concept of how to manage money.

Chapter 7

Iran

The only weakness was in Iran. There had always been opposition to the Shah, especially among the clerics and in the countryside. In 1977, that resistance intensified and began to appear in the *souks* (markets) of the biggest cities. This was different, and it concerned me. In early 1978 it became worse. Both Bob Siff and Fred Heldring started asking pointed questions with good reason. Steve Nichols was our Representative and it was fortuitous he was scheduled to bring his family back for home leave in April 1978. This would give us an opportunity to understand his relatively benign view of the unrest. Steve and Kathy wanted to visit India briefly on their way home so I asked him to visit Kabul first. We had a long time customer in Kabul, Haji Ramatullah, a rug dealer. I thought he might help us set up a courier. Not a good idea!

Steve was visiting banks on April 22, 1978. Kathy and the kids were enjoying the pool at the Intercontinental Hotel on a hillside on the edge of the city. When Steve and his hosts left for lunch they heard something hit the roof of their car several times. They got out of the car and found .50 cal machine gun shells on the ground. Then they saw

Russian planes strafing and bombing the Presidential Palace. Steve always kept his valuables with him in his briefcase (passport, tickets and US$ cash). He convinced a taxi driver to take him back to the hotel for $100. They got through two checkpoints but were then stopped at the hotel by troops that had it surrounded. They refused to let him inside. Steve started to open his briefcase and they almost shot him. He let them open it themselves, showing his and Kathy's passports but with no luck. But when he showed them his kid's passports, they relented. Steve tried to call us then but all communications had been cut off.

We learned about the coup attempt the next morning when we got a frantic phone call from Kathy and Steve's single set of parents. This started an event which taught me never to trust the US Government's promises to US citizens in a crises in a foreign country. The first thing I did was to get a map of Kabul, which suggested they were probably safe; the hotel was well away from the downtown where the fighting was going on. The State Department advised me to tell Steve, once communications were restored, to stay put. I asked them to call me as soon as they had any news which they promised to do.

After two days Steve was able to call. He told me that foreign businessmen had organized a caravan to go to the Pakistan border. It was not that far but dangerous country. He asked what he should do and I repeated the advice from State which he already had heard locally and from their parents. He then asked me again, this time asking me what I would do if I was there. I told him I would go. He did and two days later I got a call from him; he and the family were out. The whole bank celebrated. I had never had someone I was responsible for in such danger. It was an awful experience. Three days later, the State Department called me to tell me that Steve Nichols and family were safe in the hotel in Kabul. So much for relying on government help.

Steve's visit back home wasn't particularly pleasant for anyone. Our

IRAN

credit people had concerns. I had concerns. Steve was more relaxed. He described various conversations he had had, not just with Pro-Shah people but also members of what he was convinced were the opposition. He reported that while all expected the situation to continue to escalate, none saw a violent revolution. They all said that this was going to change how the government operated and it would be for the better. Steve had support for his position. The Shah had been responding to the protests with conciliatory measures. After four months of unrest things seemed to be cooling down. Everyone at the Embassy with whom he spoke said pretty much the same thing. Since my early days of the bank, given my background, I have always encouraged our people to talk not just to the economic officers but also to the CIA whenever possible. They said the same things. We might have been over-reacting after all.

Political issues were not the only reason Iran was a problem for our group. Our strategy was the same there as in other countries. Yes, we lent money to the banks for short term, six months or less but we only did so if we were able to get transaction business. That was hard to come by in Iran. Furthermore, everyone and his brother wanted to lend money for short term so the spreads became extremely thin, less than 50 basis points for a 180 day advance. That spread income hardly justified the risk. In addition, we had a large expense base in Iran and the office was not profitable. Fortunately, the increasing profitability of our Asian offices allowed me to reduce our own exposure at not much of a cost to Area 1 profitability. Our exposure had been gradually dropping over the previous three months which was fortunate.

By the time Steve left Philadelphia, we had agreed to reduce the country limit to 50 million. Our actual outstandings at that time were not much higher than that anyway, but it made senior management happier. Fred Heldring always preached the importance of financing trade whenever possible. He said his experience showed trade was always the first credit repaid after a problem. I also experienced a bit of that during problems in the Philippines a few years before, as well as the discussions that took place around Angola. Steve and I decided we would focus strictly on trade and make sure that every communication request on our loans specifically identified what products were being financed and why. In addition, we decided to concentrate our exposure to just the two banks that were giving us most of the non-credit transactions. The largest of these was Iranians Bank, which was also the bank of one of our large corporate client's distributors in Iran. We decided to continue to work aggressively with both of these companies because it gave us a clear direction of financing trade and supporting a domestic customer. I won't identify the Iranian company for reasons that will become clear later.

We did one more thing that seemed a little melodramatic at the time. But both Steve and I had learned some lessons in his recent Afghanistan experience. We purchased tickets for Steve and his family to travel first class to India from Tehran. Why India? This was an emergency plan. In an emergency foreigners and Iranians from Tehran would all be fleeing west to Europe on western airlines. We believed going east with Air India was safest. In those days, dates of travel could be changed without penalty. Our plan was to set a date months in advance and then adjust the date based on what we thought might be happening. We also provided Steve with cash although I don't recall whether it was $5000 or $10,000. I had a reputation in the bank of tending to overreact. The criticism was justified. But it was the right thing to do here.

Over the next three or four months, the situation continued to deteriorate. Demonstrations became more common and sometimes more violent. Some people were killed. The Shah started using troops rather than his secret police, SAVAK. Rumors circulated about students gone missing bringing up visions of insurgency or increased repression. Either was bad. This escalation was alarming. Steve and I talked often.

He was calm and did not focus on the increasing escalation on both sides. He was also brave, and did not want to be seen as one of the first bankers to leave Iran in a crisis. But we did shorten the dates between reservations to two weeks and Steve moved the cash to his home from the office.

By August, things took a turn for the worse. There were periodic strikes. The universities were no longer functioning. The *souks* seemed to have joined the revolution which it now appeared to be. In short, we were now in a whole new phase. We started reducing exposure as fast as possible, which was made easier by our short maturities.

Again, Steve was calm. But he was not getting the same news we were. Censorship even covered our telephone calls so I couldn't be as specific as I wanted to. Finally, I ordered Steve out of the country. He argued. I finally told Steve that they did not pay me enough to lose him and his family. Steve reluctantly agreed to leave; as I said, he was a brave man. We arranged for the office to be staffed by one person. She was instructed to say that the representative was at headquarters. As I recall, Steve and Kathy left in late November or early December. The Christmas break gave us some rationale for their absence.

In December 1978, the Shah left Iran. By the end of February, 1979 Khomeini declared the Iranian revolution over and assumed power. Over the next several months, we gradually reduced our exposure further. We knew we had to do it slowly so we renewed for a shorter term and lower amount as maturities came due. The only thing we continued to do was work with Iranians bank and our corporate customer's dealer. That family had previously learned to trust us and had about $5 million in deposits with us, illegal under exchange control rules. They weren't the only ones; most businesses and all the elite had money offshore. The office was quiet. Our exposure was about $15 million and the prognosis was not good.

By now I was less than six months away from leaving my position as head of Area 1. I had already let Joop know that Harry Hayman would be my successor. He had agreed. Now I started to communicate openly with the rest of the team. I think, at first, reaction to Harry was mixed, about half accepting and the other half questioning. There wasn't any doubt about his qualifications. He knew Asia and the business well. He could learn the Middle East. He had the support of another good manager, Doc Miller. Harry would succeed. The issues were more about style. I tended to be extremely direct, probably too much so. Harry was the opposite, holding his views close to his vest, so much so some people had a hard time understanding where he actually was on an issue. I was not an easy person to succeed. Eventually opposition began to fade and I was ready to leave at the end of the year.

But Iran was unfinished business. We needed to shut the office down. Employees had to be taken care of. And repayments had slowed. We were owed about $12 million at the time, the largest amount by Iranians bank, the Citibank affiliate. I didn't waste my time thinking Citibank would step up. We had gradually converted our exposure from direct short term advance loans to financing specific trade transactions. We continued to believe that no matter what the regime, trade transactions would be honored. But the last two maturities of these loans had not been repaid. I was getting concerned.

My first inclination was to send Harry Hayman to Tehran to see what was happening. This would be a good introduction and would also signal to the Area that there was no question he would succeed me. But I quickly realized that that would not be fair. I knew the country, he didn't. I knew the people of the large importer we were financing indirectly, he didn't. The only option was for me to go myself. Was I nervous? Yes, a little. The news reporting out of Tehran was a bit scary but news reports always were. While there was a lot of anti-foreign sentiment, no direct attacks had been reported. I had a visa that was issued by the previous government but these were still being honored. Nobody at the bank warned me against going.

I left on Thursday evening early in October, 1979. The plane was only half full. Most of the passengers appeared to be Iranians. I remember thinking at the time that some of them seemed to be so unhappy while others seemed quite jovial. It wasn't clear why. Perhaps some had been exiles and now were returning home to the New Iran while others may have been working overseas and been ordered home. On previous visits there had always been many planes sitting on the tarmac; this time there were only three. At the bottom of the stairway leading from the plane, passengers were divided, Iranians onto one bus with foreigners walking a short distance directly to immigration. As we entered the immigration building I looked to my right and saw something that gave me chills. There were three huge (perhaps 20' x 10') photographs, each of a single man from the waist up, no clothes visible, and each with a single bullet hole in his forehead, complete with powder burns. They were identified as three senior generals of the Iranian army. If this was meant to intimidate foreign visitors, it succeeded in my case.

Immigration was hostile. I was first told that my visa was no longer any good, and I would not be allowed to enter the country. After a brief set of games, they relented but required me to buy a new visa. Customs was equally difficult. They went over everything in my suitcase and even searched me personally. They were rude, aggressive and insulting. The ride into the city was equally unpleasant. Normally, Iranian taxicab drivers enjoyed scaring foreigners with their crazy driving but often were quite jovial and friendly. It was not the case this time. The driver was sullen. The only good news was that I was able to get a room at the Intercontinental, a hotel right in the heart of downtown. Over the previous three years, that hotel had always been booked and I would stay miles outside of town at the very nice but very distant Hilton.

It was late afternoon on Friday (their Sunday) and the Intercontinental reception area was deserted. There was a single man behind the counter who asked me what floor I wanted. I asked him if there were rooms available on all floors and he said yes. I asked him how many guests there were; he said three. There was me, another banker from Chase and a German businessman. He told me the restaurants were closed and there was no room service but that I could get a snack where they served tea.

The tea area was at the other end of the hotel. It had a separate entrance and appeared to have been where weddings or similar events were held. The tea room was at floor level; on either side a curved staircase took you to another seating area that overlooked the main seating area. Unlike the hotel itself, the tea room was jammed. My impression was that I was looking at the elite trying to pretend life had not changed post-Revolution. It was jammed, but in a peculiar way.. Both sides were completely full but the areas on both levels in front of the entrance were completely vacant. That seemed the obvious place to sit so I did. No one came. Eventually I got a server's attention who took my order. No alcohol was being served, quite a change from the normal Iran. When he brought my order, my curiosity got the best of me and I asked him why the unusual seating arrangement. The seat I had seemed to be the best in the room. He explained that the previous Friday a car stopped in front of the entrance and two man pulled out sub-machine guns and sprayed the tea room. The people directly in front were hurt. I debated moving but there was really no place to go and I guessed it would not happen a second time. I did eat rather quickly.

The next morning I dressed in my normal suit and tie and headed out. Again, the taxi driver was surly, even rude. He dropped me almost a block from Iranians Bank and I had to walk along the road which was designed like many French streets with a large center area and on both sides a narrow concrete divider, then anther lane for traffic. There were

IRAN

many men just standing in the street; I smiled at them but they did not return it. They were surly and angry; for the first time I felt afraid.

There was little activity at the bank but I was expected. My meeting was with someone I knew well. However, when I went to his office, his secretary, who seemed very nervous, told me the meeting would be in the board room. Very unusual. She led me there. At the head of the table was my friend, and to his immediate left a bearded man in a white tunic, On one side of the table were people I knew across from which were poorly dressed strangers. My friend did not look or speak to me. Something told me not to show any sign of friendship or even show recognition.

The meeting lasted for three hours. I was first introduced to the man next to my frightened friend, obviously a mullah and clearly in charge. Over the previous few months, Iranians Bank had repaid us some $5 million, albeit grudgingly and painfully slow. However, payments had stopped which was the reason I was there. I took an aggressive stand, berating my friend about his failure to pay. After some back and forth, the mullah stepped in and started to question me. He knew absolutely nothing about banking but was a quick study and very smart. He denied we were owed anything on the grounds that any loans we made were to prop up the Shah's regime. He claimed we knew this and since the Shah had fled our loans went with him. Not the greatest start!

Over the next 90 minutes, the dialogue ranged back and forth between lectures from him about the evils of the Shah and his secret police, SAVAK, lectures from me about the sanctity of trade finance, and interrogation by him on international banking in general. My credibility rose when I pointed out that PNB had never lent money directly to the government and had no loans to private individuals known locally as 'friends of the Shah'. I inferred this was because we did not like the Shah which was partly true.

As noted earlier, we had stopped making 'clean' advances to the banks months before, requiring documentation on what goods we were financing. I gave example after example of previous countries where trade finance was paid first before other types of loans. The mullah questioned me extensively while his aides took notes. He picked up every possible inconsistency. I explained letters of credit to him, why they would be very important to the future of the new regime. At one point he asked if we would continue to lend money to the new regime. I told him we would, only for trade, but first Iran had to recover its credibility with my loan committee, lost when they stopped repaying on time. Once those arrears were cleared up, we could resume normal lending, I said. I don't know what he believed or understood. Certainly he was smart; he did seem to accept that trade finance was different than the clean lending most foreign banks did in Iran.

Suddenly the atmosphere seemed to change. The mullah asked me if I wanted tea, which I accepted. He also served some sickly sweet buns and conversation shifted to questions about how the Iranian Revolution was perceived in the US. The meeting ended on a positive tone and I was promised that legitimate trade transactions would be repaid eventually. That sounded good but I didn't know when 'eventually' was or if he had the authority to make promises. I was escorted to the front door by my friend, who very quietly thanked me.

From there I went to our office to meet the office manager, experiencing the same angry vagrants in the street and sullen taxi drivers. I decided to ditch my coat and tie and asked our manager to find me a car and driver. He first arranged for a limousine from the hotel but I had something else in mind, hiring a student from Tehran University who drove a very old pigeon-egg blue Fiat which I used for the rest of my stay. I sat in the front seat and wore jeans and sweater. I also stopped shaving. A bit unusual but it felt a lot safer.

The landlord would not meet with me so I wrote him a letter cancelling our lease, referencing the *force majeure* clause. The manager and secretary divided the furnishings between them. They would move them out gradually after I left. For the rest of the day, evening and much of the following day I 'cleaned' the files. PNB did not lend to 'friends of the Shah', nor did we take personal deposits from them. Nevertheless, that did not stop these people from coming into the office and trying. Our meeting notes would be dangerous to them if discovered. I went through our files page by page removing individual names as necessary. Some I burned; some I flushed down the toilet. My teachers at the US Army intelligence school at Fort Holabird would have been proud!

The next day was more of the same but in the afternoon I had an appointment at the US Embassy. Embassies are always well guarded but this was ridiculous. It took me almost a half an hour to get inside. There were three separate US Marine checkpoints. But before we even got to the building itself, we had to pass through the Iranian Army unit that had surrounded the structure. They appeared to be holding back a large group of Iranians, some of whom looked like people trying to get into the embassy and others seemed to be protesting. They were periodic chants but I didn't know what they were saying. Most embassy calls were a bit over an hour; 30 minutes with the economic person and 45 or so with the shallow-cover CIA man. This time I was there for three hours, People kept coming in to debrief me on my experiences over the previous few days. They were not a happy group, had nothing positive to say about the new regime or the situation at hand.

In one of my earlier visits to Tehran, I met with the local agent for one of the national divisions domestic clients. The agent was importing a lot from our customer and I had asked them to designate our bank to receive the letters of credit from Iranians bank. That was the source of our current outstandings in Iran. It had been a real good meeting. Not only did they direct the letters of credit through us but they also opened an account on our books and the balances had gradually risen into the millions. This was an exception to our normal policy of not having individual accounts from Iranians but we certainly knew that they were not any friends of the Shah and they were very close to our domestic customer.

On the last day my student driver and I rode out to their offices. It was an interesting trip because we went through parts of the town that I had not seen in a long time. Again, a foreign face was not welcomed. We had a very good meeting. They were clearly nervous about the account they had opened with us. The new regime had demanded every individual and company give up any dollar accounts they had in exchange for local currency, at a very bad exchange rate. They wanted to know if we would keep all this confidential. I assured him we would, and he gave me an address where I should send any communications, including statements. As a matter of caution, we had already stopped sending anything directly into Iran.

I had brought with me a blank collateral pledge agreement. I wanted them to sign it in blank so I could take it back with me. This took a lot of explaining. "Why should they do that, they asked?" I explained that I could see a situation developing whereby they would be needing cash in the future. They agreed. I asked them how they could have money sent to them from their offshore $ accounts when they were not supposed to have any. If we had the documents pre-signed, we could make a loan secured by the cash deposits. I further warned them that the relationship between Iran and the US banking industry was increasingly tense and they could not expect the US bankers they knew to visit any time soon. They agreed. And they signed.

Later on that last day, I went back to Iranians Bank and once again pushed for repayment of the large letters of credit that we had refinanced and were still unpaid. Fortunately, I was able to meet alone with my friend this time. I pushed him hard, noting that he had already been paid by the importer (my friends) so he should pay me. He claimed that he had not been paid. I asked him to give that to me in writing. He did and I now had what I needed.

At 4AM the next morning my student driver picked me up at the hotel and we drove to the airport. I was nervous, especially at the military checkpoints we had to go through. When we finally went wheels up, I took the first relaxed breath in four days. It was the scariest trip of my banking career.

On Sunday morning, November 4, 1979, I woke up late after a late party the previous evening. When I finally got around to turning on the television to watch my football game, I was met with the announcement that Iranian students have taken over the US Embassy. The next morning I pulled all of the Area 1 to my desk area. I asked the question, "What is going on, what is happening here, and what will the outcome be?" Everyone had their say but the meeting was short because the opinion was unanimous, even Vic Dewan who was now handling Iran who was even more pessimistic than I was. This was only a publicity stunt and after a few days, the hostages will be released. We all agreed there was no possible way this could last a week.

When there was no resolution a week later, I brought the group back together again and asked the same question. This time there was a lot of debate. Vic led the pessimists among us. The consensus was that this was something unknown and we had to assume the worst. On Wednesday afternoon I brought in a team of lawyers from Pepper, Hamilton and Sheetz (I can't remember the senior guy's name but he was well known in Philadelphia as an international lawyer - he had white hair - was the name Bill Klaus??). The question I posed was this: Iran, I told him, would abrogate their foreign debt (or at least debt to US banks) this coming weekend. PNB had deposits from various sources in Iran of over $12 million. Following my visit to Tehran our loan were outstandings a bit less than that. How can we set-off the loans with those deposits?

Friday afternoon they came back. There was no way we could set-off - our deposits were from different sources than our loans, with only a few exceptions. At most we could set off about $1 million. My early experience with lawyers in Australia kicked in. I told Bill Klaus (?) he didn't understand the issue. I was going to set-off no matter what; his job was to justify the action. He was prepared for that. He said our justification would be as follows: Should Iran abrogate its debt to US banks, that act could only occur if an effective 'nationalization of banks **and all US dollar deposits of Iranians** had taken place. In that event, all loans and deposits were therefore now from and to a single source - the Iranian government. On that basis, we could set-off. Brilliant!

Brilliant as it was, it was still a pretty flimsy legal argument. But it was better than nothing and I could sort it all out later. What I figured was that the act of abrogation by Iran would change the legalities anyway. I did feel bad about the Iranian agent of our domestic customer. (I have avoided naming the party despite the many years that have passed. The family may still be in Iran and the regime has a long memory.) They were good people and I wasn't happy taking their money. But the refinanced letters of credit from Iranians Bank had been for their benefit so there was some logic to what we were doing. Besides, I had the collateral pledge agreement they had signed while I was there which our lawyers said would hold up. (Interestingly, this same argument was used by all banks post-freeze to justify their setting off of deposits in their foreign branches)

Late Friday I called Peter Giaccio in Operations and asked him to have the set-off documents prepared in advance, undated. The process was organized and managed by Vic who fully understood what we were doing. It was a pretty complex task but it was completed later that night. We were ready. It was November 9th of 1979.

Nothing happened that weekend. Or on Monday. Or on Tuesday. On Wednesday, about 6AM, I got a call from our London Representative Office. They wanted me to know that the rumors in London were that the Iranian banks were withdrawing their money from US banks. This action was no abrogation, or even a nationalization, but it certainly seemed to be a precursor and if successful would take all the deposits we had. Fortunately, I had Giaccio's telephone number. I told him to process the entries immediately. I got in the office at 7:15AM and within 15 minutes Pete called to tell me the set-off was complete.

My next stop was to Fred Heldring's office to let him know what I had done. While I was there, about 8:30 or so, we got a call from Joe Gordon, head of Legal. He told us the Federal Reserve had called to tell us that all Iranian assets had been frozen by the US government. We were instructed to keep careful records but to transfer all deposits to a special account at the Fed immediately. Legal wanted us to comply. I didn't. My point was that we had acted before the United States Government, and we could prove it. I was losing the argument when I proposed an interim compromise. After the set off, we had a couple of hundred thousand dollars in deposits left over. I proposed we send that to the Fed and deal with the other issues later. That worked.

In December, the Fed informed us that there was a disparity in what we had sent them and what Iran had reported we had in deposits, about $5 million worth. The good news was that Iran did not know about the company deposits we had; the bad news was that the Fed wanted its money. By this time Bill Klaus had convinced Joe Gordon that the freeze had settled our weak legal case and he was prepared to defend our action as an 'anticipatory breach' by Iran and, further, that our set-off timing was clearly documented as prior to the US Government freeze.

So started years of conflict between PNB and the Fed over Iran. I was told that we were threatened in a number of ways but senior management stuck by us, for which I was grateful. In 1980, an international commission was formed to intercede between Iran and the US. Although I was no longer in Area I at the time, Harry Hayman and Legal made the smart decision we should submit our claims as if there had been no set-off. Our hope was that if a settlement took place we could get all our loans repaid and the deposits from the Iranian company could be returned to them. The Fed could have played hard-ball here but they didn't.

In the late-1980s. I was sitting in my office one morning when I was brought business cards of two men wishing to speak with me. They were Iranian and had a letter signed by the principals of the Iranian company whose deposits we had used to set-off. The letter authorized my visitors to act on their behalf to recover their deposits **and to negotiate on their behalf.** By this time the Iranians Assets Tribunal had already settled our case; we had received all the money due us from Iran.

The gentlemen were polite, but clearly ready for and expecting a fight. They demanded their deposits with interest at the prevailing average interest rates since November 14, 1979. That was a problem for us. Although their original deposits were interest-bearing, this was the time period when interest rates had soared under President Carter. They could make an argument that we owed them principal plus interest at 10+%. The Iranian Assets Tribunal had paid us less than 5% which was public information. The difference would come directly out of our current profits.

But we had some things on our side as well. The original interest-bearing deposit agreement did **not** call for automatic renewal; at maturity proceeds were to be credited to their demand account, presumably for subsequent renewal via routine communications channels. When in Iran I had not changed these instructions because I simply had not considered them. In addition, the principals were still in Iran and a public spat was not in their interest at all. I pointed these issues out to them and they were not happy. They handed me all of their documents and I asked that they come back in the afternoon because I needed to review the situation.

The Division Credit Officer who had handled the Tribunal negotiations, Rick Emigh, and I huddled with Legal. Their documents appeared in order. The signatures on the authorization letter matched our records. Legal authorized the settlement. Next I met with my boss, Bob Siff. That took a while since he didn't know the history. He authorized me to pay interest up to 8% but we agreed to start lower. I arranged for a bank check payable to the principals with interest at 6%. When the Iranians returned, I handed them the check. They were visibly surprised. I told them the interest rate and handed them the disclaimer agreement. They looked at each other, never said a word and reached for their pens. Our Iranian crisis was over with no loss. A few months later Fred Heldring asked me to write a memo on Lessons Learned in Iran. It was the best such memo I ever did.

So far, banking had not proved to be a lucrative career from a financial perspective. When I took over the Asian group, I was making $33,000 a year. Now, at the end of my tenure, I was being paid $43,000, barely enough to live on with little opportunity to save. But I was happy that I would be able to expand my horizons and learn new things in my next assignment.

My time running Area 1 was coming to an end. But there was no job for me to go to. Not yet, anyway. I was told that it was coming but in the meantime, I was to write a business plan for a new Regional Division. My office would be in a small space on the 22nd Floor. That was ominous.

Chapter 8

Regional Interlude

THE FIRST SIX months of 1980 were some the worst six months of my career. I had left Area I in triumph. Iran resolved without loss. Profits booming. Good people in place. But I did not have a job to go to despite two years of warning senior management I wanted a change.

I was moved up to a small office on the 22nd floor of the PNB building. My loyal secretary, Ann Reardon (who I later sent to operations training, leaving her career as an AVP) had agreed to go with me. We were told to do a market study on companies with $5 million in sales to $200 million. How many were there in our market? What did they need? That sort of thing. No reasons were given for the study. Nothing about what that had to do with my next job.

A week later, all of Area 1 came to visit me, led by Harry Hayman. They presented me with a map of Asia and the Middle East. That map is now in my place in Delray Beach and I prize it greatly. Nostalgia set in.

After about a month I finished my report and submitted it to Dick

Ravenscroft, the President who had always been a strong supporter and was apparently 'in charge of 'Chuck'. He told me he needed more detail. Two weeks later I gave him more detail. He said he wanted more. My frustration was apparent but still no answers. About this time, my old boss Roland Bullard came over to me at the Officers Dining Room and asked me if I was having fun on the 22nd floor. He said I bet I wished I had come with him when I had the chance. He said it with a smile, but it might have had a tiny bit of a smirk in it.

I decided there was nothing much more I could study or write. So, essentially I did nothing. That Spring I spent more time at home than I ever had. I started looking for a job elsewhere but I was too senior for anything in New York, and another bank in Philadelphia was out of the question. Joann liked her life in Swarthmore and it was near her parents, which was important. I was stuck.

I decided to play the 'threat' card. Dangerous but worth it, I believed. Ravenscroft was especially close to the President of Philadelphia International Investment Corporation, Don Frankenfield, with whom I had worked closely in Australia and Area I also. Don liked me, but I knew he was more loyal to Dick and the bank than me. I asked Don to write a letter of recommendation to a European Bank he knew well. I had not contacted them so if he checked my goose was cooked. He didn't; he went to Dick.

Dick called me to his office. He explained what was going on in strict confidence. PNB was known as the bank for big corporations. The National Division, which Roland Bullard now led, were the elite bankers. But margins were shrinking in that market and growth was in smaller companies where PNB was weak. Furthermore, company needs were different for smaller companies (credit products, simple cash management, international collections) than for the big names (sophisticated cash management, back-up lines of credit).

Dick wanted to split the National Division into two groups, $5-200 million in sales and $200+. Apparently Roland wasn't happy about it, which was understandable. . I was told to keep my head down, keep quiet and wait. The family spent a lot of time at the beach in Lewes, Delaware with my Mom that summer.

By early Fall the new Regional Division was formed. The head, Bob Spencer, was a great credit man who had worked with smaller companies for years. His credit officer, Bill Sudhaus, was probably the 2nd best credit mind in the bank. Jay Howson was one team leader; I was designated the other one. Jay had 80% of the new division's assets, customers and people. I was expected to build my own book. It was obvious from day 1 I was not Bob's choice of team leader. Dick Ravenscroft had foisted me on him. But I give him and Bill full credit. They were ordered to both take me and to teach me corporate credit. Which they did!

To suggest that I got short shrift was an understatement. The city of Philadelphia went to Jay, as did middle market rich New Jersey and the Lehigh Valley. I got western Pennsylvania, counties where we had virtually nothing. I got Delaware, DC and Virginia where we also had nothing. I got one experienced banker, Lew Van Dusen. I got him because nobody wanted him. His customers loved him; they loved him because he never told them no - ever! As I later found out he sometimes told them 'Yes', but without actual credit approval. He was really likable just the same. I got one other officer, Donn Scott, who had only one year on the job and a couple of clients. Donn was black, the only African-American officer in the corporate group. We had one trainee assigned to us, also an African-American.

In short, when the reorganization finally took place, Roland kept most of his good people; the good ones that Bob Spencer got went to Jay Howson. I had one opening which several domestic lenders had refused. Ian Rainey was unhappy in Area I where he and Harry Hayman were often at odds. I knew he knew absolutely nothing about credit but I also knew he was a marketing genius and I thought his British accent would be unique. He joined me.

I am not going to spend too much time talking about the Regional Division. Suffice to say, I was there to learn domestic credit and I did, thanks to Bill Sudhaus and Bob Spencer. Whenever there was a difficult credit, even though it was not in my group, they included me in the meetings and often asked my opinion before anyone else. My judgment in the beginning almost always required correction which they did very directly but also very gently. I owe them a great deal.

I was in Regional for a little over 15 months, during which time we tripled loan assets. That sounds a lot better than it actually was since we started from such a small base. But we did bring in about 12 new accounts that later did pretty well for the bank. Ian and his British accent were successful. I started out in Regional with very little credibility. International had a reputation of not knowing corporate credit. While probably true, domestic bankers did not realize the bank risk we took in international carried with it the same core principles of credit extension they used. Country risk was totally foreign to them. My experience with domestic credit in Australia, coupled with what I learned from Ken Dennewald, also was helpful. Over the course of the year, both Bill Sudhaus and Bob Spencer gave me a passing grade which they communicated to others.

In June, I got a rude shock. In PNB, most people looked at everyone else as a potential rival. We each knew how long we had been in our current positions and ranks. We knew when others had joined the bank and when they had first become an officer. We knew when they had been moved into their current rank. I was a Vice President, the most senior of that title. One of Bob Palmer's mentees was Charlie Connolly.

I barely knew him but kept hearing about him as a rising star. In June, he was promoted to Senior Vice President.

I went ballistic! I let everyone know how I felt. It was my worst error in judgment of a successful career. Even though everyone did so, it was really stupid to look at these situations as a sprint. It wasn't. It was a long distance race and at any given point in time someone else might temporarily take the lead. As I got to know Charlie later on, I found out he was very smart, a good banker, and a great leader of others. It would have been so much smarter to have gone up to him and congratulated him. But I looked a bit of a fool in how I reacted. And Dick Ravenscroft let me know that too.

In retrospect, my Regional experience was extremely good for me. Aside from the credit side, it also changed my reputation within the bank. I was known as smart and a hard charger. I was also known as incredibly ambitious. The negative side of that was many people felt I did not have others' best interest at heart. But by the time I left in late 1981, I was also seen as a champion of minorities within the commercial side of the bank.

When the group was just coming together, I was out for a couple of days when Donn Scott moved from the second floor to our unit on the third floor. When I came back, I walked over to introduce myself. I found him sitting with his back to the aisle. That was unnatural. Was it because that way he did not have to face anyone? That was his general posture for the first few weeks. He rarely got out of his seat and he never said hello to anyone but was very polite when someone said hello to him. When i questioned him about that behavior he seemed oblivious to it.. So every time I walked by and he was in that posture, I pointed it out. Then we sat down and talked about it.

What we both decided was that he was feeling extremely insecure as a black man in a white man's company and industry. He told me a lot about his experiences in the training program. He felt alone. He had been assigned a mentor but there was very little communication between them. I told him a little bit about my civil rights experience and I promised to be as supportive as I could. I made sure that I went out on calls with him because so far no one else had ever done so.

A few months later our young black trainee left the bank. I did an exit interview with him and he kept saying he just wasn't comfortable in the environment. Donn and I spoke about it at length. Donn told me that all of the black employees that we had hired for commercial banking were failing. This was despite very strong educational backgrounds. That made no sense to me but it recalled something Donn said to me early in our interaction. I don't recall what it was but something he had done was wrong. We sat down and I explained it to him in depth and I was very clear that he had made a mistake. He thanked me and commented that this was the first time anyone at the bank had criticized his work, ever. That also made no sense to me.

I asked Donn to set up meetings between me and several young black officers and trainees that he knew in the commercial side of the bank. Donn insisted that the meetings be in secret. I thought that was a bit of paranoia but it also showed me how deep some feelings were. What I discovered was that none of the young black bankers were given feedback. Their white supervisors were unwilling to point out any negatives. As a result, they weren't given the instruction they needed and kept repeating the same mistakes. Eventually, they were weeded out. I talked to a couple of the white supervisors I knew. What I learned was that they were fearful to be critical because they didn't want to be known as 'racist'. "How could they learn then?", I asked.

I wrote up my observations and sent it to someone I knew in Personnel. It wasn't taken particularly well but I also worked with Donn to pair new black trainees with people that I knew would be willing to give proper feedback. The situation improved but still was not what it needed to be. Later Donn would improve the system further.

One customer that Donn brought with him when he came into the group was National Fruit. This was a company in Winchester Virginia that harvested and processed apples. Donn was given the account because he was from Roanoke Virginia, a fellow Virginian. Evidently, his supervisor at the time didn't understand that Winchester was particularly redneck and might not appreciate a black relationship officer. It was a minor relationship because they did not borrow and most of their needs were met by a local bank. I offered to give the account to someone else but Donn said that he had developed a decent connection with the owner, Frank Armstrong III, over the previous year.

One morning in the late spring, Frank called Donn. He was considering buying Musselman's, a company in the same business almost 3 times their size. Could we help? One of the things that Bob Spencer and Bill Sudhaus had made a key component of our Regional Division was the ability to respond immediately to credit requests. This made us unique among our competitors. Donn and I met with Spencer and Sudhaus to compile a list of things that we would need. We communicated those to the company and got a bank car to head south.

When Bill and Bob arrived the next day, the four of us spent an hour going over everything we had learned. We then sat down with the owner and his management team. Our questioning was very detailed and possibly somewhat harsh. After all, the company was looking to borrow $5 million and risk their survival for this acquisition. The discussions continued over lunch, some sandwiches, soup, and, yes, applesauce. Once we were done, the four of us met. So did Frank Armstrong III and his management team. We took at least an hour but wrote up the basis on which we would be willing to approve the credit. We presented that to the company after which Frank asked how long it would take to get approval. We told him he had approval. The company was very impressed but told us that our questions had made them wonder whether they should be taking this risk. They had decided not to proceed. A lot of work to no avail, but it was a great exercise which impressed National Fruit immensely. And I learned a lot.

In the banking world of today, brought about by bank regulators responding to crisis after crisis, what we were able to do in this case could never be done today. The idea that the line (Bob, me, Donn) could sit in the same meeting with credit (Bill) and reach a final credit decision just isn't done anymore. The two sides are not trusted to act together in the bank's best interest. In my last chapter I will discuss this in a great more depth. Suffice to say I believe banking has lost something but, more importantly, so have bank customers. It did not need to happen that way. I think Federal banking regulators took the easy way out. But more on that later.

By then it was dinner time and Frank wanted to entertain us at the Winchester Country Club before driving all night with a buddy to watch the Masters. Frank was a character. This turned out to be a pretty interesting experience. Donn and I had a little work to clear up, so the rest of the group, 15 in all, headed over to the club. As Donn and I walked up the entrance, he told me how nervous he was. Rednecks might be willing to have a black as a banker, but entertaining one at their country club?? I jokingly told him if things got rough, he was on his own. We had to walk down a long hall to approach the dining room which opened up on the right side first. Our table was around the corner on the left side. So at least half of the people in the club got a clear view of Donn and I walking in. Some mouths dropped.

Frank positioned Donn at the end of the table so that anyone who walked into the club would immediately see him sitting there but not the rest of the table. The reaction from many members was fun to see. Not satisfied with that, after dessert, Frank walked Donn around to many of the tables, introducing him as 'my banker'. Donn and I walked Frank out to his car, a red mustang with two coolers of iced beer. Frank was off to the Masters.

Donn and I remained close for the rest of our careers. Every once in a while he would ask for an appointment, ask a question which usually related to career options, listened, and did whatever he was going to do. Sometimes he took my advice sometimes he didn't but I believe he always knew I would give him a straight answer. Donn went far, eventually ending as an executive vice president with our buyer, First Union.

All during the time I was on the domestic side, people from International were talking to me about how unhappy they were with leadership. Joop van Vollenhoven had brought some discipline to the division but the simple fact was that he was not as smart as any of the Area Heads and he also didn't know our business. He was a New York banker with New York bank thinking. Finally, even the Dutchman Fred Heldring realized that the Dutchman van Vollenhoven was over his head.

Management had had to deal with the decision on who would take over the international division for some time. Mark Ledger and Peter Longstreth made the decision easy in the end, when they left International early in 1981 to start a new real estate company called Aegius International, which turned out quite successful. Two of my protégés, Mike Heavener and Rick Clarke, replaced Mark and Peter, respectively.In the third quarter of 1981, I was called to Fred Heldring's office and told I would be taking over the division as of December 31, 1981. I would move to be deputy international head in late October of that year, reporting to Joop.

Chapter 9

Latin America Debt Crisis

I am not sure Bob Siff, head of Commercial Banking and a former Citibanker who had hired fellow Citibanker Joop Van Vollenhoven, agreed with Heldring that Joop was over his head. Bob liked Joop's discipline and process over the innovation and creativity of we 'young turks'. Bob made that clear in my first meeting with him but, after meeting with Joop at Bob's request, there was no doubt that Joop was out at the end of the year and I was in.

Joop was adamant that I let him keep his leadership role to the end. He asked me to do nothing to undercut his position and be clearly subservient in public at all times. After a moments thought, I agreed; after all, that was how I would want to be treated were I in the same position. It was only for a couple of months, in a normally slow period. In retrospect, it gave me the time I needed to understand other parts of International before taking full responsibility, especially Latin America. It gave me time to think and assess instead of my more characteristic 'full steam ahead' approach. Would I have made the decision I did on Latin America, the most important decision of my career, without that time of reflection? I doubt it.

After meeting with all the Area Heads, and especially Operations and our New York processing center, I was left with lots of time on my hands. The first thing I wanted to learn was about our medium term lending in Latin America. Fred Heldring had always opposed it, but finally agreed a few years earlier that Area II could have a third of its exposure in medium term (5-7 years); the rest would have to be short term, hopefully but not absolutely related to trade. The spreads were three times higher on medium term, with some up-front fees as well.

As head of Area I, I had been a part of the International Loan Committee which approved those medium term facilities. One of the principal rules of lending in other countries we had been taught was the debt service ratio (short term loans and maturities of long-term debt payable in one year) should never exceed 20% of export proceeds. That was a ratio we followed religiously in the Asian group. However, Latin America never did. Their officers always said that Latin America was "different" and could sustain a much higher number. That never made much sense to me. I decided to take a trip to Latin America on my own to find out the reason.

Just before I left, Mexico devalued it's currency, something I had been told only the previous week would never happen. We discussed it at length in our loan committee just before I left. The Area officer, Kate O'Brien explained it was a one time event, never to be repeated. I recalled it had happened before in 1976 but kept quiet. We decided not to take any action, thinking that we should leave that judgment to the officers most familiar with the market. Our international credit officer, Rick Emigh, concurred in the decision but showed his skepticism. I decided to visit Brazil, Argentina and Chile to get a better sense of their economies and how vulnerable they might be.

In all three countries, I sensed that the market for new medium term loans was weakening, with rising demand but increasing reluctance of lenders to increase exposure. Further, I also learned that there might be increased capital flight, with more foreign companies manipulating their inter-company trade transactions to keep export proceeds offshore. Wealthy businessman were also trying to move money offshore. These were classic warning signs of a pending balance of payments crisis, a major concern.

The only thing local banks wanted to talk about was whether we were prepared to provide more medium term loans to their customers, or even themselves. Foreign banks, especially the major New York banks, claimed to have no concerns, but they also did not appear to be increasing their own exposure. However, they very much wanted to lead a syndication to local banks and distribute almost all of it to others, smaller US and foreign banks. That was another concern. If they weren't worried why the reluctance to taking more assets? I returned to the United States more fearful then when I had left.

The economics of long-term lending into Latin America were very favorable to the syndication managers, which were mostly in New York City or London. They would negotiate with the borrower a loan at roughly 2% over cost of funds, with upfront fees of at least 2%. They would syndicate that loan to smaller banks at 1 1/2 percent over cost of funds and a 1% fee, keeping the rest for themselves.

Let's use a $100 million syndication for a large Brazilian bank as an example. The New York syndicator would often sell all of the credit but let's give them the benefit of the doubt in this case and say they kept 10% or 10 million. The economics are that the lead bank would earn its own one and a half percent spread each year and a one and a half percent upfront fee. But they would also earn additional half percent on all $100 million and an additional 1/2% fee on all $100 million. In other words, their upfront fees were $700,000 and annual interest income was $650,000 on their $10 million loan. By contrast, a regional bank that took the same $10 million participation earned $150,000 in fees and and $150;000 annual interest income. Same risk level but vastly different return. The significance of this difference will become more clear later.

One meeting in Brazil with Courtney Haight of Morgan Guaranty was particularly enlightening. Fortunately, Courtney did not know our bank very well, so I was able to play the naïve regional banker looking for assets. He described transactions like the one above, encouraging us to join him. I asked him if he would commit to retain 30% of the syndication for their own books. That surprised him and he hemmed and hawed a bit before saying, no, that was not part of their strategy. That told me a lot.

On February 19, 1982 Mexico devalued the peso for the second time in three months. Experience told me that we were heading for a major crisis. More than any other PNB international banker, I had gone through three liquidity crises, first in the Philippines, then Angola and finally in Iran. That experience paid off. The problem was, of course, that others who had not gone through those previous experiences could not see what was happening. It did not help that I had little knowledge of Latin America, where our officers were convinced I did not know what I was doing. Only Mariana Wilson, who had a lifetime living with financial crises in her native Argentina, and Rick Clarke who had a history with me, supported my take on the situation, the latter with slight hesitation. In addition, we had just started a new financial year. If we were to withdraw from Latin America at this point, the division would never be able to make plan, risking our profit-sharing bonuses at the end of the year. At this point, it was my Division, my 1982 Plan and my bonus we were talking about!

I credit my boss, Bob Siff, for the ultimate decision. Yes, it was my initial recommendation and later decision to withdraw but, to be perfectly honest, I would not have done so without his support. He was a good credit man, student of Citibank's Henry Mueller, but admittedly had little international experience. At our meeting he never came out and said that he agreed with my recommendation but he did make it clear that it was my decision to make and I should never let profits interfere with a credit judgment. It was that latter comment which gave me the courage to proceed.

Had I gone directly to Vice-Chairman Fred Heldring instead, the man most experienced internationally, I wonder if I would have been given the same answer. On the one hand, Fred was cautious in credit and never liked the medium-term exposure to Latin America, especially Brazil. On the other hand, Fred had rarely missed plan and might have hesitated as a result. Furthermore, Fred's experience told him trade finance was safe as would be overnight placements to US-based branches of Mexican banks, of which we had $100 million. But if export proceeds were delayed by inter-company corporate games, rising capital flight by the very wealthy, and finally increasing reluctance by smaller banks to increase their medium term lending all happened at the same time, feeding on each other, then I thought nothing would be safe.

Bob Siff showed real leadership and I felt comfortable to start withdrawing exposure from Latin America. As a strong 'P' on the Meyers Briggs scale, I knew I was prone to change my mind when confronted with new data, even new opinions. I knew I would get a lot of those once I announced the decision. I decided to wait until just before leaving for a three week trip to Asia. That meeting is ingrained in my memory. It was at 4 PM on Friday, March 16, 1982.

Attending was the head of Latin America, Rick Clarke, Rick Emigh, Kate O'Brien, and Al Murphy, who handled our corporate exposure to Mexico. The topic was Mexico. There was little discussion since I had already told Bob Siff what I was going to do. I ordered an immediate pullout from Mexico, a reduction in the other countries, and left for Asia. Was I a bit of a coward not to stay in Philadelphia to face the music? Yes, but I knew myself and might be unable to resist the uproar when Roland Bullard (Al Murphy's boss and my old mentor) and the deputy heads of Latin America (Harriet Cordero and Mariana Wilson, an Argentine) heard about it.

At that point, PNB had total exposure to banks in Latin America of a bit more than $425 million. In addition, we were lending $100 million in Fed Funds to the largest Mexican banks which was overnight exposure. As I recall, PNB's total capital base was a little over 400 million. We were heavily exposed. Fortunately our proportion of medium term loans was only 33%. We could rapidly reduce the short-term loans but do nothing about the medium term. In those days, there were no secondary markets to sell medium term loans to other lenders or investors like there is today.

The rundown started immediately. Within a week, however, Kate O'Brien announced she was leaving to join Citibank. Undoubtedly, she must have communicated to them what we were doing and why. Their head of Latin America, Bill Rhodes, later became the senior US banker responsible for re-structuring Latin American debt. When he and other New York bankers selected January 1, 1982 as the date on which all lenders were supposed to base their overall exposure, I have often wondered if he had PNB specifically in mind. That date was beneficial to the New York bankers because it excluded from their base all the new lending they did during 1982 which was especially large. Why so?

In 1982, capital flight was growing rapidly and trade deficits exploding. New syndications had to be written or else Latin borrowers would run out of cash and default. The major syndicator banks could not let that happen. Beginning in May, as other banks around the world also began to reduce exposure, they needed to fill the gap to try to prevent the crisis that eventually happened. So using January 1, 1982 as the date on which the required 'new money' formula was based was at the least self-serving, at worst cynical. And both the Federal Reserve under Paul Volker, and the Jacque de la Rosierre-led IMF said nothing about it despite mine and other protests. I point this out here a bit out of sequence but wanted the reader to understand my bitterness at New York and the Fed which fueled subsequent actions. More on that later.

Each Spring, international bankers from around the world would congregate in Boca Raton, Florida for the annual meeting of Bankers Association of Foreign Trade (BAFT). Invitations for US bankers were limited, as BAFT wanted as many foreign Central Bankers and Treasury people as possible to attend. PNB was allocated three slots and I took Rick Clarke and Rick Emigh. We met before the first reception to plan strategy.

Our objective was to talk with every US regional bank and smaller foreign banker we could in order to find out who else shared our concerns and might also be withdrawing. When the three of us shared experiences at the end of the three days, not a single bank admitted they were reducing exposure and only a few indicated they did have serious concerns. The ones that did were the small European banks; US regionals and Japanese were still drinking the money-center bankers' Kool Aid. Much of the talk revolved around the new $1 Billion medium-term loan to Mexico being put together by Bank of America. Most people thought it would be a success.

I was now concerned for a different reason. My decision had already caused issues inside the division. Our Mexican relationships were upset although not as much as anticipated because they considered our actions naive and at that point not particularly damaging. Old Mexican banker friends of Fred Heldring, however, did call him to complain. While Fred did not challenge the decision, it was clear to me that he was watching my career-threatening move closely.

Shortly after the BAFT meeting, Bank of America announced that their $1 billion loan to Mexico was fully subscribed and signed. That's when I made a mistake, and it was a costly one. That week we had the last $40 million of short-term advances to two Mexican banks coming due, one on Wednesday and the second a week later, both for $20 million. Once they were paid, there was nothing more to do in Mexico; everything else was medium-term related to our domestic corporate business.

What to do? The big rescue credit was an apparent success. Maybe I had over-reacted, a trait I knew I exhibited in the past. To his credit. Rick Clarke did not push me in any way. It was entirely my decision. I told Rick to only ask for repayment of half, rolling over for another 180 days $10 million each. When Mexico finally froze all debt repayments in August that year, all $20 million was caught, half by three days and the remainder by 10 days. That was a bad day and I only had myself to blame.

However, immediately after rolling over the $20 million I had no worries. The new credit had been signed and there were no obvious signals that other banks were pulling out. That is, until we got a call from Bank of America a couple of weeks later! One of their syndication officers had not been warned to stay away from that radical regional bank, PNB. They wanted to know if PNB wanted a piece of the rescue credit loan. I don't remember who took the call but whoever it was was smart enough to just take a message. We set up the questions we wanted to ask. Wasn't the credit oversubscribed? How many banks participated? How many US regional banks participated? And the most important, how much was still left to be syndicated? While we did not get all the answers we learned enough; over 30% of the credit still needed buyers and very few smaller US banks had joined. Mexico was in deep trouble and the contagion was spreading.

Another life lesson! Earlier in this chapter I referenced being a strong

"P" on the Meyers Briggs personality scale. When confronted with new information, "P"s will often change their minds. "J"s, on the other hand, don't. I should have been a "J"!! We could have been completely out of Mexico if I had stuck with my convictions; instead we had $20 million on which we would later take a loss. On the positive side, I never forgot the lesson and would carry out management of this and future crises with complete conviction.

At the BAFT meetings over the years, I had developed some very good relationships with other US regional bank international division heads. Regional banks, both US and European, were the cannon fodder to the big money center bankers' guns (US, Europe and Japan). I don't have the actual figures but would venture that from 1978 growth in money center Latin American assets went up at less than half the rate of Latin American overall debt, with the difference syndicated to smaller banks at significantly cheaper prices than the money centers made on them.

When the crisis finally hit, governments and the IMF went to the money centers to solve it. After all, they were the most exposed. The money center banks designed the re-scheduling of debt to benefit themselves at the expense of the less-sophisticated and less-powerful, as described previously. What they ultimately did was wrong. I would make it the biggest fight of my career.

In May, I spent a fair amount of time on the phone with other regionals' International division heads. At first, there was a reluctance to share information, especially with PNB. We had a much larger International Division, one others were trying to emulate. But gradually the picture became clear. The US regionals had had enough of Latin American medium-term debt. What especially struck me was the discussions related not just to Mexico but to all the region. All of them had country limits, but most also had regional limits as well. They were selecting which countries on which to focus in the region. In that scenario, Mexico would lose; their banks had been the most demanding on rates and had insisted on using their own New York agencies to process transactions in lieu of sending that business to their regional correspondents, an economically-smart short term decision but guaranteed to turn off $ spigots when the going got tough. Mexico, I knew, would be squeezed first, but once Mexico defaulted the rest would follow. We made the decision to continue to pull out everywhere and to make no new loans. Before this, we had been slower withdrawing from the other countries. The only exceptions were being made by me.

I made my first exception in Venezuela, a big oil producer.. We had not been successful doing business in Venezuela up to that point and we had a new young officer, Andreas Bacalao, who was about to make his first trip and be trained by Banco Provincial. We received a frantic call from him on his second day. The bank had virtually demanded that we provide $5 million for 180 days to them as a sign of good faith. Our officer assured me that it would be for trade finance and not what is known as a "clean advance".

The difference was significant. There have been many country debt restructurings in previous years but in every case of which we were aware trade finance was never rescheduled. Clean advances, on the other hand were often rescheduled. That is why Fred Heldring had made trade finance the fundamental aspect of our international landing to banks. It was a good policy. I agreed to make the loan but when the documentation arrived we saw no reference to a trade transaction. I was furious. After getting no positive reaction from the bank, I called their head of international personally to demand that the transaction they changed to trade. He refused, saying that our officer had never mentioned trade. Caught between supporting my officer and protecting our position, I chose the former. Eventually, we were repaid after several rollovers thanks to Venezuela's oil revenues, with a warning that the bank would never ever work with PNB again. And this was just the start of what would prove to be a very difficult three years.

PNB's Latin American group had built a wonderful group of relationships with the region's banks over the years. Much of it was built on credit. For a regional US bank, we were in early and were quite active. Now we had stopped lending? They didn't understand it. Our officers didn't understand it. There was lots of anger, mostly directed at me. Rick Clarke did a great job trying to keep his officers under control but it was obvious to me that I had to help them personally, as it was my decision in the first place.

In early summer, I traveled to Columbia, Brazil, Argentina and Chile. I had two objectives. First, I needed to take the heat off of our officers. Second, we needed to convert all of the clean advance lending that we had been doing into trade finance. I won't bore the reader with all the technical details. Suffice to say, it wasn't easy. Our correspondent banks only had so much trade to finance and double financing on the same trade transaction was against banking rules. Our correspondents had borrowed from us by clean advances and on-lent those dollars to local companies without a specific trade transaction behind it. $ borrowing, after all, was much cheaper than local currency interest rates.

Our correspondents needed to understand what we were doing and to plan for either conversion to trade or repayment of coming maturities. On one hand, we were helped by being early. We were one of the only banks doing this and so got a healthy proportion of committed future trade financing. On the other hand, they also thought we were pretty ignorant but our officers could blame it on me, the new guy to Latin America, and still maintain their own credibility.

It was a tough trip. We had offices in Sao Paolo and Buenos Aires so they were our top priorities. The Falklands War had hit Argentina hard.

LATIN AMERICA DEBT CRISIS

Colombia had the drug cartels. The Pinochet regime in Chile bred civil unrest. Brazil had rampant corruption. Their economies were hooked on the drug of excessive US $ debt provided by the largest banks syndicating $ credits and distributing the assets to smaller lenders new to the business and very inexperienced. The previous five years had shown massive increase in debt; the newer lenders were getting nervous. It was still early days but the trend was obvious.

Central bankers in the region had picked up the market's concern. As a result, I was able to meet with people at a level normally not offered to a regional bank like PNB. I was favorably impressed with most of them, especially the governor of the central bank of Brazil, Delfim Neto. Overall, we were pretty successful in changing the nature of our lending.. Outstandings were way down in all countries and trade now made up the bulk of our shorter term loans. There was nothing we could do about medium term because at that time there was no market to sell such assets.

By mid August, I was feeling pretty upbeat about the situation. The $20 million rollover of the Mexican bank credit would be repaid at the end of the month, bringing our reduction in our standings to more than $200 million. But it was not to be. On October 17, 1982 Mexico announced a moratorium on all foreign debt, just three and ten days before our two repayment dates. We had $20 million stuck and it should not have happened. It was my mistake. .

To say that Mexico's default was a shock to the global financial system would be an understatement. Money-center banks in the United States, Europe and Japan were all heavily exposed and vulnerable. The International Monetary Fund and the US Treasury began to mobilize teams to deal with the situation. Naturally, they turned to the major US banks to lead the effort; after all, they had the most to lose. The good news was that by this point our LDC exposure was down to only 35% of the bank's capital.

Chapter 10

FIGHTING NEW YORK....AND THE FEDERAL RESERVE

BY JANUARY, MONEY-CENTER banks, supported by the International Monetary Fund, the Federal Reserve and the United States Treasury, announced their rescheduling plan for Mexico. The fundamentals were as follows: 1) A temporary moratorium on repayment of all medium-term debt 2) A requirement for banks to make new loans to Mexico based on a percentage of outstandings as of **December 31, 1981.** 3) Maintain all trade facilities at their current level 4) All short term loans were re-scheduled the same as medium term loans and 5) All loan repayments, short-term trade as well as maturities of medium-term loans made after January 1, 1982 were to be returned and re-scheduled.

I saw this as a deliberate effort to punish Philadelphia National Bank. In speeches given by officials of the money center banks, most specifically Bill Rhodes of Citibank, blame was being assigned to those institutions which had reduced exposure as the ultimate cause of the crisis rather than the economic mismanagement of the country or excessive lending by the world's banks. In other words, those of us who analyzed the situation correctly and took appropriate action were ordered to revert to the status quo. For us, that meant putting back over $220 million into Mexico. That was absolutely ridiculous.

Furthermore, they also said that the new money requirement would be based on total outstandings to the country, as of that date, including trade. That put trade financing in the same category as medium term loans, the first time this had ever been done with any re-scheduling in my experience. Regional banks like ourselves tended to concentrate exposure in trade on the grounds that it was less risky. Our spreads on trade loans were minimal compared to the medium term loans made by the money center banks. In addition, those non-trade short term advances earning a spread of 50 basis points were treated the same as medium-tern loans earning over two percent. And which institutions had these longer assets? The very ones given the charge to design the re-scheduling plan.

It was a totally one-sided set of proposals, endorsed by governments and international organizations only because they either did not understand the differences or were concerned solely with solving the problem. I certainly understood the IMF's position. They had a major crisis and were fearful of contagion for the rest of Latin America and beyond, with cause. I also understood the money center banks position, namely, being as heavily exposed as they were, the more of the resolution that could be passed on to others, specifically regional banks like PNB, the better.

The whole design, of course, was a mildly disguised attempt to convince bank investors that bank portfolios (hence earnings) were safe. 'New money' would allow debtor nations to continue paying interest on their loans. Banks would not have to write-down their loans or even show them as non-performing. It was a fiction, but one everyone wanted to believe.

The chances we would be able to influence the design of the rescheduling were dim.. We had no voice. Countries, international agencies, and academics were all focusing on the macro, while our attempt to focus on the micro was falling on deaf ears. The money center banks controlled the press. I appealed to all the New York bankers I knew and many of the international banks as well. There was sympathy but nothing concrete. The other regional bankers I talked to were equally upset but saw no recourse. Each of them, with two exceptions, told me that they had been told to cooperate by their senior management, who in turn had been pressured by Treasury and the Federal Reserve.

With the two Rick's (Clarke and Emigh) help, I presented a formal proposal to the various re-scheduling committees in New York, copies to Treasury and the Federal Reserve. The Federal Reserve was heavily involved because, should Latin America unravel, many of the money centers, especially Citibank, Manufacturer's Hanover, and Continental Illinois would be insolvent.

We proposed that repayments made prior to Mexico's formal default would stand, on the grounds that those who foresaw the crisis like PNB should not be penalized for doing what bankers are supposed to do, reduce exposure when borrowers get in trouble. We agreed to put our fair share of ‚new money' loans each year based on our medium term loans but not on short-term trade. Our argument was re-scheduling of trade was unprecedented and trade financiers had deliberately chosen to take lower spreads for less risk, hence should not be treated the same way as those who took more risk and made more money doing so.

There was one technical weakness to our proposal - What was a trade transaction and what was not? The normal process was for borrowers to specify in some detail what movement of goods was being financed. Over the years, however, as banks wanted $ to re-lend to their corporate customers for other purposes, discipline broke down and regionals, including ourselves, began to lend short-term without proper documentation. These were called 'clean' advances; they weren't trade so where did they fit? (Fortunately, PNB tightened up our process with all countries when we first began to withdraw from Mexico so our outstandings by that August were mostly in good shape). The money centers used flawed documentation to successfully persuade most regionals to ultimately go along with their plan.

Our proposals fell on deaf ears. Why? It would have meant the big banks putting in more 'new money' each year. They did not want that, and they were in charge. My plea that the difference was just a drop in the bucket was ignored and ridiculed, especially by Bill Rhodes of Citibank. He was supported by Treasury and the Fed, in part out of ignorance and in part because they had the very tough job of getting borrowers to agree to any re-scheduling at all, instead of just walking away from their debt. Any re-scheduling would severely hurt the Latin American economies and their people for years to come, as we subsequently witnessed. No one wanted to place blame on the countries for borrowing too much; it was much easier to blame banks like PNB which started the withdrawal in the first place.

The good news was that almost all of the regional banks supported our proposals. The bad news was that only three were willing to refuse to go along. My two allies were Phil Moon of National Bank of Detroit and Tony Furr of Wachovia. Both banks had portfolios quite similar to ours, a high proportion of documented short-term trade. All three of us were only able to stick to our guns because of support from our CEOs and top management. Phil Moon's boss was an old-time very tough banker named Verne Istock who, like our Morrie Dorrance, had run his bank for years. Tony Furr had the support of a man I thought the best banker in the country at the time, John Medlin. Their self-confidence allowed them to resist the myriad pressures from Treasury and the Fed. It was only after I was Chief Credit Office of the bank during the 1989-1992 Real Estate crisis that I really understood how difficult it was for Fred Heldring and Morrie Dorrance to support me refusing to go along with the re-scheduling.

By then I understood the power both Treasury and the regulators had over a bank. Then I saw it first-hand. The Iran Crisis was just a taste. In 1982 I was still a bit naive. I do know that Walt Wriston of Citibank was on the phone to both Morrie and Fred several times, as was the Chairman of JP Morgan. Paul Volker, Federal Reserve Chairman, called at least twice.

Bob Siff was supportive from the outset. As an ex-Citibanker I suspect he enjoyed tweaking their noses, most specifically Bill Rhodes whom he knew from before. Fred Heldring required a lot of convincing. Quite rightly, Fred was considered the elder statesman of international banking among US regional banks. He was one of the first bankers outside of New York to build an International Division, starting in the early 50s. His reputation extended into Europe and New York. He was well known and respected at the IMF and in Washington DC. He had travelled all over the world developing friendships with senior bankers. How hard it must have been for him to stand alone against so many friends! Morrie had no such ties; he had always left it to Fred to manage the international side.

I remember three conversations with Fred over several months discussing the issues. Each was more than an hour. Given his rivalry with Fred, Bob Siff did not attend any of them. Fred was tough. He challenged every point I made, making me repeat the same points over and over. He was very critical of some of the poor documentation we had on trade transactions which I took personally, even though that had mostly not taken place on my watch. He asked me what I thought putting new money would cost the bank and I told him we might write-off 50% before we were done. I also pointed out that bank analysts would crucify us if we agreed to put back what we had withdrawn since March. I had already told them what we had done. If that part was a non-starter, why not go all the way? It was only at the final meeting, when Fred started to talk about language we should use with the New York bankers and regulators, did I realize he would support me.

We then met with Morrie who gave the go-ahead to refuse the re-scheduling plan. Our final reply to Rhodes said PNB would agree to 1) provide 'new money based on outandings of medium-term exposure and 'clean advances' as of August 31. 1982 not January 1 and 2) we would agree to keep our aggregate trade finance lines of credit in place for at least three years. As each new country was re-scheduled we took a similar position.

Morrie was especially concerned with the public relations aspect of our decision. He did not like being virtually alone and named as a 'free rider' by New York and the press. I told him that over the previous nine months, as the issue was heating up, I had made friends with a number of bank analysts and press. I promised him we could get our side of the story told. I will never forget it! He stared down at me and said: "OK, but if you ever get quoted in a way I don't like I will fire you!" I didn't really think he would, but I certainly got his point.

Over the next five years, I was silently part of most of the major articles on the LDC debt crisis. The best bank analysts (Tom McAndless, Dick Fredericks, Tom Brown, Nancy Bush and Mike Mayo) liked what we had done and would recommend press people talk to me for background. Analysts also liked that I was the most pessimistic person they talked to, and wanted to use support from even 'an unnamed US banker' for the criticisms they made of LDC exposure. In the early stories and articles I wasn't quoted which the press did not like. Later, I agreed to be quoted, but Morrie had to approve the language. After a bit, he told be go ahead on my own but 'be careful'.

I have to compliment the integrity of both the press and the analyst community. The former always honored what was deep background and what was quotable, giving me the right to veto phrases. The latter never revealed the source of questions I suggested they ask; at least nothing ever came back to me. Morrie Dorrance's ultimate compliment came when he agreed that I could testify at Senator Paul Sarbanes' Senate Banking Committee, along with two New York bankers, one of whom was Bill Rhodes. To the Committee I was the good guy, for a welcome change.

As noted earlier and in retrospect, I know how hard it must have been for Fred Heldring that PNB take the rebel's view we did. Fred was ultimate 'establishment', so well known and respected in Europe. Publically defending our position must have been hard for him, but he did it well. A couple of years later in, perhaps 1984 or 1985, an International Monetory Conference was held in Philadelphia at Fred's urging. I was not allowed to attend as I was too junior and, as Fred put it, would be '…too controversial'. At the luncheon, Fred was host. He had Jacques De La Rosierre, Chairman of the International Monetary Fund on one side and Bill Rhodes of Citibank on the other. A common phrase, 'free riders' had been coined by Bill and used by the press and academics to describe banks like PNB which refused to provide 'new money' as dictated by New York; we were putting in new money but at a much lower dollar amount than proscribed by their formulas. Fred was horrified when the Chairman of the IMF made the 'free rider' issue the topic of his speech. Fred also got an earful about me from Bill. Fred was not a happy camper.

From the moment of Mexico's default, Rick Emigh, Rick Clarke and I took the position our first priority was to protect the bank. At the same time, we had to protect, as much as possible, the well-established banking relationships built up in Latin America over the years. We had offices in Panama City, Bogota, São Paulo and Buenos Aires. Although

Rick Clarke had lost his Mexican relationship banker over our initial decision to withdraw, he had a stable group remaining led by two women, Harriet Cordero and Mariana Wilson. It was that team that bore the brunt of animosity of our customers and I was fortunate to have Rick as their leader. The tough decisions we made were a whole lot easier than implementing them. Rick was superb.

None of us thought anything would change in the near term; it was only going to get much worse. I attended several conferences in New York to try to get PNB's position on the crisis better understood. In early 1983, there was a presentation by a relatively unknown 'paper-hanger' who dealt with distressed debt. His name escapes me and he was not the most impressive person; he never looked you in the eye. His thesis was that LDC debt would eventually be sold in a secondary market, just like previous real estate crisis assets had.been. Speaking to him afterwards, I told him we would consider selling our $20 million Mexican bank loans if the price was right, and did he have buyers? He said no but would get back to me.

Back in Philadelphia the two Ricks and I agreed that anything over 75% would be worth it, broaching the idea to senior management. Fortuitously PNB had fully recovered from a serious over-exposure to the Real Estate Investment Trust (REIT) industry whose loans were being sold in the secondary market. The man in charge of dealing with that crisis, Ernie Smith, was a believer in the theory that the first loss is the best loss and had been selling REIT assets and writing our portfolio down aggressively. He had some hidden gains he could sell to offset the $5 million loss should we sell Mexico. Frank Dyer, Chief Credit Officer, also believed in the 'first loss' theory, as did Bob Siff. We were given the go-ahead at 75% if anything developed.

A few weeks later we had an offer, at 75%. We countered at 85%, eventually settling at 80%. When I hesitated, the broker pleaded with me, stating that in distressed debt situations brokers usually earned 3-5% but he was prepared to do this deal without commission because no LDC debt had ever been sold before, and he wanted to do the first deal for credibility purposes. Maybe. I asked him one last time to improve the price and he refused but offered me some corporate shares in a Mexican company as a sweetener. Naively, I asked what they were worth; his reply was zero, but "...they might be some day." We did the deal, at 80% and 143.000 worthless shares in a Mexican conglomerate.

It felt good, reducing our LDC debt by almost 10%, in an historic transaction. Later we would see Mexican paper drop well below 40%. At that point we felt really smart! Not so fast. A few years later, the shares of Groupo Alfa reach $2.50 and I decided to sell, making a gain of over $350,000 which meant the actual sale price of the Mexican bank paper was 82%. We were brilliant!! Not so fast. Two years later Grupo Alfa's stock was $62 per share, or almost $9 million.

Morale in the Latin America area was low. They had such a difficult job, maintaining relationships with banks to which we refused to lend money, at that point even for trade finance. They needed a new spark. When I was running Area I (Asia, Africa and the Middle East) I described our RCS product to the Area II (Latin America) team. Nothing really came from it then but now we started selling it in Argentina, Chile and Brazil.

Not only did this create a new focus for our officers but there was an ulterior motive as well. I still remembered our earlier ploy which got PNB repaid in Angola. The RCS product could produce a flow of export collections, $ flows which, in another crisis, could help repay trade finance loans to the banks sending us collections. They were not formal collateral but could behave that way in a pinch.

We set up couriers and pushed the product, especially in Brazil where the economy was still strong and growing. It was first tested with the Japanese bank branches whose parents were some of our biggest users in Asia, and whose head offices endorsed the product.

At first the local banks were reluctant but, as they saw collection times dropping for our users, began to show interest. But they would only use us if we also provided short term credit trade lines. After a lot of debate we started to lend again, mostly in Brazil but more limited in Chile and Argentina.

Our Brazilian business grew rapidly especially once we arranged for DHL to pick up export bills directly at the local banks international branch offices in the heart of the business districts. We also were successful with the largest bank in Chile, Banco de Chile. It was with them that I made one of my bigger mistakes of the crisis. We had made a clean advance loan to them before Chile defaulted which was still outstanding and being rolled over every six months. I don't remember the amount but $2 million sticks in my mind. We had asked them to convert the loan to a documented trade loan several times which they ,said they could not do because the $ had been on-lent to a corporate borrower which had not repaid it. As their collections sent to us grew I suggested they designate the proceeds collateral for the loan. They refused. So when their demand account reached the amount of the loan, I repaid our loan. They were furious and told us by telex that they would never do business with PNB again.

A mistake, in retrospect. Why did I do it? It was still early in the crisis. Bank analysts were focusing on Latin American outstandings of US banks. The issue of whether short term clean advances would be rolled into a long term loan was still unresolved. Bob Siff knew what I had done and agreed. Perhaps he never told Fred Heldring. A few years later, when much of the crisis had passed, Fred asked me accompany him on a Latin American trip to assess the damage our posture had to our relationships. I did not schedule a visit with Banco de Chile because they had closed their accounts. But Fred knew senior management at the bank and wanted to meet (or perhaps he did know what I had done?). After they told the story their way, Fred turned to me and said I should never have done it. Later he said my actions lacked integrity. The rest of the trip was chilly at best. I asked Fred if he wanted me to put the $2 million back but he did not come back to me on the question. Eventually, years later after most of their senior management had retired, Banco de Chile became a major customer again. Perhaps the name change to Corestates helped.

By late 1983, Brazil began to show positive balance of trade numbers and our RCS business with local banks was growing rapidly, While our medium term loans to Brazil (Resolution 63s) were stuck in the re-scheduling morass, our short term trade loans seemed pretty safe. These were tied to our product sales and created a flow of cash from our borrowers that gave us some security, albeit no formal agreements existed. We became increasingly comfortable with our business in Brazil, both product sales and trade finance. For several years everything was positive.

By mid-1986, Brazil had a monthly trade surplus exceeding $1 billion and reported reserves of $11 billion. Their new Cruzado stabilization plan was working so well that in 1985, Finance Minister Funaro persuaded lenders to re-schedule $4 billion of term debt without simultaneously requiring a formal IMF agreement, with its attendant discipline conditions. In retrospect this was a mistake, as the price freeze aspect of the Cruzado Plan sparked a consumer boom boosting imports and threatening traditional exports. Central Bank secrecy, however, hid the growing reality from the public, including ourselves.

By late-1987 the monthly trade surplus was less than $200 million and exchange reserves had fallen to $4 billion. Inflation was now over 20%. Brazil needed new money to continue servicing debt. Lenders, known now as the Paris Club, were reluctant without a new IMF agreement which would have been a sharp reversal for President Sarney's political posture. A stabilizing force was Central Bank Governor Fernao Bracher, who still retained foreign banker confidence.

In early February 1987, Treasury Minister Funaro fired Bracher with Sarney's blessing, a precursor to a politically popular stance directed against the foreign banks. There was a precedent. Eighteen months earlier, Peru had taken a similar position, limiting any debt repayments to 10% of exports. Foreign banks reacted quickly, isolating Peru from any international financial support. Brazil evidently decided they were too large and their debt too high for the same thing to happen to them.

On February 21, Brazil suspended interest payments on all debt, a total surprise to New York and ourselves. For a few days, we were pretty calm. Our trade finance loans and collection business seemed safe. We had recently begun lending to Banco do Brazil, a government commercial bank with by far the largest export business in the country. One of our sales arguments had been that it was safer for them to concentrate collections with PIB than New York banks with much larger loans to them.

Then Banco do Brazil informed us they would not be paying us interest on our trade finance loans. They said they were precluded by law from doing so, noting that the moratorium decrees made no differentiation between trade finance and any other loans. This put our entire strategy at risk. We suspended all new loans to Brazilian banks and I was immediately on a plane to Brazil.

It was a very tough trip. Banco do Brazil was adamant; they gave me a copy of an instruction from the Central Bank that no interest should be paid on ALL debt. Our other customers were furious at our suspension of new loans, claiming they had no such instructions from the Central Bank. How could only Banco do Brazil have that order and no other banks did?

The first Central Bank official I talked to denied any such instruction existed. The people we knew there had left along with Bracher, who I knew from discussions earlier, understood and supported the distinction with trade finance. After another meeting I showed the official what I had been given by Banco do Brazil. He left the room. Ten minutes or so later he re-entered with another gentleman, who told me that communication should never have been shown to me and I was not to show it to anyone else. I asked whether the instruction had been rescinded. He said no but that it was not official policy yet. He would not answer if it was going to be. After giving my speech on the sacrosanct nature of trade finance over all other debts, I left.

I was in a quandary. All our banking relationships were furious at our lending freeze and threatened to stop all business with us. No one else was cutting back trade. I asked an economist friend of the bank who knew Bracher well to find out what he thought about including trade finance in the moratorium but got no clarity. Before I left Brazil I shared the Central Bank communication with some key banker friends who were incredulous but not quite willing to see it as an adequate justification for our position.

We decided to hold firm until things were clarified. A few days later, we got a call from *Veja*, Brazil's *Time* magazine which wanted an interview. Thinking this would be a good way to get our position into the public eye I agreed. Big mistake. After clarifying what was *off the record*, and their agreement to run any quotes by me before publication, I made our case. They asked what the consequences of the moratorium might be and I was pretty tough in response with respect to trade finance.

No call back. The published article had nothing about trade finance, contained made up quotes and made me look like the proverbial evil foreign banker against whom Sarney was campaigning.

I don't remember exactly when we started lending again but I do remember that for the first time the credit side, including Rick Emigh and Bob Siff, did not support me when I recommended starting up again. Sarney fired Funaro in April but the final chapter wasn't written until November. Our business was damaged but in a year or so we were able to fully recover and expand. The RCS product and our New York operations team were that good.

Angola, South Africa, the Philippines, Iran and, of course, Mexico 1982 had all taught me that quick and aggressive action was the best course in a credit crisis, lessons I used as Chief Credit Officer during the 1989-1992 real estate debacle. In retrospect, however, less would have been more had I not immediately flown to Brazil when I did and seen a copy of that missive from the Central Bank to Banco do Brazil. The attempt to include trade in the moratorium was probably just a trial balloon through the only government commercial bank. Other local banks kept paying. Had I stayed put we would have had a month or so of heartburn but little else and our business would not have been hurt.

The LDC debt crisis was certainly a threat to the banking system, and even more so for individual banks. Regulators were all over the issue, but prepared to temper what could have been their response just to protect the system. Bank analysts, however, were less kind, although at the outset some had less understanding of the scope of the risk and the nature of the problem. Over the next five years I had regular contact with all of them and believe built a level of trust that served us well during the early 90s real estate crisis.

Had PNB's exposure been what it was in January 1982, we would have been treated like everyone else. Our total LDC loans would have been greater than our capital. However, having reduced our exposure by almost 70%, we were not seen as much of a risk and I thought might instead become a source of information. However, as a target of criticism from New York, I had to build credibility with analysts first. I was convinced most analysts did not understand the difference between short term trade finance assets and the term loan exposures of New York banks. I had to establish credibility and educate analysts on the differences.

Over the next few years I met with all of them explaining the differences in our portfolio, providing them questions they should ask New York banks. Gradually, many began to listen and trust me. The sale of Mexico proved to them that I at least believed it likely that future losses would exceed 20%. As the secondary market developed with other regionals selling, the prices continued to drop, adding to our credibility.

Increasingly I was invited to speak at conferences with Bill Rhodes to debate the issues. In turn, more analysts used me as a resource, as they discounted more and more of New York portfolios. Tony Furr of Wachovia was my major ally; he played the 'good cop; with New York and I played the 'bad cop' but we got our position across. The annual meetings of the Bankers Association of Foreign Trade (BAFT) were an especially useful forum. At one meeting I was invited to a luncheon with Bill Rhodes, Courtney Haight, Don McCouch of Manufacturers Hanover and Paul Volker, among others. Bill probably was hoping I would be cowed by Volker into keeping quiet. I was aggressive with Volker and asked him to change the 'new money' formula to PNB's proposal. I did understand that Volker was trying save the system, and my view was a parochial one. I knew I had got to him when he turned to Joann (wives were invited) and commented on her double chin, a dirty shot unbecoming of the man.

FIGHTING NEW YORK....AND THE FEDERAL RESERVE

At the time, I was the favored candidate of the regional banks to become BAFT president. However, the New York bankers, led by Bill Rhodes, vetoed me in favor of a more malleable regional division head, The consolation prize was to be named a BAFT Senior Fellow in 1984, along with Bob Bench, Comptroller of the Currency. I got my revenge sitting next to Bill at the Senate Banking Sub-Committee chaired by Paul Sarbanes of Maryland where I was praised and he was criticized. It felt good.

By 1986 we had made more asset sales, taking losses, and our exposure was way down. PNB's loan loss reserves were in good shape and we began to raise reserves on our remaining assets, writing down most term assets by over 40%. The analysts loved it and started to do the same with their estimates of the value of New York international loans. Although most of the bank analysts were openly supporting our posture, especially Dick Fredericks of Montgomery Securities, the dean Tom Hanley of Solomon was more circumspect about our write-downs. He suggested we might have gone too far because, in January 1987, the aggregate secondary market price for LDC assets was slightly under 74%. My point to him at the time was supply from sellers was low given that none of the big banks were in a position to sell. If they chose to do so, supply would overwhelm demand and prices would collapse. By the end of 1987, prices were down to 45 cents on the dollar.

On May 18, 1987 Citibank (Bill Rhodes' bank), and the world's largest LDC lender, made a bombshell announcement. They made a special provision for LDC debt of $3 billion, 25% of their total and wiping out the entire year's income. Over the next six weeks bank after bank did the same thing. Despite not being sufficient (they only provided enough to cover the inflated secondary market values as discussed above), it was a courageous move which met with accolades from bank analysts. I like to think that the steps PNB had taken played a role in their decision. To a small degree it probably was but the primary catalyst was Brazil's suspension of interest payments on their medium term debt.

Brazil's goal was to create a debtor's cartel.and force lenders to forgive a portion of the old debt. Brazil was actively soliciting the support of Mexico and Argentina; they already had the support of an earlier rebel, Peru. Although the big banks, supported by Treasury and the IMF, led by Citigank , had acted to squash Peru promptly, as leaders of the re-scheduling and 'new money' efforts they knew they had a problem. There is an old banking adage that if I owe you $1 million and can't pay I have a problem; If I owe you $50 million and can't pay, you have a problem. As long as the big banks did not recognize reality borrowers had increasing leverage and New York was starting to figure that out.

While a lot still had to be done, I believe the action Citibank took was the end of the Latin American debt crisis. Economic value of the assets could be set eventually and banks could act as openly as they wished. This was not lost on governments as well. Secretary of the Treasury Brady proposed a plan which called for banks to take haircuts on the principal of their debt. In July, 1989 the Robert Morris Associates commercial lending newsletter interviewed me on the Brady Plan which I called "a step in the right direction." It was one of my better interviews. Tempting as it was to point out New York was finally facing PNB's reality, I decided to take a swipe at governments instead and defend the big banks. The Brady Plan was urging the banks to take big losses without also providing a form of regulatory forbearance to ease the pain in the near term. Furthermore, I said, the biggest lenders to the LDCs were in fact the governments. Why weren't they prepared to take their own haircuts at the same time they were asking the commercial banks to do so? This made me a little more popular in New York but less so in Washington DC, although some people in the OCC quietly applauded

PNB's reputation was established as a small but successful player in International Banking. Our experience further reinforced Fred Heldring's adage of only financing trade and my penchant for pushing international processing business instead of credit. Eventually, our successor institutions, Wachovia and Wells Fargo, would become the largest international processor of banking transactions in the world, surpassing both Citibank and UBS.

Chapter 11

NEW MARKETS....NEW TACTICS

I DON'T BELIEVE I suddenly had an epiphany lead me to the goal of getting to the top. It was there from day one at PNB. I certainly did not have it at Westtown or Tufts. It started - the competitiveness - during my involvement in the 1964 political campaign, then the Army. When I joined the bank I was introduced to all the young trainees hired just before me - Peter Longstreth, Peter Burns and Mark Ledger of Area II, Howard McMorris of Area III and Bob Chase in my Area I. There were already very smart young officers in the Division, Chip Levengood and Roland Bullard, both in Area II and the International Division heir apparent, 30 year-old Bob Palmer.

I have always believed that a level of insecurity drives one to win, be the best, perhaps to prove insecurity is unjustified. In that group - most with MBAs and more business experience - I was justifiably insecure. The previous chapters reflect the drive maybe stemming from that insecurity. I was not warm and fuzzy. I wanted to win.

Becoming Division Head satisfied a ten year ambition. The Debt Crisis seemed almost intended to thwart my advance. But in the mid-80s, the

Division continued to grow. Profitability surged in Area I and recovered in Area II as product sales rose. Only in Europe were we weak, and it was Europe senior management (Siff, Heldring and Dorrance) watched.

Chip Levengood had turned our New York bank, PIB, into a very efficient operating bank for international transactions. The only product we could sell in Europe was Dollar Clearing, which we had been doing for a number of years. Clearing was the settlement of foreign exchange contracts and repayments of dollars borrowed by banks from all over the world, mostly from London but increasingly in other European cities and tax havens like Luxembourg and Nassau.

In the early days, banks might have up to a hundred transactions a day, communicating with each from where to expect to receive $ and where then to pay $, an operational mess in the days of telex communications from different time zones. Big New York banks were notoriously weak at processing them and errors were common, with corrections and overdraft charges being very expensive. Area III had had some success convincing small European banks in London to concentrate their payments at PIB, sending the one bank a list of payments we would receive each day and a similar list of payments to make. We generated deposits and income from dollars that stayed for a few days before leaving. These were the days before explicit pricing and balance reporting.

This product was the future of Area III growth and profitability. We needed volume to gain credibility in Europe. One way we could get bigger was by selling the product to all the Japanese bank branches in London, at least those who did not trust their own New York branches to do work considered menial and beneath the concern of branch managers wanting to make corporate loans. Other Asian banks were also opening in London or other cities. Area I officers starting calling in London. Volume rose rapidly and so did the attendant credit risk.

The credit risk from clearing would occur when we made payments for customers and the covering $ did not arrive. An overdraft would result. Many payments came from the big, and inefficient, New York banks. Finding and ultimately receiving those funds could take a few days. Sometimes several large payments would not come and the overdrafts could be tens of millions of dollars. Our daily payment volume was over one $billion a day so overdrafts were common and each overdraft had to be approved over the phone by either Rick Emigh or me. Bob Siff and Bob Murray, the Chief Credit Officer, did want us to sell more product , which only increased the risk. . We needed a more automated payment system to meet the 4PM Clearing House Interbank Payment System (CHIPS) deadline.

Our head of both Operations and Technology was an extremely smart Indian, EVP Bipin Shah. Most technology budget dollars was being spent in automating Operations, a clear conflict of interest in my view. In addition, Bipin was also interested in the retail business. He and Bob Palmer had pioneered a payment network they called MAC which allowed customers of one bank to use an ATM from other bank members of the network, the first of its kind in the US, a concept Palmer copied from New Zealand banks which shared use of expensive capital technology years earlier. I had been fighting Bipin for several years about automating the RCS and Large Dollar Payment (Clearing) products with zero success.. Fortunately, pressure from the credit side got the approval to automate Clearing.

Rick Emigh worked on the specs for our new clearing system, meeting with me weekly to discuss them. During one such session we made the key decision that put us ahead of many clearing banks. The programmers had specified that the system would make payments in the order that they were received, matching receipts as they arrived. Very logical. But we did some tests and realized that doing it this way we might not make a lot of small payments if sent in late. That would infuriate our customers; a very large overdraft they could understand, especially when we explained that a non-receipt put them at risk as well. Furthermore, failure to make a large number of small payments would result in a reconciliation nightmare.

We decided that the automated system should pay all the small ones first and leave the biggest to the end. This would also greatly reduce the number of calls we got to approve overdrafts, improving efficiency. When it was tested it worked very well, satisfying the credit people who gave us the OK to expand our volume. By the end of the decade, PIB was the 10th largest clearing bank in New York while only the 25th largest bank in the country. As our volume grew, so did our ability to attract larger European customers. When Area I won the clearing business of the Central Bank of the Philippines, our reputation in Asia surged; other Central Banks followed. Although LDC write-offs hurt division profitability, senior management looked past that when evaluating our performance. They understood the success we were having and rewarded us accordingly.

Meanwhile Roland Bullard was running the large corporate market and butting heads with Bob Siff. Bob saw no sense in extending large back-up lines of credit to big companies, which would only use them at the very time our bank would be in the worst position to lend. The credit side agreed. Roland was also fighting with Bipin about technology needs for the cash management business vital to Large Corporate. I don't know how Siff orchestrated it but got Roland moved to Operations, reporting to Bipin as a career enhancing move. Siff gave me the Large Corporate Division.

Although Bob Siff had a high opinion of me from my handling of the LDC debt crisis, I don't think his move of Roland was intended to clear a path for me. Rather he might have objected to Roland pushing credit products first and cash management second. Bob's fair-haired boy was

EVP Bill Fenimore, who ran Cash Management and ran it well. In retrospect, had Bob Siff become CEO, his ultimate ambition, he would probably have made Bill head of corporate banking, not me.

There was a lot of talent at PNB. The Office of the Chairman included long-time CEO Dorrance, Heldring and long-time designated-heir Dick Ravenscroft. The next tier was Bob Palmer, head of Retail, Bipin and CFO Greg Dillett. Next level was Roland, Bill Fenimore, and Charlie Connolly, protege of Bob Palmer in Retail, later EVP in charge of Regional Banking. As a new EVP, I now joined that level, although if Roland Bullard had not been reporting to Bipin he would certainly have been in the higher group. Everyone, including me, saw him as the top wholesale banker.

Shortly after becoming EVP, Fenimore approached me to argue that cash management should get all of corporate banking's technology budget, and asked for my support in exchange for a veiled hint of future career support as he advanced. His argument was that International would never be able to compete with the big banks. Bill was smart and really knew his domestic product as did his very competent deputy, Perc Moser. But he was wrong about International and I told him so.

There was one other extremely smart guy, Terry Larsen, but he was only an economist and no banker. Still, he had saved the bank when we mismanaged our asset and liability mix by funding too short (liability maturities much shorter than asset maturities) when rates rose. Banks often do that but set formulae that can forecast earnings impact accurately under differing rate movements. We had them - but they didn't work as forecasted, severely hurting earnings. Terry was called in to solve the problem which he did within a few months. Early in his review he called me in to talk about my short funding experience in Australia, thus beginning a series of impromptu meetings as we complained to each other about all the things wrong with the bank. That proved fortuitous.

One of the first concepts I learned at the bank was that of reciprocity, essentially you send me business and I send you business in return. As an international trainee i would research what business (letters of credit, collections, payments, credit extensions, etc. we sent to banks and use that information to ask them to send the same to us. Both parties tended to ignore the fact that most such business, with the exception of credit extension, was directed by the corporate customer not ourselves. Since most foreign banks concentrated their US business at the big New York banks, we were at times able to use the reciprocity argument to grow some relationships. But overall the concept of reciprocity was our enemy; the big banks had all the corporate volume to send and we were peanuts compared to them. It was only when we began to focus of the inefficiencies of New York bank operations and the high cost of correcting mistakes and soothing angry domestic clients were we able to expand market share. In International, RCS was the best example.

It was no different in domestic US banking, at least for the Large Corporate market. Most major companies used we local banks for local needs but went to New York for their big needs, especially back-up lines of credit. Fortunately, big bank processing transactions for large US companies was no more efficient for them than for foreign banks. As a result, regional banks, including ourselves, began to develop payment and collection products (cash management) to compete with New York. Rapidly rising interest rates in the the late 70s made faster collections and slower payments a premium. Bill Fenimore and Perc Moser had made some real headway with our products but many were dependent on a good Philadelphia Post Office, an iffy thing. Also, before any successful sale, there was the inevitable demand for a larger line of credit as 'reciprocity'. Our product competitors among the regional banks were also much larger than PNB, with larger credit capacity.

Those were not the only issues with which Bill Fenimore and Perc Moser had to deal. The biggest was cultural. The Large Corporate banker was the elite, not only at PNB but in all banks. Ours was made up predominately of the sons of the Philadelphia elite; Morrie Dorrance and Dick Ravenscroft came from Large Corporate. Long liquid lunches, elite conferences and entertainment was the norm between banker and customer. Ranking was based on which credit tier you were in. The biggest goal of a business call was to get past the Assistant=Treasurer or Treasurer, to the Chief Financial Officer (CFO), Chief Operating Officer (COO) or even get Morrie invited to meet the Chief Executive Officer (CEO), the holy grail. This is what I found when I took over Large Corporate; the similarity with early International was clear.

The previous year I had also been given responsibility for the domestic correspondent banking division which was a natural extension of the businesses I had run in international. It was a processing business; processing checks for smaller banks all around the region, competing with the Federal Reserve.

Before taking over Large Corporate, however, I had to make a decision as to who would now run international. The smartest and most creative officer within the division was Steve Nichols, now based in Hong Kong and beginning to sell outsourcing of international processing for other US and international banks of collections involving China trade. Steve was everything you would want, with one exception. He tended to get lots of people very angry with his intensity and drive. He had also angered Bipin Shah who ran technology. For me, working with Steve was like looking in a mirror.

Another superb manager was Michael Heavener, head of Europe. He had been our first Philippine rep and fully understood Area 1 products and our goal of growing them in Latin America now. He was intelligent, sophisticated and both a good judge and motivator of people. Everything pointed to him as the best choice. I had one hesitation.

Significant changes were happening to our business and we needed to change how we did business, and quickly. With extremely high interest rates our profitability from float created by the RCS product had been huge. But now rates had fallen. The New York banks had also started to introduce overnight balance reporting to their correspondents. That was a significant risk to us because we relied on holding deposits for several days. Balance reporting would mean funds moving much quicker, directly impacting profitability. Product pricing was no longer based on float but now based on individual transactions at mutually agreed prices. Our officers were not used to that. They had to change. Steve was tough and I knew he could force the change quickly because he would not be particularly concerned with how the officers reacted to his dictates. I chose Steve, and that was not a popular decision.

Steve got it done but in the process made more enemies. Eventually both of us realized that something had to give. Steve and wife Kathy loved Hong Kong. Steve also believed there was a huge further opportunity for insourcing in Hong Kong. I replaced Steve with Mike Heavener and Steve returned to Hong Kong, eventually building one of the best parts of our International Division, processing transactions for almost 100 US and foreign banks in Hongkong. At our peak I believe we had over 500 people doing this work. That was all Steve; all I did was make sure he had all the resources I could give him. As far as Steve was concerned, it was never enough but it was all I could do dealing with Bipin Shah.

My first moves at Large Corporate was to try to change the culture, urging our officers to call at lower levels of our customers to identify their issues and needs, and then design products to help them. The highest levels of any major company would always be focused on credit and in that area we were too small to compete effectively. On this Bill Fenimore and I were aligned. But the old culture was ingrained and resistance to change palpable. There had to be another way.

Large Corporate, like International, did have administrative assistants (AAs) but they were mostly used to arrange meetings, do correspondence, and other menial tasks. They also handled small operational issues and it was here I pushed the officers to expand the AA role. There were always small matters that our customers wanted solved and would call their relationship banker to resolve them, a low priority task in the account officers' list of things to do. But for the AA the tasks were interesting and fun, quickly becoming their highest priority. Naturally in those days all the AAs, many with the same degrees as the officers, were women. At first, the officers insisted on calling the customer with answers directly but, gradually, the AAs began to make the calls and establish good contacts among comptrollers and other mid-level management. Over time, officers would take the AAs on calls with them. Once this became routine we were able to get their job grades increased, even to junior officer level. Operations training became mandatory. To further enhance their credibility, I made it a point to stop by their desks to chat when visiting the division. Later I would hold group meetings with them to find out what our customers were thinking.

Bill Fenimore and I could have been a great team. We thought a lot alike. The problem was that he thought himself superior because he became an EVP way ahead of me, and he had Bob Siff's unconditional support. I thought my international resume and credit experience, of which he had none, made me his equal. Our first confrontation was over allocation of the wholesale technology budget which he controlled. I lost hands down. In his early days Bill made calls with Large Corporate, as did Perc Moser. Any cash management successes came from them. Over time, Bill was able to get approval to hire other 'experts' to help, some from Operations and others from outside.

Our next confrontation occurred when he wanted to hire his own sales people and bypass my officers. I fought it long and hard until a fateful meeting with Bob Siff at which, after my explaining how this approach would have ruined the successful strategy developed in Asia, he asked me one simple question: "What makes you think you could ever turn our large corporate officer corps into product sales people?" Frustrating as it was, he was right. In Area I, I had hired most of them and they were trained from scratch. Only the outside hires knew anything different. PNB's large corporate bankers were a whole different kettle of fish. I conceded, much to my people's chagrin. I was now 0-2 with Bill Fenimore.

My Large Corporate Division did not include all of the larger companies in our customer base. Shortly after he arrived, Bob Siff had taken a page out of Citibank's playbook by forming what he called a Specialized Lending Group. It was a great move. Certain industries required very specific lending skills outside the norm. The average corporate officer sitting in a geographically based structure could not expect to be proficient in all industries where industry knowledge was paramount in evaluating credit. In addition, these industries also had very specific product needs and the specialized officers were expected to understand those needs as well as credit which fit very well with Fenimore's product initiatives.

Units under Specialized included Real Estate, Transportation and Equipment, Telecommunications (primarily Cable Television), Finance Companies, and Leasing. Gradually, the best people began to migrate there instead of Large Corporate. That was where the growth was. It was headed by Ernie Smith who had worked PNB out of its Real Estate Investment Trust (REIT) debacle. Of all the positive things that Bob Siff did for the bank, this was the finest. At this time in my career, however, I did not appreciate it, seeing it as robbing me of the people I needed to get my job done. My attitude probably was the start of souring my relationship with Bob, who had been a good supporter for quite a while.

Bob's second major contribution was in revamping our credit culture and processes. I got a taste of it when he first arrived. He attended one of our International Credit committees and ridiculed our country write-ups. Most of the Division, including me, thought it was a shot across the bows against Fred Heldring and his protege Bob Palmer, who we all admired but were obvious rivals of the newly-arrived Siff. The result, however, was a completely revised analytical process of country and bank risk in the Division and a much improved product. Still, it was cumbersome and took a great deal of time to prepare each report.

Bob Siff was a protege of Citibank's credit gurus, George Moore and Henry Mueller. Citibank was the best in the industry, until two successive CEOs weakened the role. As part of his restructuring, Bob added Credit Officers to each group giving them the highest credit approval authority, some equal to the group Heads themselves. There was initial resistance, especially after he said that any credit over the certain amount required both the unit's credit officer and the Group Head. Bob diminished opposition by having the credit officers report to the group head, with a dotted line reporting to the Chief Credit Officer and not the other way around. This was genius. Previously, credit approval authority came with rank alone. Unfortunately, rank and title do not always go along with credit skill.

In fact, the most successful line officers were often great salesmen but not as strong in credit. Conversely, some of the best credit minds were not people you want often in front of customers. This system allowed each skill set to have a valued place. People who could do both equally well were few and far between. Over time, workload required the addition of more and more credit officers, especially in Specialized.

As both relationship officers and credit officers became experts in their industry, the bank's credibility among specialized customers grew so we began to play a lead role with customers in some cases, or, in the larger ones, given a major position under the New York bank's lead. One of the best examples of this was in Telecommunications. In the mid-70s we made our first loan to a John Malone cable deal; we lent Comcast's Ralph Roberts his first dollar. Once we consolidated all these credits in one unit, its Senior Credit Office Jim Brooks became an industry leader. Later he was moved to Real Estate but more on that later.

This credit structure gets described in more detail in my final chapter. Raising the stature of the credit decision makers in the bank while still embedding them within the line structure is no longer permitted today by the regulators, even though a far cry from the credit officer-less, line dominated approach of the past. Regulators view was that the line units would always dominate: therefore there should be a total separation between line and credit. In our case that was simply not true. The key was to build a credit culture, which respected both responsibilities, credit and sales. That's what CoreStates did. As long as the CEO respected that process, and as long as the board made sure the CEO did so, the system worked and was good.

By the later 80s I was becoming frustrated, We were profitable and growing, especially International, but it was slowing. Budgets were tight; more and more resources were being put into Specialized and Cash Management. Regional was growing rapidly under Bob Spencer and Charlie Connolly, a longtime rival. I was no one's mentee or favorite. I don't like to blame that on my incredible intensity and drive, but in retrospect it was certainly a factor.

With increasingly limited resources I began to look for ways to improve productivity. I had already expanded AA roles, which allowed officers to handle more accounts. I began to hire more women who were, sorry to say, cheaper than men. (Readers will have to understand that these were different times than today. Also, ask yourself whether, if salaries back then were equal, what opportunities would male bosses have given women) But the biggest opportunity for improvement was in the credit process because that was where so much of the officer's time was spent.

The Siff credit process entailed a lot of paper and a lot of detail. Country reports were usually 20+ pages, much of it basic economic information available elsewhere from a number of sources. The content from our officers only made up a small portion of the text. For countries with high political risk and questionable economic statistics I had no quarrel with what we were asked to do. I applauded it. Providing that same level of officer input for countries rated highly by Moodys and Standard and Poors, however, seemed a waste of the officers time. Furthermore, Credit required an equal amount of information on AAA-rated US companies with which we were only placing overnight Fed Funds deposits, again, in my opinion, with little value.

Time and again I railed against these requirements in loan committee headed by EVP Bob Murray, a Bob Siff favorite. Murray was chosen from the Specialized lending group where he had the reputation of handling the most difficult credit relationships in the bank, ones that required very careful analysis. I started to instruct my officers to ease off on the detail for names with AAA ratings. That did not go well, as we were often required to re-do our work by the loan committee. That required even more time than if we had just done what was expected of us in the first place. After a few months of this I finally 'lost it' in loan committee. I spoke for almost ten minutes lambasting our credit process, calling it bureaucratic and irrelevant in terms some might have called 'disrespectful'. And it probably was. A few days later I got a message from Siff's secretary to report to the boardroom on the 7th floor. I knew I was in trouble.

The boardroom had a very large round table. As I walked in, two people were sitting on one side, Bob Siff and Dick Ravenscroft, COO.

Dick, one of my long term supporters, took the lead. Bob, my boss, did not say a word the entire meeting. Dick began by admonishing me about my outburst, specifically my language and lack of control and noting the bad example I set for others in the room. He then gave a long lecture about credit discipline, and the need to adhere to our credit culture by everyone. I was silent. He then asked me to explain what my objections were which I did, forcefully. I told him that for top-rated credits and overnight lending we could be using published rating material, instead of the full-blown analysis we do for a highly-leveraged transaction or a regional credit name. I talked about bureaucracy and efficiency. Neither made any comment. Then the bombshell hit.

Dick said I was being removed from my Group. He said that since I was so opinionated on what was wrong with the credit process I would be given the chance to make improvements. I would move to Credit and become the Deputy Chief Credit Officer under Bob Murray. I would stay there for one year, after which Bob Murray would move and I would take over. I was stunned. On the one hand, I was leaving a group that I knew well and loved. On the other hand, the Chief Credit Officer (CCO) job was much higher up in the pecking order. In retrospect, I had forgotten the maxim I gave every mentee over the years, that when one is completely comfortable in a job it is time to move to one where you are totally uncomfortable. That way you again started to learn. I was being given a piece of my own medicine - in spades!

I never really knew what Bob Siff's motive for this move was. On the one hand, Bob Murray might have been frustrated with the CCO position (who wouldn't be) and might have been pressing Bob for a change. Possibly, Bob may have seen this as a positive move for my broadening experience. Then again, it may have been time for Roland Bullard to return from purgatory, most likely at Dick's insistence. Finally, he may have been removing a threat to Fenimore's advancement, giving Bill free rein over cash management strategy in Large Corporate. It was probably a bit of each, as Bullard was given all of Wholesale Banking at the same time. I was given two weeks to say goodby to my International team.

Chapter 12

CHIEF CREDIT OFFICER

THE SIMPLE FACT is that I was totally unqualified for the job of Chief Credit Officer. On the positive side, I knew country and bank risk better than any other candidates for the job. I also understood how to manage a crisis and working out a bad credit situation better than most. However, I had minimal credit experience, doing less than two years in Regional despite good training from Bob Spencer and his credit officer, Bill Sudhaus. We only approved one highly leveraged transaction in that time on which I only observed, while they did the work. I knew virtually nothing about specialized lending where most of the credit risk was, especially Cable TV and Real Estate. I was going to be a fish out of water. That was also the general consensus around the bank, especially, as I learned later, among the credit officers.

Bob Murray was a godsend. He obviously wanted out of credit and knew that unless I was able to step up, he would be extended. He taught me so much. For the first four months or so, he made sure I attended every credit meeting for approval requiring CCO signature, other than countries or banks which I took over from him immediately. CCO approvals were not based solely on $ amount; many policy exceptions, of which there were many (excessive leverage, term, industry concentration, weak covenants were just a few), had to be signed off. I also attended 'pre-approval' meetings where line officers and Group Heads would take Bob's pulse and get his suggestions. They were invaluable. For some time, I was totally silent, but followed up with Bob afterwards for his thinking. He was very patient, even forgiving.

Credit Officers reported to the Group Heads and not the CCO, which was a 'dotted line' relationship. Bob met regularly with them to test the culture. Was the drive for growth to meet plan (read 'make bonus') causing stress? Bob was a great listener which I needed to learn. The approval meetings gave me the opportunity to assess the credit officers and Bob and I shared these assessments. Bob also met with credit officers individually, at which he focused on the relationships with Group Heads and profit tensions within each group, He made sure no credit officer felt bullied by their group head or that a group head was pushing line officers too hard. When he did, we discussed his reasoning and he met with the Group Head privately, but he always explained to me what went on. That was invaluable as well.

The most important thing he taught me was that a CCO did not have to know more than anyone else about an industry or credit. He needed to know the homework was done, all key questions asked, 'what-ifs' analyzed. More leeway went to the credit officers he trusted the most.

Despite what I thought at the outset, the CCO job was management, not staff. You had to manager people who didn't report to you, manage a culture not a unit, manage behavior more than actions, manage by nuance, inference not direction, not a Chuck Coltman strength. This I learned over time by trial and error, but learn it I did.

Bob let me take on the challenge given me when first appointed. With help from Internationals's Rick Emigh, and credit officers Dottie Motz and Jim Brooks, we re-designed credit approval process for the best credits. Dottie Motz, one of three best credit minds in the bank, was skeptical at first but eventually embraced the concept and was invaluable in its creation. The other, Jim Brooks from Specialized, was helpful too but few of the credits in his realm qualified for this treatment, except for healthcare and Insurance. Nevertheless, his common sense approach was especially helpful.

We used Moody and Standard and Poor ratings and write-ups as base documents, focusing relationship managers on making comments on that analysis. Only AAA or AA ratings and the highest rated countries were permitted this approach. Everything else required a complete analysis. When either agency downgraded a name, a further review and comment was mandated. Immense time was saved.

As said earlier, the general consensus among credit officers was that I was, at best, too inexperienced for the job or, at worst, unfit. Many Relationship Officers (RMs) shared those views and voiced them openly. My reputation in the bank was being aggressive, although given good grades for handling of Latin America. Bill Sudhaus was supportive of my Regional Banking credit work but no one, including me, thought it sufficient.

Fortunately, numbers seemed to speak to me, so in many cases I was a quick study but that was not going to be enough. I had to win over the credit officers first, but also had to diminish the 'chatter' among the RMs, especially those who handled the toughest loans. Support of the two best lenders, Dottie and Jim, was crucial, which was why they were asked to redesign part of the system with me.

A brief explanation to non-bankers on the role of a bank CCO. Obviously they are the final signature of the largest credits but, more importantly they are the final authority on the toughest credits, some of which can be quite small. Banks build up extensive libraries of policies over the years and making loans that violate these policies usually required credit officer approval, many by the CCO alone. The latter included highly leverage transactions or acquisitions. In other words, the CCO had to approve deals with which I had the least experience.

I asked Dottie and Jim to alert me when a tough transaction was being considered. In such cases they would often have one or two, even three, pre-meetings before final approval, at which additional information or better structure was considered. I asked to sit in the pre-meetings, to which both reluctantly agreed, if I promised to never say a word. Later I would sit with them and go over why they asked, or did not ask, what they did, I learned a lot. The first shift I noticed was when I sensed they were were no longer using the meetings to teach me but rather to persuade. When they started to ask me questions in the pre-meetings it felt like I had arrived.

Convincing the better RMs took a bit longer. PNB gave up Loan Committees as an approval body when we moved to the Credit Officer system. That was a very good thing. Loan Committees, in my opinion, had three flaws. First, they allowed decision-making to be defused and responsibility hidden. "The Committee said 'No'" was too easy for an RM; a customer wanted to know who said no and why. Second, a Loan Committee was made up of different levels, including Group Heads who might wish to score points against a rival. Usually all heads pointed to the senior person present and started nodding. Open argument against rank was too risky for most. When attendees included two or more of the same rank things could get sticky. Finally, they were often a waste of time because the involved Group Head would have had a private meeting and made the decision, so the Loan Committee was often just a staged formality.

Committees, however, did have one very important benefit; they were a wonderful training tool. You can learn accounting in a book. You can share credit experiences in case studies or 'Learning from Lending' seminars. But you can't learn credit judgment from anything but debating the pros and cons, then watching the outcome. Murray and Siff had retained the Loan Committee for training, post establishing Credit Officers. It was a post approval review process. Committee was headed by the CCO and composed of a majority of rotating credit officers with the rest being line officers, also rotating, from all the groups. A few days before each committee, members would receive copies of the approval document to review and determine if it was necessary for the RM to attend to defend his/her work. Sometimes line officers were brought in because the decision was tough. Other times it was because the credit was fine but the work sloppy. The approving credit officer was not required to attend (but often did) unless specifically asked or when one or more committee members .thought the credit should not have been approved in the first place. Most often that happened for Specialized credits, where industry knowledge was most germane.

Bob Murray had stopped attending Loan Committee, assigning a credit officer to serve as Chair in his place. I was designated to serve as Chair going forward, giving me a perfect opportunity to both learn and eventually alter the perceptions of my ability. I made it a point to read every write-up and prepare a list of questions, ticking them off as they were asked by others. For the first couple of months I said nothing, with the exception of banks and countries. Then I began to ask credit officers on committee why they had not asked the unanswered ones on my list. Eventually, I started to ask them myself, sometimes even starting the questioning with what I thought the toughest issue. Over time, my credibility rose with both credit officers and the line. Some even said later they were glad when I was unable to attend Committee, a compliment to be sure.

The role I chose on Loan Committee took a lot of time. We had two committees each week. Homework I described in inches of paper. Six inches was a light committee, 12-15 the norm. Most I read at night, consuming 3-4 hours, and 8 hours each weekend. In the early years I justified my hours to wife and kids as necessary 'úntil I became more senior'. My absence from their lives now was not easily explained and would have consequences.

Not long after I became the Deputy CCO, the most significant re-organization of the bank in my career took place. Morrie Dorrance had been CEO for almost 20 years and was approaching retirement. Years before he had set up an Office of the Chairman, made up of himself, Vice-Chairman Fred Heldring and President Dick Ravenscroft, his designated successor and my mentor. While Dick was extremely smart and capable, he had little direct responsibilities in his role, spending much time in his office instead of taking a direct management role. His customer contact was limited as well. Tension between Morrie and Dick had risen, perhaps in part because of the obvious talent in the next level. Bob Siff had made it known that he might be a better candidate as well. But all of this was pretty well hidden from the rest of us until the blockbuster announcement.

In May 1986 we woke up to a bombshell. Dick Ravenscroft was leaving the bank. Morrie Dorrance would retire in eighteen months. In the meantime four executives were named as potential successors. Bob Siff was not one of them and he left shortly thereafter. The four named as possible heirs included three very macho males, Bipin Shah head of Operations and Technology, Roland Bullard who would run the Wholesale Bank, and Greg Dillett chief financial officer (all of whom were named Vice Chairmen of the holding company). The fourth was a big surprise. Terry Larsen, the economist who now headed asset and liability management, was named Chief Operating Officer of the new holding company.

Another surprise was that Bob Palmer, Head of retail and Fred Heldring 's protégé was not included. Many had thought for some time that Palmer might be in the running. That ended with this announcement. Although ostensibly Terry Larson's position was the most senior of the four no one really thought that meant anything and he was handicapped by most observers as being in fourth place.

For me, this was not a positive development. I had been fighting with Bipin for quite a while and while Roland certainly respected my abilities I was not sure he had ever really forgiven me for my decision not to join him years before. Greg Dillett and I had a mutual disrespect. On the positive side, my relationship with Terry Larsen, who I thought the least likely candidate, was good. We often spoke about things that were wrong at the bank and discussed better options for the bank's direction many times. I think Terry should have been as surprised as anyone about his elevation. Office location is often a visible indicator of power. Terry was not asked to take Dick Ravenscroft's office in the former office of the chairman location which was a further indicator to me that he wasn't the chosen one. It was only very recently that I learned Terry had been told the job was his to lose.

At that point, and with further moves during the year, it was apparent that the new holding company was now where all of the real power was. The visuals did not look particularly good for me. By the end of the year, Corestates Financial Corp had one COO (Larsen), six Vice Chairman (including Heldring as PNB's CEO) and the senior executives of our two acquisitions Hamilton Bank and New Jersey National Bank. Significantly, Bill Fenimore was made CEO of Hamilton Bank, a move designed to give him direct banking experience. Also, there were 14 EVP's in the holding company, one of which was Bob Murray. There were only four at the bank level, of which I was one, now the Chief lending officer of PNB. The only possible interpretation was that I had dropped significantly in the overall power structure and was not seen as a future top leader at that point.

Fortunately, now being on the credit side, I was not in the middle of the fray. The credit side continued to report to Siff until he left, and then directly to Morrie. My sources at the wholesale bank reported that Roland was being quite cautious, perhaps because of his past conflicts with Bipin and Greg. I didn't hear much about how Bipin and Greg behaved within their own groups. Terry acted in a low-key manner. Both Bob Murray and I kept our heads down.

There was still 18 months to go before Morrie would retire. A lot could happen. I had so much still to learn about credit and I dug into it, probably with a bit too much intensity. The many one-on-ones I used to have with Terry diminished after his elevation for obvious reasons. He was a lot busier and I was reluctant to take his time without clear reasons. Several times he asked me about the credit process and I know he had similar discussions with Bob Murray. I also noticed he had more interactions with Greg Dillett which made sense and Bipin Shah which did not.

Later that fall, Terry asked me join him and Greg in a meeting. It proved not to be a good one. Greg spent most of the time asking me questions, mostly hostile and even insulting. In retrospect I suspect Terry wanted Greg to share Terry's positive opinion of me, and knew Greg did not like me, hoping the meeting would resolve our differences. It did not work and left a bad taste in all mouths.

When Terry took over the funding of the bank a few years before, he had observed that while Corestates was active taking deposits in the London Eurodollar market from banks, often the deposits came through brokers instead of directly, at a slightly higher cost. Why so, he asked, when we had so many close correspondent banks all over

Europe? I told him I did not know that side of the business but surmised that it was probably a combination of our size (small), location (non-money center like New York, Chicago and LA) and the fact that our relationships were transactional and not based on credit.

I don't remember if it was Terry's or my idea but we decided to pursue a five year stand-by line of credit from banks out of London. Terry had another motive too. He spent years in Texas and friends there told him about the impact dropping oil prices had on local bank loan portfolios; some corporations even questioned whether they should take their money out of banks, not something someone responsible for funding the bank wanted to hear. He asked me to put it together.

There were conflicting goals. On the one hand, the facility was going to cost us money and an objective was to have the lowest possible interest rate. The lowest rate also meant we were a strong credit, something we wanted the world to see. My other objective was to make sure that the banks in the credit were the absolutely finest in the world. Their presence would say to the market, "CoreStates is a quality institution". The lead bank was key. Greg wanted a top US bank to lead because of his domestic background, and he knew some of the top bank CFOs in New York. However, I was able to convince Terry that if we needed to get European banks to place Eurodollars directly with us, it should be European-led, specifically by Union Bank of Switzerland (UBS).

UBS was known as the most conservative bank in the world at the time. They were an established lead bank for European companies but had not yet done much in the US as lead. They also had never led a consortium for a bank. All discussions took place at UBS's offices in New York. I asked them to tell me why Corestates should have a UBS-led syndicate rather than Chase or Citibank and why doing so would not eliminate Credit Suisse joining the facility which was also important to us. Their answers helped get them in a marketing mode.

My last requirement was that we had to have final say on which banks would be allowed to join. This was the toughest 'ask' but UBS's head office eventually agreed.

I can't remember the final number but we did increase the credit size based on strong demand. Credit Suisse came in as one of two second tier lenders along with, I believe, Chase or JP Morgan. I had given UBS a list of the world's best banks in credit quality to approach first, and most participated. I only vetoed two banks which UBS wanted in, probably for their own reciprocity reasons, but which I thought might weaken the syndicate. The ultimate result, post credit, was that Corestates became an established Eurodollar borrower as we had hoped.

I accompanied Terry and Greg to London for the signing, which was followed by the traditional lunch. I thought lunch was a disaster. Greg seemed to take the lead role I had expected Terry to assume. Greg only spoke with the US bankers present during cocktails. UBS sat at the head of the table as expected but Greg assumed the seat at the other end reserved for Corestates. UBS formally thanked us. Perhaps it was my fault for not briefing them ahead of time but instead of the expected brief acknowledgement Greg proceeded to talk for close to ten minutes about how Corestates was so much better than other US banks. He morphed into a CFO talking to bank stock analysts. His arrogance was embarrassing. What a contrast to how Morrie Dorrance and Fred Heldring would speak to world bankers at our International Monetary Fund dinners in Washington DC!

Terry believed that the changing attitudes at the Federal Reserve gave commercial banks the opportunity to enter investment banking in the future. He was certainly right about that, but his interest in joining competitors setting up UK investment banks in London did not excite. London costs were prohibitive in my view, and most such entities were extending huge credits to companies, few of which would offer us the collateral transaction business which was the basis of our Large Corporate and International strategy. Most such borrowers were not even our customers, which made less sense to me. Terry and Greg spent a week in London, after which an ex-Citibanker Jim Hildebrand came to visit to meet various executives.

Shortly after the visit, Terry asked me to come to his office. . He wanted my opinion of Jim and also on the idea to create a *de novo* investment bank in London led by Hildebrand. I knew he wanted my honest opinion but also my support for a venture he was committed to do. Looking back, I believe this moment was a crucial one in what eventually became an enduring relationship between the two of us. I told Terry Jim was born and bred a Citibanker and would have unrealistic expectations of what the much smaller Corestates could do for him. Furthermore, the potential customer base was not ours and the expense base would never allow an acceptable return. Terry was not happy and it was some time before we spoke again. Nevertheless, I believe this meeting established the principle that I would tell him what I thought even if it was something he did not want to hear. I think we owned Philadelphia National Limited about two and a half years before shutting it down.

I mention the above two experiences because they were the only two I had with the four candidates from May 1986 until the final selection late in 1987, aside from a couple of credit meetings with Roland. Greg Dillett certainly acted like he would be the chosen one and nothing I had seen negated this view. Knowing I could never work for him my focus turned to learning as much as possible about the credit side of banking to fill out my resume.

Even before I took the credit job, the country was experiencing severe problems from what later became known as the savings and loan crisis. It's origination went back many years and I attributed it to a logical political decision made to equalize the interest-rate yield opportunities for the average consumer compared to the much higher rates that institutions and wealthy individuals were able to receive on their deposits.

Savings and loans were set up years before to make mortgage loans, which they did at rates slightly higher than the regulated fixed deposit rates given the average consumer. However, during the high interest rates of the late 1970s, market rates rose into the mid teens while the average consumer continued to receive rates around 5 or 6%. This was unfair and Congress (Bernie Franks) resolved to eliminate it. First, they eliminated the interest rate cap on small deposits. This was problematic, of course, because most of the assets in the savings and loans were at fixed rates. Rising rates put their portfolios under water. This had to be fixed. Savings and Loans had to be given an alternative way of making money. Congress did so by permitting savings and loans to make consumer and commercial loans.

This seemed like a good idea at the time and actually worked for a few years. However, with the federal government guaranteeing all deposits via deposit insurance, there was no restraint on savings and loan gathering new deposits. Many of them grew rapidly and invested their deposits in very risky but highly lucrative commercial real estate loans.

Over the years I have given a number of talks on the Savings and Loan crisis. The main point I make is making loans at 80% of value at a small spread over a fixed cost of funds doesn't take a genius. In fact, that doesn't take much skill at all. However, when all of a sudden, the local Savings and Loan is faced with losses caused by rising rates funding a fixed rate loan portfolio, and they now have the opportunity to invest in real estate development projects, that is a huge temptation. And real estate development is a whole lot different than what they had been doing. Deposit insurance also meant that there were no restraints on their ability to acquire deposits and make more and more risky loans based on projections not worth the paper they were written on. In turn, that naturally led to more opportunities for fraud.

Although Corestates had no exposure to the industry itself, we were exposed to big commercial banks all over the country, many of which, in order to compete with the savings and loans, began to make their own equally risky loans. This first signs began to surface in a serious way in Texas. The Federal Reserve and OCC were slow to act but, once they began, proceeded to put incredible pressure on the Texas banks which concerned me.

In retrospect, by 1987 the economy was in a period of froth. At the time it was less obvious but there were many major acquisitions of companies using debt with very little equity. We were making these loans also, although our officers would suggest our credit policy was still relatively tight. The Federal Reserve and OCC issued new regulations governing highly leveraged transactions (HLTs). Approving HLTs at PNB now became a credit policy exception, which took the approval process up to Bob Murray and me. Fortunately, we had some incredible credit officers like Dottie Motz, Bill Sudhaus and Jim Brooks who formulated excellent analytical tools to evaluate these credits. My knowledge was limited here and I spent much time to fully understand the risks.

While I knew all of the regional bank international division heads and regularly shared information and opinion with them, I had no such contacts among senior credit officers from those institutions. Bob Murray was kind enough to let me attend the Credit Roundtables for the industry. These were held in some nice places, including the Breakers in Palm Beach. I had the opportunity to meet some pretty talented people and learn from them. I knew absolutely nothing about retail credit and absorbed as much as possible from several sessions on the topic. But the one topic I remember most vividly was a discussion about the Texas real estate crisis and how the Federal Reserve and the OCC were aggressively pressuring the Texas banks. I had also heard some rumors about the Bank of New England's heavy concentration in New England real estate and elsewhere around the country. I made it a point to get to know their top credit man, who was both friendly and open.

A few months after that credit roundtable, news articles appeared suggesting many of the OCC bank examiners who had been in Texas were being moved to New England. I decided to spend a day in Boston with the major banks in that city. I visited five banks arranging my final visit to be Bank of New England. My appointment was at 4 PM, but when I went to the chief credit officer's office, his secretary told me that unfortunately he had been called up to the chairman's office to discuss a new real estate deal that the chairman was negotiating. Really! The chairman of the bank actually negotiating a credit transaction? This was a fundamental breach of good credit policy CoreStates had been following for years. From that moment we decided not to continue business with that bank. More ominously, all of the banks confirmed that the OCC was all over New England real estate portfolios.

The American bankers Association (ABA) also held annual meetings in very nice locations. Generally, for most of us, they were boondoggles, although when I was first made responsible for domestic correspondent banking they were quite useful. In the fall of 1987, the ABA meeting was held in Texas and I decided to attend, with wife Joann, given my concern about what was happening around Texas real estate and the banking system there. It was in Dallas where the Texas state fair was being held simultaneously.

We left Philadelphia late Friday afternoon. The stock market had taken quite a tumble that day but nothing really seemed out of the ordinary. There were some nice events over the weekend and I was even invited for the Monday night football game between Dallas and Washington which was exciting even if it was during the NFL players strike and both teams were using replacement players.

On Monday we went out to the Texas state fair. In early afternoon I was walking by a booth and heard a news report that the Dow was down over 200 points. That was a huge move down at that time, almost 10%. What was happening? I found a payphone and called the office. No one knew very much so it didn't sound like something that I needed to be concerned about. An hour later the market was down over 300 and, quite frankly, I panicked. I got on one of the buses to take me back to the hotel so I could call (pre-cellphone days) more easily from my hotel room. That took about 40 minutes. I turned on the television as soon as I walked in the room and saw that the market had closed down more than 500 points, over 22%. I packed my bags and immediately left for the airport. After checking in for my newly arranged flight, it suddenly occurred to me that I had forgotten something. Where was Joann? In my panic mode I had completely forgotten about her. She did forgive me but it took a few days.

I walked onto the trading floor around 7 AM on Tuesday morning. There were already quite a few people there. The European markets had essentially been frozen from the start of trading that day. It seems the world was waiting for the US to act. Although the equity markets have no direct impact on the bank, a crisis like this hurt cash liquidity on which the bank was fully dependent. And when I arrived on the floor, nothing was moving. Nothing. No buyers!

Terry Larsen was obviously the man in charge. He was very calm and was directing people to focus on specific things. One can tell in these situations when leadership is trusted and when it is not. In this case, Terry Larsen was trusted. He was waiting to see if the Fed would act to provide liquidity into the market. Exxon and IBM were two of the most liquid stocks in the market at the time. At a little after 11AM, some trades of them came over the ticker for the first time that morning. Terry was convinced that the Fed was behind these purchases even if they didn't do them directly. His confidence rose, as did all of ours. This was the point when I began to believe that Terry Larsen would be our leader going forward. There were others on the trading floor who shared that opinion but certainly it was still not widely held around the bank. But it wasn't long afterward that Morrie Dorrance named Terry as his successor and retired at the end of the year.

Consolidation of the banking system had been going on for some time. Many of us in the bank were worried that CoreStates was falling behind, in part because of archaic state banking rules in Pennsylvania. Nevertheless, our two recent acquisitions of Hamilton Bank and New Jersey National Bank had started us on the acquisition path. The benefits of consolidation are most apparent when two large banks with overlapping branch banking systems merge. A major player in Philadelphia was the First Pennsylvania Bank, certainly our largest historic competitor.

First Pennsylvania was vulnerable. Over the previous decade, they had aggressively pursued a strategy of trying to overtake CoreStates as the largest bank in the city. One way they chose to do that was to bulk up on long-term investment securities and fund them with shorter term liabilities which yielded a very nice spread but exposed them to interest rate risk. When rates rose, they started to bleed. In response, they started to lend much more aggressively and we later discovered that loan opportunities Corestates turned down, especially in real estate, were subsequently made by First Pennsylvania. A lot of our new business in the regional market was coming from First Pennsylvania, making them even more vulnerable.

Nevertheless, most of us were a bit surprised when we heard the announcements that they had agreed to be acquired by Marine Midland.

That company had recently been acquired by the Hong Kong Shanghai Banking Group (HSBC). Not only were they a New York bank, but the international power and presence of HSBC would have caused some real competitive issues for us, especially in International, even though no one else I talked to had that concern. A key point in the announced deal, however, was that there was no large break-up fee as often seen in deals like that. This suggested First Pennsylvania wanted to entice other bidders. Perhaps it was because the HSBC bid was for cash, which would be a taxable transaction for the First Pennsylvania shareholders. And they soon came knocking…..but not on our door.

One of the most aggressive acquirers in eastern Pennsylvania over the previous five years was Meridian Bancorp, the successor institution of American Bank and Trust of Reading, Pennsylvania. With the purchase of some defunct S&Ls from the FDIC in the early 80s, and subsequent purchase of Central Penn of Philadelphia and then First National of Allentown, Meridian had grown to almost 6,000,000,000 in assets. Never a shrinking violet, its CEO, Sam McCullough, decided to try to bite off a target much bigger than he was. It made good sense for Sam. If he didn't and we did, or even if Marine Midland was successful, his path to future growth was shut off.

For CoreStates, First Pennsylvania was a wounded giant, vulnerable to our active solicitation especially in the middle market. The news that Meridian Bancorp had acquired the right to purchase the bank from Marine Midland was not welcome news to us. First Pennsylvania was the the only institution which we might acquire that would allow massive synergies. With Meridian's purchase, that opportunity would be lost forever. The powers that be were rightly concerned. Although I was not included or aware of it, due diligence began shortly after the information became public.

Bob Murray was put in charge of evaluating the credit risk of the acquisition, should we decide to proceed. Bob briefed me early and I was given total authority to evaluate and value First Pennsylvania's International portfolio, a simple task. I was also given their real estate to evaluate, quite a compliment from Bob. Although Ernie Smith, EVP was in charge of all specialized lending and his background was in real estate, it was Dennis Courtright, SVP and Jim Brooks, senior credit officer, who helped me review the portfolio. Their support was invaluable, as real estate was no strength of mine.

Everyone knew we had to do this deal. If we did not buy First Pennsylvania we would eventually be bought ourselves. No one wanted that. The key question was what the price would be, and what we would estimate the total losses on their portfolio might be when everyone also knew there was a coming recession. I had already been talking to Terry about what we were seeing happening in New England so real estate was especially important.

I have to admit that I went into the due diligence with the mindset that we had to do the transaction. In the beginning, I leaned toward a more optimistic assessment of possible losses. Thankfully, both Jim and Dennis pushed against that tendency. While we compromised often, I also began to move more toward their position. The reason was that both of them were very familiar with the loans they were looking at. Why? They had already turned most of them down.

A good example was a group called Linpro. Linpro was a national real estate development company that started in Philadelphia. PNB was one of its original lenders. We knew it well. As they grew, they became too big for us and we gradually became a bit player. Ernie Smith had an arrangement with them that we would see their easiest credits, from which Ernie could pick and choose. He had emphasized to them that CoreStates wanted to lend only in geographic areas we knew well. In my view, this was one of Ernie's better contributions to the bank. He had chosen well and we were quite comfortable with our Linpro portfolio. However, most of the transactions that we turned down from them were done by First Pennsylvania.

When Dennis, Jim and I submitted our final estimates of possible losses, I was still uneasy, realizing that I had pushed both of them to agree to some more optimistic assessments than they were comfortable with initially. To compensate, I did something that later turned out to be a lifesaver during the worst of the '89 to '93 real estate crisis. CoreStates has been selling our International Portfolio for some time, and I really believe we knew the market as well as anyone. Distressed sale prices are always the worst, but as a bank's loan loss reserve strengthens, the need for those sales diminishes. I saw signs of that happening. We already had an unrealized gain on our written-down LDC assets of about 25 million dollars, which I thought would rise in the next year.

When I submitted the mark to market on First Pennsylvania's international loans my number left another potential $25 million of future gain. Terry Larsen was the only person who noticed. He asked me if my haircut wasn't a bit rich. I said, "Maybe a little". He let it slide, perhaps knowing that Meridian would have absolutely no idea what the market was and would probably take a worst-case scenario, whereas mine had built in some optimism. In any event, a couple of years later those gains gave us the flexibility to avoid a second special loan loss provision, which would have severely damaged our credibility with bank analysts.

The merger was announced on September 18, 1989. It was valued at $730 million, ostensibly well below the offer by Meridian bank, which on that day would have been 813 million. The difference between the two bids was that Corestates was willing to commit to a dollar value, whereas Meridian's based theirs on a specific number of shares. Therefore, if the Meridian share price dropped on the day of closing, their purchase price would also drop. Our price was fixed.

Because Meridian had purchased several banks more recently than Corestates, their share price drop was likely to happen. Furthermore a recession looked inevitable. First Pennsylvania made the right decision. Meridian was now blocked to the east. Bank analysts liked the deal; after all, dilution was less than 7% and the acquisition would contribute to earnings by late 1991. Of course, all of this assumed that our estimate on losses in the First Pennsylvania loan portfolio were projected correctly. One negative that I do not believe we considered was that, without First Pennsylvania from which to take relationships as we had been doing, our regional banking growth would suffer by comparison to previous years.

During the negotiations and in the early days after the merger, Terry Larsen, Bipin Shah and Greg Dillett spent a great deal of time together. They were obvious reasons: Bipin had to consolidate two quite different processing platforms and Greg had to do the initial financial analysis, as well as monitoring its progress. Greg had been quite critical of my estimate on losses in real estate, and although Terry never said a negative word to me, we hadn't spent much time together recently. Shortly after the merger, Bob Murray moved out of his position of CCO and I took over the role formally.

About six months after the deal was announced and shortly after its close, a situation developed that Terry did talk to me about, specifically about credit. Shortly after the merger, we put First Pennsylvania's larger loans in the 'review' bucket for loan committee as a way to better understand the First Pennsylvania loan portfolio, and also to evaluate each newly acquired lending officer. The largest commitment facilities were put on a quicker review process. One such credit was The Money Store, First Pennsylvania's largest and most profitable relationship.

The Money Store was a high risk consumer lending company operating throughout the country. What banks would not do, they would.

CHIEF CREDIT OFFICER 169

They did not have a funding base, so they sold their loans into the secondary market. Although the reader knows this is extremely common today, at that time they were quite unique. During the review meetings, what I and others did not understand was how the company committed to take back bad assets from the portfolios they had already sold safely. Were there any limits to what had to be taken back? If a loan was taken back, how was that loan then valued? One of our best young commercial bankers, Dan Aboyan, was starting to look at the securitization business. He and both retail credit and commercial credit people were asked to spend the next two weeks evaluating every part of the company's processes and report back with a recommendation.

Once we received the report, which actually did not have a group recommendation, I called for a meeting of everyone in the Green room on PNB's seventh floor. My memory is that there were about 15 people. The head of First Pennsylvania's commercial lending gave an impassioned plea to retain the business. But no one could really explain the buybacks the Money Store had offered to buyers of their loans.

They would sell a group of consumer loans and agree to buy back those that had defaulted. Initially, they offered one time buybacks, but more recently were offering unlimited buybacks. Most assets that they bought back this way were re-written to bring the borrower current, at least for the moment, and then resubmitted into portfolios sold for a second time. Since those loans had already in default once, they would probably have to buy them back again but not for 90 or 180 days. In other words, it was like kicking the can down the road, the 'can' being a bad asset. Unsaleable loans like this were called "tails" and carried at face value on the balance sheet. Nothing had been written down. That total was a multiple of existing capital.

The meeting lasted almost 2 hours. At the end of it, I asked whether anyone could estimate what the actual value of the "tails" was. No one raised their hand. I don't remember if I made the decision at that moment or a couple of days later, but the bankers were eventually instructed to end our relationship with The Money Store. Since we were eliminating a pretty large income source from the acquisition, something not considered during due diligence, Terry Larson asked to speak to me about the decision.

This was a critical moment for me. I also think it was also a critical moment for the bank itself. Terry was a new CEO who did not have the 18 years experience of working with the credit process Morrie Dorrance had. In fact, he was not even a banker, but an economist. No matter how good a credit culture might be, every CEO can destroy it in six months, if he decides to do his own thing. Why? Only his board has the authority to stop him or her, and only the Fed or OCC could force the board to do so. Terry asked lots of questions. His tone was measured. He thanked me for the meeting and I never heard anything else from him about it. This was the point I decided Terry deserved my complete respect.

The best specialized lenders were more than bankers. Over time they became consultants to their customers because they understood the industry as well as the individual company . From our specialized lenders we began to learn of the coming recession, and it's probable depth. All across the bank, with the possible exception of our credit card solicitations, the credit officers began to tighten up. Terry Larsen with his economist background understood the environment better than most and made no objections.

We weren't alone. Other banks were doing the same and it was starting to have an impact on the overall economy. Banks are easy targets , easy to blame by politicians. Someone had to take responsibility for the coming recession; the banks were chosen. The Wall Street Journal did a front page story in March, 1990 called "credit crunch". Our public relations people asked me to take a phone call from the writer, David

Wessel. I did so but knew I had to take a delicate balance between being a cautious lender to keep the regulators happy but also somewhat reluctantly cautious, to keep our customers satisfied we weren't overreacting to the pressure.

Wessell's key theme was that the credit crunch was really being caused by the regulators' pressure on the banks. I remember the interview pretty well. At least three times Wessex tried to get me to support his opinion. I'm sure he tried the same thing with all the banks, but no one else agreed to be quoted. So he was left with me as the one banker to comment in the article. What I said was, "…the industry has to be careful that by tightening our standards we don't create the very problem that we are trying to avoid. I think we are in danger of that". I thought that was a nicely worded statement because it actually never really said anything. But the comment also made clear every bank was being pressured by the regulators.

The news out of New England was not good. The OCC was all over the banks, requiring massive write downs on the real estate portfolios. Most bankers in the Bankers Credit Roundtable felt it was being overdone, myself included. The Bank of Boston was the best bank in New England. We had a very long and close relationship with them, and I knew their international people very well from the old days. I asked if they would share with us their experience in real estate with the OCC, starting from the very first days and bringing us current to today. They agreed.

Dennis Courtright, our head of real estate, Jim Brooks, senior credit officer of real estate and in my opinion the best lender in the bank, and I spent an entire day at Bank of Boston. It was held in one of their conference rooms, starting at 9 AM. We left at 4 PM. They shared absolutely everything. There were at least 20 people in and out of that room, from some small towns around Boston and from the real estate group at headquarters. I fully expected them to be furious at the OCC. They acknowledged that at the outset, they were. However, they now believed that the OCC was correct which was quite a surprise to the three of us. In all my years of banking, I have never seen such incredible cooperation from a competitor. I wish I remember the name of that chief credit officer, but I don't.

As we left the conference room, the three of us said nothing to each other while we waited for the elevator. When the elevator came, we got in quietly. About 2/3 of the way down, I think it was Dennis who said "…those poor bastards. Thank God that will never happen to us!". Jim and I nodded. I set up a meeting with the three of us the next morning. We brainstormed everything we had heard, using that invaluable tool, the flip chart. Once everything was up on paper we sequenced by date of occurrence with the earliest warning signs listed first, followed by the later ones. The final list contained three full pages on the flip chart, which stayed in my office for months.

The three of us would met regularly, but it was probably three or four months later that we revisited the list in depth. We all agreed that at least the first few items were now being seen in our own markets. A few others further down were as well. Our conclusion: it was now happening to us. We had been wrong. We decided to go into crisis mode. Dennis and Jim briefed Ernie Smith who, having worked out the real estate investment trust crisis, understood. I briefed Terry Larsen.

Some real estate lending was still being done in the branches and in the middle market. Bank of Boston had warned us about that, because the regulators in Boston had found underwriting away from headquarters much weaker. We ended that. Every one of our real estate customers was visited and given our assessment of what was coming. We told them we would continue to finance the commitments we had made but there would be no more. Essentially, we asked them to shut their operations down. Some agreed and some did not. Those that did, we committed to support through the crisis. We knew that it would eventually end, and they needed to carry their top people through it. This was especially true for the small homebuilders, many of which were in New Jersey.

We had stopped lending for commercial buildings in Center City Philadelphia a couple of years before, when Ernie Smith began to be concerned. Elsewhere we had continued to some degree; that was now shut down for new ventures. Ernie used his good relationship with Linpro to ask them to take us out of some of our credits. As I recall, we were early enough that they could find someone else to lend but that only was possible for a couple of deals. All in all, we were in lockdown.

It was pretty obvious, if we were experiencing this, so were the other banks. And if the other banks were, the OCC would not be far behind. Jim Brooks took charge of an assessment of our entire portfolio with Dennis and his people, using the criteria that the OCC had imposed on Bank of Boston. The results were not pretty. Using OCC criteria, our nonperforming loans and write-offs would jump dramatically. Our loan loss reserve was going to be deficient. Terry Larsen had to know.

I went over the numbers again and again. I knew we would have to make a special provision, but I thought it would be less harmful to our stock price if it was not an excessive one. The larger the special provision, the more concerned bank analysts would be about our overall portfolio because, by acting now we would be the first bank outside of New England and Texas to address the problem. We still had some flexibility in the international portfolio but it would not be sufficient for the losses we were looking at in real estate.

I asked to meet with Terry. He asked George Butler, former CEO of First Pennsylvania and now chairman of Corestates, to join us. I was glad, and a bit surprised, he did not ask Greg Dillett, CFO as well. I went over everything from the beginning, from the Bank of Boston meetings to what we saw happening in our own markets, and then our assessment based on what we assumed would be coming from the OCC. I told him that we needed a special provision of $140 million in the fourth quarter of 1990. It was now September. I did not want to do it for the third quarter because I needed time to make bank analysts more comfortable with the idea that we would be acting ourselves and not under OCC direction. They would have a hard time believing we made such a provision without being forced to do so.

I think Terry would have been satisfied with that number, as was I, but George Butler, to his credit, was not. He said in his experience things always ended up worse than originally expected. He pressed me hard, and I had to acknowledge that in a number of cases while evaluating the portfolio, I had taken the optimistic choice, not a pessimistic one. With his advice, not only did we increase the fourth quarter special provision to $180 million, but we also chose to write down more of the LDC portfolio well below current secondary market prices. This would allow us to increase our gains on sale of these assets in later years to offset more real estate write downs, if necessary. We already had a cushion and this made it bigger. They were needed, and we used those gains to avoid a second special provision later, much to the delight of bank analysts.

Our fourth quarter 1990 loan loss provisioning and write offs alarmed both our regulators, each for a different reason. The Federal Reserve did not like the huge write down of the LDC debt portfolio because it put significant pressure on the biggest banks in the United States. The OCC, on the other hand, was alarmed at the special $180 million provision caused by our assessment of our real estate portfolios. They were not used to a bank taking preemptive action. They were used to being the one that forced a bank to act. We were the first to act ahead of them. Therefore, the regulators who arrived at Corestates in early 1991 from New England had the pre-conceived view our real estate problems must be much worse than anyone else's.

Their attitude and arrogance made me very angry. Fortunately, Jim Brooks handled most of the interaction with them. He was more calm and ultimately his credibility won the day. The key to value in real estate of investment property was the "cap rate". The higher the cap rate, the lower the value. When we went through our portfolio to arrive at the amount of special provision we needed, we used high cap rates, consistent with what the OCC had been using in New England. Even though the OCC saw what we had done, they required us to redo some of these at even higher rates. It was very frustrating and after that examination, we ended up writing off more than we needed to in some instances. Nevertheless, they did leave having a healthier respect for our process. Bank analysts had also been waiting to see what would happen. When we were not required to take additional reserves, their respect for our process rose.

I don't think the average CoreStates banker really understood the extent to which bank analysts impact the bank and our actions. Some analysts are good and, of course, some are not. There is a herd instinct among them and some tend to overreact, especially if numbers do not match the arbitrary forecast that they made in the first place. All of this was something I experienced with the LDC debt crisis, an experience which certainly helped navigate the real estate crisis. Fortunately, we had some of the best covering our bank.

As Chief Credit Officer, every analyst wanted to speak with me after they spoke with Terry Larsen. In some cases they spoke with me without speaking to him. My approach was to give them everything they asked for, and more. All the bad news came out immediately. I even began to forecast some possible future non-performers. If I could give them a few months forward negative projections, they were happy. In the early months, and even into the first full year, they tended to penalize us since other banks were not as forthcoming as we were . Terry was fine with that because he no longer worried about our stock price, knowing that there would be few if no acquisitions taking place at that point. I took the same approach with the board which, I believe, gave them some confidence we were on top of the issues. Periodically I would call our primary OCC regulator contact and gave them similar reports. In the beginning, they were quite skeptical of what I was telling them, but over time began to have some faith in our forecasting ability.

I remember one specific incident midway through the crisis.. Our transportation and equipment group begin to be concerned about one credit that was not on our non-performer list, not even on our watch list. As I recall, it was over $25 million, which would have been a pretty big jolt to our quarterly numbers. I called up a bunch of our bank analysts and warned them about what might be coming. At the end of the quarter, I gave my regular reporting on non-performers which did not go up at all, and some of them asked me about that particular credit. I told them things had turned for the better. After that, I noticed a distinct change in their attitude, which became much more favorable and there were fewer and fewer questions about our problem credits from then on.

About this time I also started to sell our remaining LDC portfolio which had significant gains, using the proceeds to write down our real estate loans even more. While our gross charge off numbers were quite high as a result, the net number was still low as a result of the offsetting gains. Our past history of aggressively writing down LDC debt in the past satisfied both analysts and regulators. In this real estate crisis, however, one problem I did have with regulators was they thought I was being too aggressive in our write- offs and asked me to justify the numbers which, with the help of Jim Brooks' creative analysis, I was able to do.

In hindsight, it is obvious I had underestimated how bad the recession would be. Each quarter, it was a very delicate balance between what Loan Review wanted to do and what I could do safely as far as the analysts were concerned. I remember one night thinking that maybe our $180 million special charge wouldn't quite be enough. Fortunately, a couple of credits went off non-performing at that point and we were able to ride through without taking a second special charge to the loan loss reserve.

Another lesson learned from the LDC Crisis helped in this situation. By acting aggressively early, we were able to start lending again in Latin America ahead of many other banks. We did the same here, especially with medium-sized home builders which had done what we asked early in the crisis. Many of them grew rapidly over the next years and stayed with us even when other banks again started sniffing around.

At the height of the real estate crisis, we were approached by Al Lerner to acquire Maryland National Bank. Although Terry had an aversion to expanding toward the south, he did not consider Maryland as truly southern and decided he wanted to look at the opportunity. Although both of us knew they had significant real estate loan problems they also were one of the early adopters of affinity credit cards, which was particularly attractive. We took the train down to Baltimore and met with Lerner in a hotel room. I wanted to talk about his real estate portfolio. He did not. When we next started asking questions about the credit card business Al informed us that that would not be part of the deal. He intended to spin that operation off and become chairman and CEO of the new entity. That killed the deal for us. In the end, Al Lerner's creation became the highly successful MBNA, and Maryland National itself was purchased by Nations Bank in 1993.

In the fall of 1990, I had a very interesting confrontation with Terry on a credit issue. It was actually the first and last I ever had. The city of Philadelphia was in deep financial trouble. The state legislature had lost faith in Mayor Wilson Goode and Moodys had downgraded its debt. Racial overtones were fierce. The city was unable to meet payroll. Terry had organized the other Philadelphia banks to provide a temporary cash infusion and wanted to talk to me about how to get this done. I told him he couldn't. What he was proposing broke too many credit policies and I was not prepared to approve them. He told me he had to do it anyway because it was in the city's, hence the bank's, best interest. We agreed that if he wrote the appropriate memos and signed the appropriate tickets any action of his, as CEO, would get done. He asked me what the consequences would be and I said as chief credit officer it was my responsibility to report to the board any violations of credit process and principles by the CEO. So that is what I did. As I was presenting this to the board, Terry was quite calm. Fortunately, someone asked me the appropriate question, namely what would I have done had I been CEO in Terry's place? My answer was simple: The exact same thing! The board approved Terry's action after the fact and Philadelphia eventually repaid the loan.

I bring up this example because, as will be discussed in more detail in the final chapter, this is an example of a proper credit process, the role of the CEO and the role of the board ensuring the CEO does the right thing. Unfortunately in subsequent years banking regulators were unwilling to impose these requirements on Boards of Directors.

Chief Credit Officer was not the hardest job I ever had. It was not the most emotionally challenging. It was not the most painful. It was not the most draining. But if you put all of those into one, then chief credit officer was the worst of that combination. It caused the most damage to my health, my emotional well-being and certainly the worst impact on my family.

Chapter 13

CULTURE CHANGE

I PLACE THE start of Corestates' culture change as December 18, 1990. That was the day Terry Larsen made his annual Christmas address to the officers. There were earlier hints at the change but few of us, including me, read the tea leaves properly. The 1990 advertising theme was a different one - *People are at the Core of Corestates.* Many of us thought it was a pretty corny theme, and virtually none of us thought it had any application to us personally.

Even after Terry's address very few of the officers appreciated its significance. I know I didn't. I was just angry at Terry for not including International among the core businesses that he described later in his talk. I kept a copy of his speech. It is one I have read quite a few times over the years. Each time I do, I realize Terry Larsen was a man before his time. The goals he envisioned then have come to pass across much of American business. In retrospect, he was too early and I believe it ultimately hurt his career.

A third of his way through the speech, Terry described what he thought that phrase meant to him. He said it meant a sense of family, people caring about each other, being supportive and respectful with mutual trust. It meant teamwork and team spirit.

One short paragraph stands out: **In the Corestates I envision everyone will be treated with respect and courtesy and caring — whether they work at one of our banks or at the holding company, man or woman, black or white, whether staff or line — everyone will be well treated.**

He went on to describe more of what he meant, each time ending with the catchphrase, "We Will Do It Because It Is Right". He then said: **The Corestates I envision is not the CoreStates you and I see every day when we arrive at work.** That comment stood out on its own with a pause before it was made, and a pause afterwards. There was no further explanation but it made some of us think.

Bob Murray had left the credit side to me a few months earlier, reporting to Terry in an undefined position. During the speech Terry named him head of the Peoples Task Force, reporting to him. He also spent time praising the new head of human resources, Les Butler, who had previously run first Pennsylvania's branch network.

There was one other interesting vignette in that speech which became significant five years later. Terry was talking about potential acquisitions in the future. Again, he brought up culture, saying culture should have a major part of any acquisition strategy in the future. The example he gave was particularly interesting in retrospect. Specifically he said, New England is a natural area for future expansion of the bank. Culturally, he commented, their customers and employees are very much like ourselves. Contrasting that, he noted that it would be extremely unlikely if Corestates would ever expand to the south.

So what was it like working at Corestates in 1990? Certainly many of us thought ourselves successful as we looked at the numbers. But it wasn't a fun and happy place. Internal competition was fierce, within each unit and between each unit. There were wide divisions between wholesale and retail, with the former absolutely certain, with some justification, they were far superior. All line units felt vastly superior to back office staff. And it showed. Behavior to people from different units was the opposite of what Terry sought — respectful, supportive and appreciative.

Women had made great strides within the international division in position, but not yet in pay levels. The branch system and human resources also had some senior women but virtually nowhere else in the bank. This was especially true in finance and operations, areas led by Vice-Chairmen Shah and Dillett. African Americans had made little progress, at least in the wholesale side of the bank that I knew. Bob Murray had his work cut out for him.

After Terry's speech and the holidays were over, we started back into a new fiscal year with nothing changed. Few of us thought about what Terry had said and there was nothing that really came out of the Peoples Task Force in the early days. It was business as usual.

So what was CoreStates's culture at this point. Aggressiveness and toughness was rewarded. Winning was everything. That was how I was raised, and felt comfortable with it. In hindsight, it was a male dominated culture, although at the time that just seemed normal. As noted earlier, with the exception of International, few women and no African-Americans were in positions of authority. Although we were hiring many young talented women into the training program, the good male trainees were most sought after in each wholesale group. Women congregated into the product sales side but were rarely accepted in the credit businesses. Again, this observation is all in hindsight

In technology and in the operations groups, it was completely white male-dominated. The same was true in finance. People were not treated particularly well in those groups. Some even suggested there was an oppressive culture where people were often yelled at and publicly embarrassed when things went wrong.

I did not have much contact with Terry during most of that year. I was completely focused on the credit process and how to minimize risk in the bank and deal with critical analysts. I do remember, however, in October Terry broached an unusual topic in one of our routine credit discussions. Terry asked me what I felt had changed, if anything, in both Finance and Operations. I told him that while I had no direct knowledge, my impression was that nothing much had changed. I asked him why he asked me that but he changed the subject.

In early December, he asked me the same thing and then went on to talk about Bipin Shah and Greg Dillett. He said that he had named both of them his top two lieutenants the year before with the understanding they would take his comments on behavior to heart. He then said he intended to fire both of them. He was not asking my opinion; he was simply telling me his intention but it was obvious he at least wanted a reaction. I made no objection which, as he knew, was my indication to him that I understood his reasoning and would support it. After appointing both just a year earlier, it was a courageous move that would have repercussions both inside and outside the bank. I left that meeting in shock wondering what role Bob Murray had played in the decision.

At the end of the year, Terry fired Bipin and Greg. The bank population, and I imagine the board as well, were in shock. No single act could have meant more to make everyone realize Terry was serious about his culture change. Terry had made made behavior change a condition for Bipin and Greg's designations and when they were fired the oppressive environment in Operations and Finance was still present.

In March 1991, Terry announced that Rosemarie Greco, a top officer of Fidelity Bank Corp. and CEO of its major operating subsidiary, would leave them to join Corestates. Senior managers moving from one Philadelphia bank to another rarely happened, although when Frank Reed was made head of wholesale after the First Pennsylvania acquisition Roland Bullard left for Fidelity. Perhaps that was why Rosemarie came to us. In this case, however, I believe it was Terry who wanted to bring a senior woman into the corporation to further send his broad message of diversity. Greco had risen at Fidelity from the absolute bottom and was highly regarded in the business and political communities. For a bank like CoreStates, however, with a surplus of talented senior managers, there were some who questioned the move, especially in the wholesale side of the bank. From what I heard, the retail side had the opposite reaction and were delighted. Later that year, she was named a Director of our major subsidiary, CoreStates bank NA while I was named Director of the much smaller New Jersey National Bank subsidiary.

I don't remember exactly when the Peoples Task Force .announced its diversity initiative. Yvette Hyatter-Adams, an African-American, was hired to lead the initiative, reporting jointly to Terry and Bob Murray. It's primary focus was to be women and people of color, primarily African-Americans. Initially, diversity was focused on making sure managers considered women and African-American in both promotions and position decisions. I don't recall much resistance; the idea was incorporated in regular processes fairly easily. What was less successful, however, were the actual numbers of women and African-Americans who were being promoted and put in positions of authority. Yvette attributed this to long established prejudices and norms of white male managers. Unless those at the top changed, she said, nothing would really change, despite best intentions.

At the time, I did not consider myself part of the problem. After all,

I had grown up in an environment where I was someone discriminated against, a white man among the brown people of Thailand. I had been active in the civil rights movement. I had been a leader in the International Division advancing women into positions of authority. I had helped African-American wholesale trainees get better mentoring. How could this initiative in any way impact me?

Over the next three years there were several 3 day off-sites with senior management and selected teams of women and people of color. The training started out with general teachings about how both groups felt marginalized in a white male dominated culture. Some of it was pure theory, mostly rejected by the senior white males in the room. However, there were many stories told by women and people of color of their personal experiences at Corestates. These had an impact, but most of us tended to assume it was about other people and 'not me'. Each new offsite, however, increased the learning. Eventually about half of the senior white males realized that this was a serious problem and needed to be addressed.

A few years into the program, the four white males at the top were given a small team of advisers to help us understand better. My team was made up of junior-level officers: one white woman and two African-Americans, one female and one male. They were well chosen by Yvette. I had connected with each of them in previous off-sites and they were comfortable telling me exactly what they thought. Some of it I really didn't want to hear. I am especially thankful to each of them, one in particular. They made me a better person.

One of the core principles which Yvette taught in these session was about dominants and subordinates . In virtually every setting, there are dominants and subordinates, and in those settings there is dominant behavior and subordinate behavior. Unless dominants take the initiative to ask, they will never fully hear and listen to what subordinates feel or believe. It was with these teachings that I began to realize I was part of the problem.

Yvette made us tell stories of times when we were in a subordinate position. In my case, it began on the streets of Bangkok as a kid but also when I attended a Jewish service, and another time when I met with an African-American church group. She made me describe how I felt and how I acted. When I began to describe my feelings and behavior I recognized I was describing the subordinate behavior previously taught. The lesson sunk in.

But it wasn't until 1996 when I saw the movie, *A Time to Kill*, that I could truly say I now understood. Late in the movie there is a scene where Matthew McConaughey and Samuel L Jackson are speaking in prison. McConaughey tells Jackson they are friends. Jackson tells McConaughey that he is no friend, no matter his intent and his helping but is really one of "them". I had always thought of myself only as an individual, and a relatively open-minded one at that. I think then I really understood that to women and people of color, I will always be a white male first and an individual second. Furthermore, the higher I rose in the organization, even to other white males I was dominant first, and an individual second. That was a hard lesson.

Terry Larsen never received credit for focusing on the importance of diversity in 1991. No other bank had done anything of the kind. It was a courageous act which I believe cost him credibility with his board and with his peers. CoreStates had a good board but most of them were also white males, with the same prejudices and behaviors Terry was trying to eliminate in the bank. None of the opposition was in the open but it was there.

In the early 1990s, Terry was included as a slightly junior member of an elite group of regional bank CEOs: John McCoy of Bank One, Tom

O'Brien of PNC and Terry Murray of Fleet. The group golfed together often. All were very strong personalities and powers within the banking industry. I don't know what any of them might have said to Terry about the diversity initiative, but several of their subordinates made some pretty disparaging comments to me about it during the Bankers Roundtable meetings I attended.

Many bank analysts also didn't know what to make of it all. They certainly didn't give him any credit, and some criticized what they termed a waste of focus and resources. Female analysts were more circumspect, but I don't recall any single one of them praising the effort. One analyst in particular, Nancy Bush of Dean Witter, was highly critical of it in a meeting I had with her. That surprised me. I thought she was the strongest and smartest of the bunch and would have expected neutrality at the very least. Nancy spent her early years with Butcher and Singer in Philadelphia and my personal opinion is that she had maintained close relationships with some of the people who Terry had either supplanted or replaced. She never liked Terry. A couple of years later, in 1995, Nancy successfully killed the potential merger of equals between Bank of Boston and Corestates. In retrospect, that could have been the perfect deal for the bank, and especially our employees.

In 2022, when this is being written, I believe our nation is going through much of what CoreStates did in the early 1990s. There is just as much resistance to the teachings but, while quiet and mostly hidden today, the opposition appears in thousands of Facebook pages every single day. The political implications are alarming but in retrospect it is probably something that has to take place.

Since this book is being written mostly for my descendants, I'm going to share an opinion that is probably not particularly popular today. I do recognize that change tends to occur with a pendulum effect, often going too far before swinging back to a level everyone can accept. Today

I think that particular pendulum has gone too far. One of the new tenants of diversity trainers is that people of color can never be racist themselves because they are the victims of racism. That is ridiculous. Racism and prejudice exists in every group. I have witnessed and experienced racism towards me by African-Americans and other groups.

A game we played over three days at one of our later diversity off-sites illustrates this point. The game involved handing out colored circles to each participant. There were three or four levels and each level had its own color. The most circles were in the lowest level and the fewest circles, the purple ones, at the top. The exercise was for each level to try to move higher and become purples. Most of the white male participants were placed at the lower level with more women and people of color in the higher levels so we white males had a chance to know what it feels like to be at the bottom. I don't remember all the details of how one moved up or fell back but I do remember that the single white male purple circle was quickly shoved out. One clear lesson was that those who started at the bottom tended to stay at the bottom. If you were able to break through the obvious glass ceilings, that was usually done at the expense of someone else.

What I remember most vividly is, at the end of the game, Yvette made the observation that the people in the top group, the purple circles, which at that point were mostly women and people of color, were behaving no differently than how white males behaved at senior levels in Corestates. My impression was that this surprised her a little. Those in power pick people like themselves and seek to stay in power, whether they be white, black, brown. Racism and dominant behavior exists in every single group. Unfortunately, it is a human condition.

Terry Larsen and I became increasingly close while I was chief credit officer. When I was given that job, one of the requests I made was that my office be right next to his, as a symbol of the importance of the credit role to the management of the bank. I had read an article of how, at Citibank, the legendary George Smith was right outside the CEO's office. Over the years, his and successors' locations were moved away and even onto a lower floor. Does that partly explain the deterioration of Citibank's credit culture?

Our relationship wasn't always perfect. Sometimes when Terry wanted me to do something, and I resisted, there was less access. But it never lasted long. One example was when loan demand was particularly weak, Terry suggested that we substantially increase exposure to the better quality companies we banked even though it would exceed our concentration limits. He well understood the negative impact on our ROA but felt the marginal increase in earnings was worth it. On that I'm sure he was right. However, concentration limits should not be violated. Again, as I said, these periods never lasted long and our relationship was close.

Our regular meetings each week were scheduled for an hour but sometimes went over as conversations ranged over a wide group of topics outside of credit. He expected me to know what was going on all over the bank. Sometimes the discussion was about people and often about strategy. Terry had two broad concerns we talked about. First was the bank's tendency to carry weak performers. We simply did not fire people. We tended to move them on to some other department. The other issue was our very high expense ratio which was a partial result of his first concern, but also a consequence of duplicate processes and excessive layers of management. Over the next two years this was a discussion repeated often.

In late 1993, when the economic recovery was well underway, Terry told me it was time for me to look around for my successor as chief credit policy officer. Despite my tendency to whine about the job, I liked its prestige. I wasn't sure I really wanted to leave but Terry was insistent. He had a project for me.

I was never really sure whether his primary motive was the project, or whether he thought it was time to get me out of the credit job, possibly fearing that my experiences of crisis management might not be the right mindset at a time that demanded aggressive growth in commercial lending. There had been other times where Terry believed I had been too conservative and this might be another. I never knew.

There had been broad resistance a couple of years earlier when I had taken lending authority away from group heads, giving it to the senior credit officers who reported to them. No one was more resistant than that of my old rival, Charlie Connolly. After all, Charlie was an outstanding commercial lender and he knew it, even if he was also one of the most aggressive lenders we had. I decided to designate him as my successor and Terry agreed.

If Terry had expected Charlie to oversee a looser credit policy and process, he was disappointed. Culture is often a misused word, and credit culture is not really understood by many bankers, certainly not by bank regulators. CoreStates and PNB had an outstanding credit culture. When explaining it to bank analysts , I used to say that they could interview any of our officers with at least five years experience and ask them the same questions. They would get the same answers.

Everyone understood what our credit culture was. Charlie was a very aggressive lender, often pushing the envelope. I remember about a month after he took over one of my former direct reports told me the general consensus was that Charlie was tougher than I was. Culture!! Charlie knew his role as a lender. He knew his role as chief credit officer. He did both supremely well. As soon as he went back on the line I knew he would revert to the aggressive lender he was. That's culture.

In the 1990s, both the Federal Reserve and the OCC forced many changes on banks' credit process. Their assumption was that to avoid credit losses a bank had to totally separate line and credit responsibilities, in so doing making the assumption that the line could never be trusted to ultimately make the right credit decision. Line are salesman and credit are policeman, they reasoned , and separation of those functions totally was their solution to reduce excessive risk in bank loan portfolios. So that is exactly what they did.

The credit culture we built at CoreStates and PNB forced both line and credit staff to work together. Although the ultimate credit authority did remain with the credit officers, those individuals also reported to line managers not to the chief credit policy officer or chief lending officer. Credit officers were a part of and helped build each line unit's financial plan. Credit officers met with customers regularly, and at times that familiarity gave them the confidence to stick with a customer in hard times rather than take the easy way out of withdrawal and or liquidation. I do understand that there are some bankers who really only should be salespeople and others who should only look at numbers but if both work together well they fulfill corporate customers needs, which is what a banker should be doing. That's what we built at CoreStates/PNB and that's what Charlie Connolly exemplified when he took over the task.

I think both Federal Reserve and OCC regulator policy was shortsighted and wrong. I also believe it has negative consequences and has brought with it a diminished role of banks in funding commercial risk within the economy, a role now assumed by venture capitalists and private lenders. Theirs was certainly a simple solution, easy to implement. Far harder it would have been to help build the kind of credit culture Corestates/PNB had where loan loss numbers would stand close to the top in any peer review covering 1985 to 1999. There will be more to say about this in the final chapter.

CULTURE CHANGE

The fashion industry is not the only place were styles come and go. Corporations can also fall victim to spending resources on the latest trendy idea. Most are only long lasting and bring value if they are incorporated naturally into day-to-day routine. Empowerment fits this category. So does, in my opinion Diversity. Reengineering evolved from a massive event to a routine ongoing expense management process.

Others rise momentarily and then disappear into the outbox. The One Minute Manager comes to mind. So too does TQM (Total Quality Management), when applied across an entire corporate structure instead of in specific departments that would benefit most from specific applications, like manufacturing, operations, and systems. But I learned that too late.

My next assignment was to implement TQM throughout Corestates. In late 1982, Terry sent many senior managers to visit corporate customers, which had a reputation for quality customer service and giving customers what they wanted. In his 1992 Christmas address, he spoke of the importance of focusing on the customer first rather than ourselves, giving them what they want not what we think they want. These are certainly valuable points and his ideas eventually morphed into my TQM project.

I was given an isolated office and one vice president to help. It reminded me of the 22nd floor after I left Area I of the International Division in 1979. Using readings from several writers on TQM, the two of us came up with some basic principles which we shared throughout the bank. The only one that was really taken up was the one that was most important to Terry. We started using agendas and time limits for meetings, locking meeting doors when people were late.

One of the core principles of TQM was that errors resulted in re-work which resulted in higher costs. We tried to explain that across the corporation but got little support in operations and systems where it would do most good. Another principle was that instead of the 20% planning and 80% doing that most organizations did time spent should be the reverse. Again, that got little support. Although Terry's annual Christmas speech and subsequent publication emphasized quality, there was little understanding in the company. The one aspect that did have some traction was putting the customers first and meeting their needs rather than our own. All in all, I was really not successful in the effort. Looking back I realize I was just too passive, too reluctant to demand adherence.

Partly as a result of the acquisition of First Pennsylvania a few years earlier, the management structure at Corestates at this point was extremely unwieldy. There was a 13 person office of the chairman in which all decisions were concentrated but, as one of the best bank analysts, Tom McCandless of Paine Webber said later, obtaining a consensus from 13 people made for a very slow decision making.process. In my judgment, Terry also did not have equal levels of confidence in all members of that group.

In early August 1994 things changed. Evidently Terry had not lost confidence in me from my failures in the quality initiative because he named me President and Chief Operating Officer (COO) of the corporation responsible for all the support functions including human resources and finance. Simultaneously, he named Rosemarie Greco chief executive officer of the lead bank, responsible for every activity, including commercial lending. Bob Palmer had previously announced his intention to retire at the end of the year. Frank Reed, formally of First Pennsylvania Bank and head of wholesale also announced his subsequent retirement. The office of the chairman shrunk to five, Terry, Rosemarie, Charlie Connolly as chief credit officer, Bob Gilmore as head of operations and systems, and me.

Although in the 1994 annual report I was listed second behind Terry, he had made it quite clear to me that it was his intention to name Rosemarie Greco as his successor, which would have made her the first woman CEO of a major bank in the country. I wonder if he also told her that at the same time he told it to me? If so, it is hard to explain some things that happened later.

I can't say I was very well suited for this new position or that I did it particularly well. Terry had strong opinions about human resources and finance, so he tended to dominate actions within those groups. I felt a little powerless in the role. In one area, however, I was actively involved in every discussion CoreStates had with potential acquisitions and even banks that might acquire us. Over the next five years, there were conversations with PNC, Mellon, Bank of Boston, Meridian and First Union. The sequencing of the early discussions is a bit fuzzy now but will describe them as I think they took place.

There are routine dynamics that take place during merger negotiations between banks of similar size. These were: What name survives? Who is the CEO? Where is the corporate headquarters? What is the composition of the new board of directors? There is really nothing true about the phrase "merger of equals ". Someone is going to win and the other is going to lose. The closest thing there is involves one of the two CEOs becoming the new CEO for a year or so, followed by the other then taking over permanently. I never saw a merger structure like that that did not have the second CEO's board members form the majority in the new company. That was to ensure that no one could reverse the original agreement.

It might have been early 1994 but before I had been named COO Terry called me into his office. He said he had been approached by Tom O'Brien, CEO of PNC Financial Corporation. O'Brien had proposed a merger of equals, with him retaining the CEO position for a couple of years and then relinquishing that post to Terry. Headquarters would be in Pittsburgh. The new board of directors would have a majority of PNC members. What did I think of it? He told me to go away and come back the next day with an opinion, but if that opinion was a negative one, what should CoreStates' longer-term strategy be in that case?

This was probably the point where I realized Terry knew I would keep my mouth shut. It also suggested that he thought I would give an honest opinion. I don't know why but I kept the handwritten notes I made at the time. At the top, three words, "PNC or not?" There are three columns at the top; pluses, minuses and ?'s. That is followed by notes on my opinion of the industry direction and what CoreStates' longer-term corporate strategy should be, including M&A strategy. Finally, I posed four questions to Terry, noting at the end that I would support him whatever he decides and work for the best deal for Corestates after the merger, especially for our people. My last sentence was "This commitment only has a limited life". I quote it now only because it ultimately became our agreement, post First Union acquisition of Corestates.

On the plus side: (Our) future course is clear
                         Culture closer than most
                         Shareholders get much premium
                         Terry apparent # 2
                         Wholesale dominates combined company

On the minus side: City (Philadelphia) will lose badly
                         Employees will sense failure
                         Culture direction lost
                         OOC (Office of the Chairman) 'sellout' image
                         No future options open

????????   Is Terry really # 2?
                         Do we (you) trust O'Brien?

What move is next?

Do we still have time?

Do we (you) have the management team to hold out and grow?

CLC Opinion: Do not trust Tom O'Brien!! - Society (was) offered same deal

He and (Jim) Rohr too close - are wholesale bankers who will never give it up to us

    Culture piece real shallow

    Premium still available in future

    Will disrupt our (wholesale) momentum for 3-5 yrs

    Management team never trusted again

    4th largest city needs bank headquarters

    Culture initiative will be lost

    Still have room to grow, cut costs

    "Need" to merge unclear for now

    Concerned (about) PNC earnings momentum

    Will continue to acquire and dissipate CoreStates role

    Your vision of industry future not shared by O'Brien

On the industry direction I believed whoever controls information technology will dominate their market. Consolidation would continue, but questioned the cost of acquiring retail customers. Wholesale business would bring faster profitability and growth. Banks would be buyers, but so would investment banks and insurance companies. Foreign banks, which exited with the credit crisis, would return, at least until the next one which might come as early as three years from now. CoreStates should focus on insourcing and outsourcing, national asset-based lending and transaction processing. My prejudices were showing.

In general, I opposed any bank acquisition strategy other than dominating our own region, mentioning Meridian by name. Processing companies and asset based lenders, however, should be targets. I did think we should start to identify good potential acquirers, defined as very strong retail banks without much wholesale strength like Banc One or Norwest. We should also identify possible foreign 'White Knights'.

I ended with four questions for Terry:
> Do you have the team you want to do what you want done? If yes, tell them. If not, change them, and don't worry about (bank) analysts.
> Are you prepared to start telling us the direction you intend to go and for us to decide whether we wish to come along?
> Do you trust O'Brien?
> Are you getting frustrated that others don't understand your vision?

I think it is obvious from the tone that I was against this merger. I was not a great fan of Tom O'Brien; smart he was but he was also, in my opinion, an arrogant macho male who would never fit with the culture Terry was trying to build. My real problem, however, was with Jim Rohr, Tom's right hand man.

As international division head, I attended the BAFT convention in Boca Raton each year. I had establish good relationships with most of the regional bank International Division heads, including PNC's. Unfortunately I can't remember his name. He said his boss, Jim Rohr, wanted to meet me. I assumed he wanted to question me about our strategy, but instead Rohr took the whole half hour to talk about his international vision, investing in minority holdings in some European banks. I remember he was most excited about an investment he was going to make in an Italian bank. Afterwards, the international head told me he was hoping I would be able to talk Jim out of doing it. I laughed, and told him, " You got to tell me these things first, not last". A few years later I was told about PNC taking a huge loss in an Italian bank.

My friend, who died shortly thereafter, took the fall. It was none of his doing. My primary concern was that Jim and Tom were extremely close, of similar background, and I could not conceive that O'Brien would sacrifice Rohr for any deal

Terry never shared his reasoning with me but he decided not to proceed. Today some old CoreStates employees might wonder whether that was a mistake. After all, PNC survives and we did not. In my opinion, it was not a mistake and PNC's subsequent survival was for the wrong reasons. Concerned about PNC earnings momentum from the beginning, I was not particularly surprised when that showed up fairly soon after our discussions ended. PNC's response was to attempt to build a specialized lending group. That was a little late, and they were left taking some pretty high spread and high risk credits, especially in the telecommunication industry. A few years later that started to cost them. With nonperforming loans rising rapidly, O'Brien and Rohr then made a horrible mistake. They moved $762 million of bad assets off their balance sheet and into a special purpose subsidiary designed to hide them from both investors and regulators. The technique was totally outside accounting rules and they were caught. In early 2002 they were forced to restate 2001 earnings and were put under regulator monitoring which limited much of what they could do.

As a result, PNC did not participate in many of the excesses that hurt so many banks, ending with 2008. They were not permitted to do much of anything by the regulators. By 2008, their portfolio was much improved and they were not only able to avoid major write offs that hurt so many others but their stock price was substantially better than many competitors. They were able to make acquisitions when others could not. By then, Jim Rohr was CEO and he eventually salvaged his reputation. Perhaps this would not have happened had the acquisition taken place in 1994 if, post acquisition, they turned over all the wholesale business to CoreStates people to run. But I have real doubts that would have happened.

Of course I was very happy at being named a Co-President with Rosemarie Greco. I would have much preferred to have her role running the banking businesses than the support functions. But the roles made sense. Rosemarie needed exposure to the wholesale side of the business and that left me with the staff units. I had often advised others that once they knew a business well to move to something totally different. Terry was giving me some of my own medicine. Rosemarie was priority one as his designated successor. That may not have been part of the announcement but I was told I was number three.

Not too long after I became COO Terry informed me that he and I would be meeting with Frank Cahaoet of Mellon Bank and his number two. Apparently one of our directors was close to Frank and indicated that Mellon might be willing to be bought by us. I don't know who the Director was but it might have been Ray Smith, CEO of Bell Atlantic.

The four of us met in a small hotel room near Philadelphia International Airport. We talked for about an hour and a half but it never really went anywhere. Something seemed off. Terry and I were approaching it as if we were buying them. My impression was that Frank thought he would be buying us. That was also Terry's evaluation of the discussion so we put it down as a waste of a couple of hours. Unfortunately, that was not the last time we had to deal with Frank Cahouet and Mellon Bank. They were the people who forced us to sell.

At one of our meeting in the summer of 1994, Terry asked me how much money we might be able to save were we to initiate an expense control campaign. I remember responding quickly that $50 million

CULTURE CHANGE

would be a piece of cake. He asked me to think about it some more, doing what research I could. There wasn't much to go on but I was given access to profit center reports. At our next meeting, I suggested $75 million. He did not argue the number but made reference to an article he had read about a major re-engineering at a bank in the Midwest.

I took his comment as a suggestion that I research re-engineerings. A few months earlier, a new book by Paul Allen called *Re-engineering the Bank* was published which formed the basis of my research. Allen knew banks and he had done it successfully. We brought him in for three days after providing him with what he needed to evaluate Corestates. At our final discussion he gave us his conclusion; he could take out close to 20% of expenses and increase revenues as much as 10%. He said his process would take six months, and agreed when we said that it would be highly disruptive to our day-to-day operations.

Terry's decision to proceed was not an easy one and he struggled with it for some time. On the one hand, bank earnings were good, as was ROA. On the other hand, our expense ratio was high and bank analysts were all over us about that. What finally convinced Terry was a more strategic issue. Despite our high earnings, our stock price earnings ratio was weaker than many other banks, and stock price was the currency of acquisitions. Without a higher stock price we would be forced to pay too much to acquire other banks large enough to benefit from economies of scale we would need to survive. Yes, we were able and did acquire smaller banks but none of the bigger ones. First Pennsylvania cost us a lot and anything else of size needed a higher stock price. Terry decided to go ahead and asked me to lead the effort.

Strategically, it was the right thing to do and it was successful. In retrospect, we did not anticipate our campaign would be seen by many in the bank as counter to the culture we were trying to instill. I don't know if we ever really recovered from that impact. As part of the program, we offered a very lucrative early retirement package. Again successful, it also resulted in losing some key individuals we did not want to go. There was also a cumulative effect of loss of corporate memory, which was problematic in subsequent years. Again, in retrospect, we should probably have taken the time to explain in more detail why we were doing what we were doing, and also why our actions were not inconsistent with the concept that people were the core of Corestates.

Paul Allen's process for re-engineering was a detailed and complex one. It involved taking out top people from all around the bank from their regular jobs to work full-time on the reengineering. He asked for 26 people, and insisted they be SVP's for the most part. Getting managers to give up these individuals was not easy. Most complied under pressure but a couple tried to give up weaker individuals, most of whom were rejected by me with Terry's support. The 26 were to serve on 13 teams evaluating 13 separate segments of the bank. One rule which disconcerted many was no one could serve on a team evaluating an area of the bank in which they worked or had worked in the past. Paul's opinion was that by evaluating groups with which they were not familiar there would be fewer personal prejudices and as a result more open minds. Nevertheless, as the program wore on, teams began to talk to each other about their home groups. In the end, I think the initial rule was a good one. Paul had about six people serving as advisers to the teams. His best people were put on operations and systems.

Over the years I had become an aficionado of the Myers-Briggs personality types. Myers-Briggs break personalities into 16 different groups but the two broad categories were NTs & SJs. NTs were intuitive thinkers, out-of-the-box types. SJs were sensing and judgemental, needing to see something to believe it and then, once seen, strong in their beliefs. SJs were organized and disciplined people. In other words, the two types were polar opposites. Paul Allen agreed with me that putting one of each on a team would give the widest range of thinking through the process, if they didn't kill each other first! I only had to replace one of the teams because they were not able to get along with each other, failing to respect what the other brought to the table. And it certainly took a while to get there for everyone else. What made it work was the mutual respect they developed, having recognized that the bank considered their partners top people.

The first phase of the project required everyone in the bank to come up with ideas for saving money or eliminating positions. It was hard and generated a lot of opposition. Many employees saw it strictly as a way for the bank to eliminate people. Paul's team had their own list of "ideas" which they gradually introduced to each of my teams. Many of them were excellent ones, but some were quite radical and hostility quickly developed between his people and mine. My role was a referee but generally I had to support Allen, because without those ideas the project would flounder. My popularity within the bank diminished as a result. I had always thought of the toughest job I could ever have was the chief credit officer role but now there was a competitor!

As an idea was approved by each team, it would be sent to me before being placed in the "idea book". I remember one early one vividly; it was so simple and so obvious it gave me confidence in what we were doing. About 10 years before, a human error which had never happened before on the retail side caused a write off of $500,000. A team was established to come up with a solution to avoid any such loss in the future. They did. The new process cost about $200,000 each year. The process was still in place 10 years later and we had not had a single similar situation. Over 10 years we had spent $2 million to prevent a $500,000 write off that had never happened before and probably would never happen again.

Paul Allen's central theme was to flatten the organizational chart, increasing the span of control of each remaining manager. That would mean many current managers would have to leave. Paul Allen was right about this and there were two primary reasons for it. The first was a result of our own internal job evaluation system. Salaries, promotion and title were never easy to get at CoreStates. In order to justify either of these, one had to become a "manager". As a result, senior managers seeking to retain their best people justified managerial roles and smaller spans of control. Only in later years did the bank begin to reward specific skill sets that needed to be retained, such as top credit people, salespersons, relationship managers and industry specialists.

The second reason was a result of acquisitions. During negotiation between an acquirer and the acquired, promises were made resulting in retention of individuals, many of whom were duplicative to the acquiring bank. Too many compromises led to unnecessary and expensive structures. That was especially true with what are termed "mergers of equals". As we later saw with First Union's acquisition of Corestates, the more efficient approach is for the very big to buy the little, ignoring most of the politics of a "merger of equals". I am not saying that was the best way, just the most efficient. Had First Union been able to assess their own weaknesses and Corestates' strengths honestly our acquisition would not have been the disaster it was. But in 1994, we still had remnants of decisions made with our acquisition of Hamilton Bank but more so with the acquisition of First Pennsylvania. In 1991, CoreStates Financial Corporation had 56 Executive Vice Presidents and above.

By early March 1994, the ideas and recommendations were complete. Each segment of the bank presented them to the five member Office of the Chairman. As I recall it, the first ones we looked at, approving most of them, did not include organizational structure. It was there that the majority of the savings would occur and involved eliminating many senior positions. Paul Allen made sure the first phase was easy. Once that was done came the hard part. Some of the people who anticipated their replacement took the early retirement package. Others did not and were fired. One of the hardest jobs I ever had to do was to fire one senior vice president who joined the bank in the international division shortly before I did. He was a talented individual but in a position that could be readily assumed by someone less senior. There were a number of instances of similar situations. I don't remember all of the details but at least half of the 56 Executive Vice-Presidents and higher positions in the bank in 1994 were eliminated.

I will comment on just two. The first was a man who took the early retirement package who we did not want to leave, Ernie Smith. In my judgment, Ernie was one of the best commercial bankers we had, one who could be extremely aggressive but always retained a deep appreciation of the importance of maintaining credit quality. After all, he was the man who got PNB out of the REIT Crisis years before, a dilemma not of his own making. When Ernie informed us that he was leaving, it caused a shudder in the commercial side of the bank. I talked to him twice and eventually asked him to explain his thinking to Terry. He could not be convinced. The only good news was that he agreed to stay for a while before leaving.

The second was Joe Drennan, originally from First Pennsylvania Bank. The decision to remove him was made quickly, without any objection. It was a big mistake. More than any other, Joe Drennan's removal caused consternation, frustration and anger in much of the bank. He was the most respected former First Pennsylvania senior officer in the bank. Not only did he have a strong following among original First Pennsylvania executives, but he had earned the respect of many PNBers as well. I have to take responsibility for the mistake. Even though I had little exposure to him because of his retail background, I should have known better. For several years, Terry had counted on me to understand what was going on in all parts of the bank. On this one, I failed him and the negative consequences persisted.

In a financial sense, our reengineering (called BEST for Building Exceptional Teams Together) was a tremendous success. We identified $180 million in expenses savings and $30 million in revenue enhancements. The actual layoff numbers were better than we originally thought, meaning we had less than expected. Even though we reported more than 2300 job reductions, there were less than 900 layoffs. Unfortunately, but as might be expected, the press focused on the bigger number.

As we approached the formal announcement I believe Terry Larsen made his one mistake that was to have major implications over the next five years. When I was presenting the final numbers to him, I suggested that we not announce our totals but hold some in reserve to give us more flexibility to report higher than expected results in the future. I was pretty sure that the bank analysts were only expecting a little over $100 million from the project, and we could subsequently positively surprise them quarter after quarter, always a good thing for a stock price.

I know that Terry thought about it long and hard, but ultimately decided to report the full amount. His concern was that he knew, despite approval of the ideas by senior management, there was much resistance to some of the ideas among middle-management. If we announced a lower number, it would be too easy for the middle managers implementing the changes to let many slip. He felt he needed the pressure of having to reach earning projections to get the changes made. Terry may well have been right about that, but neither of us realized that the subsequent acquisition of Meridian Bank made some of the proposed ideas impossible to complete. As a result, for years after that acquisition we consistently failed to meet analyst expectations, despite earning top Return on Asset and Return on Capital numbers among the top 25 banks in the United States.

CULTURE CHANGE

The public announcement went well. Bank analysts were happy and the stock price rose even higher than it had just before the anticipated announcement. Within the bank, however, there was a fair amount of unrest. Even though many of the actual layoffs were of weaker performers, there continued to be a belief the entire process was in conflict with the diversity and people initiatives started three years before. Right from the beginning of the culture change, Terry had emphasized the need for continued performance, but that message seemed to get lost as BEST was implemented.

I was exhausted and a bit depressed from being the recipient of many of those negative feelings towards the human impact of what I had led. For many years I had had the same work habits, arriving very early initially by train but, once I qualified for a parking space, would drive, arriving between 7 and 730. When I left my home at the edge of Ridley Creek State Park in Newtown Square, only my daughter Beth was stirring.

April 21, 1995 started out a normal day. As usual I had KYW news radio on. While on 95 near the Corestates Center, an announcer broke in with a news flash describing a very serious accident in Ridley Creek State Park that would shortly involve a medevac. My momentary alarm quickly dissipated as I remembered that Beth does not drive to school.

When I was alone at my desk the phone rang and it was my son, Clayton. He said that a neighbor had come to the door saying she thought there was a serious automobile accident and that the car involved looked like the one that Beth drove. Joann, Charlie and Clayton were not permitted to get closer by the police but were told she was going to be medevaced to either Jefferson or Penn. I told him I would be going to Penn.

When I hung up the phone I screamed. Within a few minutes Terry's secretary, Ro Murray, rushed in, followed by Charlie Connolly. Charlie took charge. He would not let me drive myself. He kept me together. We were driving west on Market Street toward the river when he pointed at a helicopter landing on the roof of University of Pennsylvania hospital building. Charlie dropped me off three minutes later, saying he would make sure the Terry and others know of the situation.

I ran inside and asked the receptionist where the trauma unit was. She gave directions and I got pretty far before I was stopped by guards, who would not let me go any further. It was early in the morning but I knew the two doctors I knew from Penn would already be there. I first called John Hirschfeld. John attended Westtown School with me and also lived in Swarthmore; we played softball together Sunday evenings. He ran Penn's heart unit. Dr. John Glick headed Penn's cancer unit and was also a Swarthmorean. Hirschfeld's nurse took my message and reported he would be down momentarily. It was at least 10 minutes, but I realized later it was just John being thorough, getting a status report before talking to me. I wanted to go into the trauma unit itself where I had seen them taking a gurney a few minutes before. John talked me out of it, telling me, "You have to let them do their jobs". Then he left and I paced.

I was in a little open area in front of a door looking down the hall towards the trauma unit. The door had a half glass panel so I could see anything that moved. Today, as I think back, I believe I really knew the truth of it all standing at the door looking down that hall, when I saw two people come out of the room. They were talking to each other and I remember thinking that both of their shoulders seemed to slump; they had no energy. That's when I knew.

When my family arrived, John returned and escorted us to an upper floor which appeared to be a wing of the regular hospital but quite isolated. There we went through a process which I guess would call grief management. At first nothing was said of a particular negative nature. It was all about hope, and what miracles can be performed. But it was certainly clear the situation was very serious. Gradually, the messages changed and it was John Glick who delivered them. After his second more pessimistic description I was now absolutely certain Beth was not going to make it. I remember feeling almost as if I was outside of myself, observing the scene.

In mid afternoon, John Glick came in again. His face was very somber. He went immediately to Joann and held her arms just below her shoulders tightly. He told her that there was no hope. At impact, Beth hit her head on the roof of the car so hard she was now essentially brain dead. Joann screamed, pounding her fists on John's chest saying "no" again and again and again. It was the worst moment of my life.

When we left the hospital the bank limousine was waiting to take us home. Our two cars, one from the hospital and the other from the bank garage, were already there. . Our street was only a couple of hundred yards long and ended in a cul-de-sac at our house. The neighbors had set up a checkpoint to make sure we were not bothered. We let Beth's boyfriend, Ryan, stay to help us select songs Beth liked for a tape Clayton wanted to make. We needed to keep the boys busy. Charlie wandered from place to place trying to comfort everyone as he is prone to do.

About an hour after we got back, a neighbor said there were two couples in a car who wanted to visit. Both were from the bank, Gene and Susie Feinour, Harry and Robin Hayman. One of the worst things you can say to someone who has lost a child is "I know how you feel". No you don't. You might think you do, but you don't. My worst experience was when a woman started to pet my arm, telling me she knew how I feel because her dog had just died. Today, having loved a dog myself and having had to put him down, I understand a bit better. I also understand that all she was trying to do was share grief, but there's no way she had any concept of how I felt. Only the Feinours and Haymans understood. The Feinour's had just lost a daughter and the Hayman's had just lost their son Brad, a friend of Beth.

Harry Hayman was invaluable. He contacted the funeral home despite it being late on a Friday afternoon. He contacted Westtown School where we intended to have her service. He contacted the press, knowing that my status would generate more than the typical obit. He helped us write it, he helped us design a handout for the service; simply put, he did everything.

Beth died on April 21 and her service was held on Saturday the 29th at Westtown. The meeting house holds about 500 people in general seating, and another 150 stood in the aisles. One Westtown teacher, Tim James, explained to attendees Quaker meetings are never planned. People speak if they wish or are silent if they prefer. Funeral services are no different. When Tim sat down there was silence for about five minutes. Then one of the kids spoke for maybe 15 seconds, telling the audience that Beth was her best friend. At least 10 other said the same thing. The deluge began, speaker after speaker after speaker. Joann tried to speak early but broke down and had a friend read what she planned to say. Clayton got through most of his but it was heartbreaking to hear him. Charlie is a good speaker and showed it here. The service was supposed to be an hour and after more than 100 minutes I decided to wrap it up.

All of us felt an incredible let down by the end of the day; there was simply nothing left to say. The next morning, Joann packed her bags and left for our house in Bethany Beach. She did not return until October. Statistics say almost 80% of marriages fail after the loss of a child. There are many reasons; different ways of grieving, anger, guilt. Neither Joann nor I ever expected it would happen to us. It was a number of years later, but eventually it dId

In the early years after Beth's death lack of concentration became the norm for me. Unless engaged in a very specific project, which I tended to take on in a 'manic' way, depression took over. I was simply not effective doing routine most of the time. I would lose focus, and when that happened got angry, at everything and everyone. I was not performing. I knew it and so did everyone else, including Terry.

Chapter 14

ACQUIRE, MERGE OR BE ACQUIRED

Just as BEST was ending, we were approached by Ira Stepanian of First National Bank of Boston to consider a merger of equals. I simply don't remember if we had announced the BEST savings at this point or if it was just prior to that. Ira certainly knew he would be combining with a slimmed down bank. This was the kind of task I could sink my teeth into.

As COO, one of my jobs was attending analyst conferences many of the major houses would hold on banking. It was fortuitous that the coming weekend there was one such conference being held on Nantucket, a place I had never been but was looking forward to doing so. Unfortunately, I never really got to see it because immediately after my presentation I was on a small private plane to Boston.

Meetings lasted for almost a full day. My shepherd was the chief credit officer whose name I still can't remember. He was the one who organized our trip a few years earlier when Boston shared everything they could share about their experiences with regulators and real estate lending. I had been impressed with him then and more so now. The key department heads were brought in to explain their businesses. My main concern was international. I knew that they had handled their real estate well and it was mostly resolved at this point. I had a lot of confidence in the chief credit officer and the culture he had instilled. International was a different issue.

Banco Do Boston is the largest bank in Argentina, not one of my favorite countries from a credit perspective. How much did the head office fund that portfolio? And that was only the first question. I only had about 15 minutes or so with Ira Stepanian at the end of the day. Obviously, the key discussions would be between he and Terry, not with me. I left Boston feeling upbeat about the deal in virtually every respect.

From start to finish, I don't think this episode lasted more than three weeks. On July 24, 1995 CoreStates dropped its proposed merger negotiations with The First National Bank of Boston. Purely in retrospect, I believe now that decision ended CoreStates' chances for survival as an independent institution. Unfortunately, much of what I will describe below is speculative since I was not present for the key discussions between Ira and Terry, and also between Terry and Nancy Bush who I blame for killing the deal. I will describe what I do know, and give a little speculation on what I don't.

Why did I think it was such a great opportunity for Corestates? Admittedly, they were the opposite of what I had previously advised Terry to look for; a strong retail bank where we could add significant value to the wholesale businesses. The First National Bank of Boston had a decent retail network but was essentially a corporate bank, having dominated that sector for decades in the Boston region just as PNB had in the Philadelphia area. So what made me look at this differently?

Culture was first. It was not only the credit culture that could work very well together but also the importance Boston placed on relationship banking. Their corporate relationships were deep and long lasting. So were ours. They were not 'deal' people, they were 'relationship' people. They were pretty far behind us in their diversity initiative, but at least they had one while many other banks did not.

PNB had set up our Specialized Banking Division in the 1970s, which was early compared to many banks. Boston was the original specialized lender. Many of the famous movies Hollywood produced in the 1930s and 40s were financed by them. They had specialties we did not. We had specialties they did not. There was some overlap but not enough that we would be forced to divest assets. In fact, in some cases we could actually become the lead bank when we combined our exposure. They had good cash management businesses, in which they also used specialized sales professionals. They used administrative assistants the same way we did.

There would be conflict between their businesses in Latin America and ours. They ran strong retail banks in several countries, and smaller ones in a few more. The point is that they acted like a "local" bank in these countries. CoreStates could not sell our collection products to banks if we were competing with them. I assumed we would have to choose what kind of bank we wanted to be within each country in the region. A complication, not a problem.

I did not have the concerns about earnings momentum I had previously had with PNC. Boston was coming out of a earnings debacle caused by real estate lending losses. That was mostly over, and I could tell from the chief credit officer confidence they had written assets down below likely value. Like us, they had some reserves. Our earnings momentum would come from BEST. Merger savings would come from operations and systems consolidation, as well as elimination of duplicate staff structures. What would make this work was something that bank analysts and investment bankers in particular did not like. To make it work it would have to be a true merger of equals, without the premiums investors were looking for.

When I got back to Philadelphia I presented Terry with an extremely positive report. We activated the due diligence merger teams and started to work. My immediate reaction to the early meetings was that there seemed to be lethargy among our people. Perhaps the structure of a deal looked problematic to our people; it may have looked like we were being acquired without a premium even though Terry Larsen would be CEO. I never figured out whether it was opposition to combining with Bank of Boston or whether it was exhaustion from BEST and unfortunately had little time to find out. I only learned recently that there was opposition within the wholesale Bank from managers who were concerned about which bank might lead the specialized groups. My source on this is impeccable. It was very shortsighted thinking.

I believed that the biggest challenge the bank analysts would have for this transaction was Boston's huge activities in retail banking in Latin America, something Corestates did not understand. I thought I would be able to explain how we would manage the business, but first I had to be assured how Boston funded their Argentine business. Was it really all retail peso deposits or did Boston have large dollar currency exposure? As a result, I headed to Buenos Aires.

Normally, I would have been picked up by our Argentinian representative, Santiago Elizondo, who also was the brother of Mariana Wilson who had left the bank a few years before to raise her family much to my chagrin. However, we could not let anyone know what was happening so instead I was met by Banco do Boston. A good day and a half was all I needed to be comfortable how the parent company funded the unit with local deposits. They did have some dollar exposure to borrowers who took the dollar risk and could generally afford the exchange risk.

Full of confidence and very excited about our prospects, I called Terry to report. He never let me talk. He said it was over. We would not be proceeding. The deal was dead. He did not want to talk, just told me to get on the plane and come home. I did.

I don't know what happened. I wasn't there. Again in retrospect, there might have been opposition within our board, but if so I don't know from where. I do know that a blast from bank analyst Nancy Bush was the death blow to the deal when Corestates did not have a good response. I had always been a fan of Bush, meeting with her in the early days over the LDC debt crisis and subsequently as CCO over the '89-90' real estate debacle. She had made a name for herself back then by putting a sell rating on Bank of New England. I believe that a contributor to that assessment of hers were discussions the two of us had following my first visit to New England as CCO, described earlier. Had I been in Philadelphia instead of Argentina, could I have countered some of her arguments? I don't know. Certainly she made no effort to reach out to me, so perhaps not.

The collapse of the talks with Boston caused immediate pressure on all of us, most certainly Terry Larsen. Our stock price was up as a result of BEST. But for how long? We had to do a deal. The logical candidate was our previous rival for the acquisition of First Pennsylvania Bank, Meridian Bank led by Sam McCullough. This was a combination that had been talked about for several years, and I had always made it a point to talk to their people at various banking symposiums. At one bankers roundtable meeting Sam McCullough has actually come up to me for a brief chat, which I duly reported to Terry at the time. The two of them were not close, so in August 1995 Terry asked me to test the waters.

The talks began over lunch with their chief credit officer who I had gotten to know during my time in that role. It was a pretty nondescript

ACQUIRE, MERGE OR BE ACQUIRED

meeting until the very end, when we started to talk a bit about the future of banking. I made the point of the importance of economies of scale and he countered with the power of strong community banks under a central leadership such as Meridian. I recall ending lunch by telling him that should Meridian ever decide they needed to merge, CoreStates would be interested and a good partner with which to do so. We agreed to keep in touch.

Subsequent details are less clear to me now than they probably should be. I recall the next contact was him calling me and another lunch, at which he asked what I thought would be the value of such a combination. We talked a bit about the strengths of each institution and I urged him to get our two bosses together for more detailed discussions. A couple of weeks later he called and said that Sam did not want to do that but would be willing to meet with me. Under strong tutelage from Terry the talks continued. In the early discussions, Sam wanted to talk about their value to a combined institution. He was especially high on his senior woman officer, Sue Perroty. There were at least two subsequent conversations between just the two of us, perhaps three. Each time, Sam was really talking directly to Terry and vice versa. I was just a conduit. Eventually Sam agreed to meet with Terry.

It had been pretty clear to me that Sam really didn't want to sell. And I don't think he was a particularly good fan of Corestates or Terry Larsen. Something was pushing him, however, and I really couldn't tell what it was. He had been a very successful acquirer over the past 10 years, combining some medium-size banks and buying a number of smaller ones. He had done them well. Was he getting tired? Did he want to cash out? Or was it something else? Only later did we discover that his board was pushing him.

As usual, price became the sticking point. Sam, if he was having to sell, wanted a price that made him look like a tough negotiator. Terry, on the other hand, had to be careful about dilution. Final negotiations went back-and-forth, with Terry in one room and Sam in another, with me shuttling between the two, playing the arbiter. Goldman Sachs was advising Meridian and were tough. The deal was struck on October 10,1995. The combined banks would make the 19th largest bank in the United States. The social issues were all on CoreStates' side. It was an acquisition.

Analysts liked the deal but, of course, they were expecting it. We were very concerned about dilution and not at all confident regulators would approve the deal without some give-backs to avoid excess concentration in some markets. We were also concerned about announced savings from BEST being in conflict with what we would attempt to do in savings from the acquisition.

Both proved problematic. Although we tried to communicate these issues to bank analysts, most just added 100% of BEST to 100% of consolidation savings without adjusting for the forced sale of branches needed to satisfy regulators. As a result, for the next three years, we consistently failed to satisfy projected earnings targets, despite having one of the highest return on assets and return on capital of the top 25 banks in the United States.

1995 was not a productive year for me despite the success of the Meridian negotiations and subsequent acquisition. My performance rating from Terry reflected that. As COO of the holding company I was responsible for all of the support functions. I knew too little about what they had been or should be doing.

Until now these units had reported to Larsen. He had selected both Dave Carney, CFO and Les Butler, Human Resources head some years earlier and they reported to him ever since. He had history with them; I didn't. At first I resented his criticism I was too weak on my direct reports, believing he should have acted himself. In hindsight, he was justified. I was simply not performing at a high level at that point.

In April 1996, Rosemarie Greco was named successor officially and I took over the wholesale banking functions with the exception of Regional Banking. Charlie Connolly was released from the purgatory of Chief Credit Officer to run his first love. I don't know exactly how all this came about. It felt like something I asked for and was given. But just as easily I might have been replaced for not doing a good job. Either way I was ecstatic, now also running my first love.

The next two and a half years were the most enjoyable of my career. I had a great team, the best by far in my career. They knew their business. I had also almost learned how to empower, something which did not come naturally as many of my previous direct reports will attest!

In addition to the wholesale businesses, I also assumed control of Technology and Operations replacing Bob Gilmore who left the bank. Both groups have always been a very important part of what I have done in the past both in large corporate and international. In 1994, CoreStates had purchased Nationwide Remittance Services at which time we formed our wholly-owned subsidiary Questpoint.

Questpoint centralized all of our remittance businesses and check collection operations, essentially combining all of what was previously called corporate cash management. Based on the original MAC Network, as well as our check collection services provided to local banks in our market, we had been actively growing our ability to be an outsourcer for other banks, building on what Steve Nichols had started in Hongkong. Part of the purpose of the Questpoint acquisition was to bring in a strong manager to run these businesses. Joseph M Loughry fit that bill perfectly. He was a very imaginative and creative individual who developed the businesses well.

Regionally, we had always been strong in providing check collection services for local banks, but it was not until we sold Morgan Guaranty on the idea did we start to become a national player. While we were certainly not as big as many other cash management banks, the outsourcing we did gave us the scale we needed so that each incremental customer provided increasing profitability due to the lower marginal cost of servicing. This, along with international processing in Hong Kong, was the primary reason that even though our revenues grew just under 15% a year, income rose 18% in 1997 over 1996.

Joe Loughry's processing business was fed by a singularly focused Large Corporate group under Paul Geraghty, and an outstanding corporate cash management sales team led by Ana Southern. These three worked incredibly well together, despite the natural frictions one might expect between operations and line units. I might hear about issues during my individual meetings, but I almost never had to intervene or was even asked to do so. That is a tribute to the leadership of all three.

A few years before we had been able to get human resources to value top sales people, of which we had many. They also participated in the corporate bonus programs and while I think we led many banks in compensating cash management sales people, some might say that we still didn't pay them enough. And that was probably true. Ana's team attended many of the national cash management programs given several times a year in various locations. Our people spoke on key topics and were recognized as true professionals by the industry. I was always pleased when Ana invited me to attend the sessions, although I knew it was really mostly the title they needed rather than my personality. Still I enjoyed it, and I think they enjoyed having me there.

Cash management services for the corporate client was a pretty standard product family for the banks that made it a priority. Pricing was competitive and became increasingly so as the product became more common. Banks wanted to provide a highly standardized product while most companies wanted one or two special features based on their own operating needs. There was a regular tug and pull between our operations and the salesforce on this issue. More than most banks, Corestates was prepared to do some specialized handling in exchange for higher volume or being the exclusive provider for the company. When we were able to do so, our operations and their operations became somewhat integrated. To accomplish this, we often gave discounted visible penny pricing in exchange for the higher volume, knowing that over the longer run it would be increasingly difficult and expensive for the company to switch providers. Since virtually all of our primary customers in this category were growing faster than banks as a whole, our volumes benefited accordingly. To compensate for the lost penny-price income, we increased our float skim and interest rate skim. Ultimately, these became issues during First Union's consolidation of Corestates.

The best example of this successful strategy was the Vanguard group. My memory is a little hazy on how things started, but as I recall it started slowly. Vanguard was a Philadelphia company so it was natural that they came to us first. Even in the early 90s we would have regular meetings between our operations and theirs to go over what was working and what needed to improve. By 1996 those meetings were held twice a year with as many as 15 to 20 people from each company. We certainly made a lot of concessions for them around specialized processing but with their tremendous growth in their industry we benefited as well. In 1998 Vanguard was CoreStates' most profitable customer by a very wide margin, absorbing very large amounts of fixed costs.

By the time I came back into wholesale Banking, International was running like a well oiled machine. Mike Heavener had been running the division for some years. All three areas were growing rapidly. Latin America was almost fully recovered, and as a result we could add good quality short term assets at reasonable prices. Product sales were strong and we were broadening into countries previously ignored. In Europe we had become a powerhouse in the dollar clearing business, starting with London branches and then broadening out to medium-size banks all over the continent. The Asian offices were going from strength to strength and most observers put Corestates in the top five correspondent bankers in the region.

Mike Heavener did not need any of my help in running international other than parading me around in various markets to show senior management support of our strategies. However, in one case I gave him a bit more than he needed. Beginning in late 1995, debt levels to the southeast Asian countries had risen too high, peaking in mid 1997. CoreStates' exposure rose rapidly as we needed to provide lines of credit to support volumes of trade transactions being sent to us. Fortunately, these were short term credits and mostly trade related although we had started to fall into the trap of providing "clean advances" as well, something we learned not to do in Latin America.

All of the people who lived through 1982-1985 were no longer around, with the exception of me. I ordered a substantial reduction in exposure in Thailand, Indonesia, Malaysia, and South Korea. This hurt our business, but our team handled it well, benefiting from the fact we were the first to reduce and so not considered all that important to those countries. By the time the crisis hit in late 1997, our exposures were down to manageable levels. One of the few benefits of the First Union acquisition was it permitted me to reduce their level of "clean advance" loans while increasing our relationship based trade finance. In retrospect, however, in this case I probably acted too fast and too aggressively. Sometimes experience is not always the best teacher.

Hong Kong, however, was in a class by itself. Years before Steve Nichols had broken the foreign exchange cartel which the Hongkong banks, HSBC and Standard Chartered, had controlled for years. New entrants to Hongkong joined the cartel because they liked the guaranteed profits. These were mostly very big banks that had regular flows of trade transactions from their domestic customers. We did not. So Steve cut his prices and, aided by the Japanese, broke the cartel. Since then he had built an outsourcing powerhouse where our operations center, now in Kowloon, was processing transactions for more than 50 banks around the world.

It was more than just doing the business for them. In their annual reports they would list their Hong Kong operation. Each customer had their own dedicated telephone line which was answered by us. They could service their customers at essentially no cost and we could benefit from the foreign exchange income and transaction fees. Steve was aggressive and tough. When one of his prospect correspondent banks was reluctant to use our services, he had no compunction on calling on their major importing customers directly. Often the customer would direct collections through us which was sufficient incentive to get their bank to join us. For innovation and creativity, Steve Nichols had no peer.

The 1990s saw many of the largest banks in the country converting their wholesale businesses from a traditional relationship banking model to the investment banking approach. The latter business was especially profitable when the major New York banks led syndications and it also resulted in a mentality that was deal driven, not relationship driven. (That also led to excessive risk-taking, which the regulators should have addressed far earlier than they did) Our entire wholesale strategy, however, was based on relationship banking. How to operate in the changing market? I did receive pressure to hire some New York investment bankers but was afraid of what it might do to both a relationship strategy and salary structures. We decided on a homegrown model.

Dan Aboyan, one of our best commercial bankers, had played around with various capital market products for a while. He was given responsibility to expand and build an operation using some mid-level hires out of New York, but mostly our own people, Rick Clarke, among others. A complication was how to compensate the capital markets group while at the same time give the proper incentive to the line groups to use them. We worked out a double counting system in which both teams were given credit for the fees from investment banking deals. What made it work was Dan's credibility within the wholesale side of the bank where he was originally from. He had had less exposure to the Specialized Landing groups but very quickly they learned he could greatly enhance their relationships by leading or co-leading major syndications. Dan and Charlie Connolly worked especially well together, and Charlie's regional relationship bankers were able to prevent many of their customers from moving to New York when their credit needs outgrew our capacity. That had been a major issue for years.

Capital markets income grew 40% in 1997 and 100% in 1998, although in actual dollar terms it wasn't significant to group earnings. However, the benefit to earnings in the other groups and the enhancement of those relationships was substantial. Some critics have suggested we should have gone to New York and hired a team. Many other regional banks actually did that, including First Union.. However, that would have destroyed what I believe was our major strength, the mentality of a relationship banker.

Specialized Landing had been around a long time, originally developed by Ernie Smith. In the beginning what differentiated that group was having officers develop an intimate knowledge not just of companies but industries, which was quite different than the generalists we had in the rest of large corporate banking. An early obstacle to the strategy was the fact that our officers were banking not just one customer in the industry, but multiple ones, including competitors of each other. Over time, however, our customers began to value more highly our knowledge of the various cycles within their industry and learned to trust the discretion of our officers about competitors.

One of the early specialties was in telecommunications. We were fortunate to have developed an early relationship with Liberty Media and also to have our next-door neighbor, the Roberts family and Comcast. We became a strong second tier player in that market, to which was added the digital phone group as the industry evolved. It also didn't hurt that we had the CEO of Bell Atlantic on our board, Ray Smith. What made all of this possible, however, was the incredible knowledge and expertise of Jim Brooks, by this time one of my direct reports. He was regarded as an industry expert even by the biggest lenders in New York and Chicago.

Two other specialties deserve special mention, led by Ed O'Donnell. We had been lending to finance companies for years, mostly on the equipment side. Gradually we had expanded to a national marketplace using our expertise in finance company accounting to discriminate between solid borrowers and the less creditworthy. Our reputation within the industry grew but also with other regional banks, which decided to follow us taking good chunks of our syndications arranged through capital markets.

Another strength was Transportation, most especially the trucking industry. Again, we gradually turned this into a national market and used capital markets to lead or co-lead major syndication. Neither of these industries gave us too much opportunity to sell our strong cash management array of products. However, two others, insurance and healthcare, gave us much less credit opportunity but strong non-credit income growth.

Dennis Courtright was another of my direct reports. He had run real estate through all the previous difficulties and was an outstanding manager of real estate risk. Growth in his portfolios were significant during these years because we benefited from having supported a few key players during the downturn who in the improving market were able to expand substantially. We grew with them. Generally, syndicating real estate loans were not particularly popular because of other banks concerned about the risk. Nevertheless, Dennis did start doing some, which generated growing fee income.

As I wrote earlier, this was the best team of managers I ever worked with in my career. We were hitting on all cylinders, growing over 15% in 1997. So when finally forced to listen to First Union, their promise they were buying us for our wholesale business made sense. Did they lie to us? Absolutely!!! As the reader will see later, that merger was doomed to fail, although not apparent immediately. It was clear, however, within six months, but it was too late to do anything about it.

The middle Atlantic region has always been a slow growth region for banking. The business groups described above were able to generate above average growth in earnings primarily because they were operating in the national market rather than just locally, with credit, cash management and international processing. Charlie Connolly's regional banking group was growing above local market norms, but still a little below the national arena. He was increasing market share in a slow growth market.

Since mid 1996, however, CoreStates had failed to meet analysts earnings projections. Each quarter there were a host of firms lowering their estimates, citing sluggish revenue growth, lagging technology and ongoing digestion problems from the Meridian merger.

The premium generated by the BEST announcement was quickly dissipated. Possibly we failed to communicate properly that as a result of the Meridian merger some of the projected savings from reengineering would not be possible. More likely the analyst community simply did not want to hear it.

Another criticism some analysts made was that we were not making enough money in trading, given the high spread between very short and very long interest rates. That is normally an environment where banks can do very well, but only if willing to take the rate risk required for holding a large trading portfolio. As the reader may recall, CoreStates got severely hurt being on the wrong side of interest rate risk a number of years earlier, and Terry Larsen had been brought in to correct it. Just as I was reluctant to take real estate and international lending risk based on my experience, so too was Terry reluctant to take excessive interest rate risk.

Over that time, Larsen had become increasingly frustrated with bank results. Periodically he would push me to generate higher earnings and we did what we could to increase loan totals despite the negative effect on ROA. For example, in early 1997 international loans grew almost 50% as did our corporate banking totals. While some of this came from taking larger pieces of syndications we were leading, the majority was lower margin short term trade finance and corporate money market loans which did little to the bottom line. He knew the wholesale side was doing well, but he became increasingly frustrated with retail and trust.

Sometime in the early summer of 1997, Rosemarie Greco asked to meet with me. We normally had monthly meetings so I could keep her abreast of what was going on in the wholesale side, but this was not one of those regular get togethers. Because of what took place later, I have often thought about that conversation. She started the conversation by admiring what was occurring in the wholesale side of the bank, emphasizing how good I was at the business and how obvious it was I loved it. She then went on to suggest that I seemed to be taking a less active role in the business and political world of Philadelphia itself. She further noted that I did not spend a lot of time communicating with bank directors. I remember acknowledging she was probably right and that I didn't particularly enjoy that part of my role compared to winning new business. She pointed out we complemented each other's strengths; she more active and confident in the external role and me on the internal, her in retail and me in wholesale. She also made it pretty clear that if the two of us were running the bank, she would be the CEO. I told her I understood that.

I never fully understood the reason for this conversation. After all, Terry had already told me sometime before that she was number two and I was number three. I knew he wanted her to replace him. Why would she need to clarify that? Maybe she had doubts, thinking that I might not support her? Surely she understood that I would never publicly directly go against what Terry wanted.

On August 11, 1997 we woke to the blockbuster news that Rosemarie Greco was leaving Corestates. She said it was for "personal reasons". Terry said that he felt "sadness" and a "sense of loss" at her departure. Analysts were in a frenzy, but neither of them said anything else. Some speculated that this suggested a sale of CoreStates was imminent which was rejected by others, although CoreStates' stock price rose. Several commented that it was a sign of management instability and not a positive development. In the aftermath most of Rosemarie's responsibilities were divided between Charlie Connolly and Sue Perroty, the best executive from the Meridian merger.

Shortly thereafter, Terry asked me whether I would be willing to take over for him when he left the CEO job. His only condition was that I would have to commit to stay a minimum of five years from the time he left. He said he expected to stay for another five years. I was 54 and to agree I would have to be willing to work until 64. My dad died at 52, and I had always expected to retire before I was 58. I said no. In retrospect, given that I am 79 as I write this, I wish I had said yes. Perhaps we would have fought harder and possibly even successfully fend off the wolves.

Chapter 15

THE WORST ACQUISITION IN BANKING HISTORY

WITH THE ANNOUNCEMENT, there was blood in the water and sharks were circling! Increasingly, analysts put Corestates on the list of most likely banks to be acquired in the next year. Sluggish earnings were the stated reason. Only a few, like Tom McCandless and Dave Barry, would point to our high return on equity and return on assets compared to competitors. For most, the only thing they counted was earnings growth, and those high expectations on that metric for us were still out there. The board asked tougher questions in the September meeting and I detected a distinctly different level of tension in the room. Sometimes the board had executive sessions at which only board members attended and the rest of us were excused. In October there was a long one.

In late September and early October a number of firms again dropped their estimate for Corestates' earnings. With that, the sharks attacked. The reader will recall previous descriptions of talks between Mellon and ourselves. Larsen had been told by one or more Corestates' directors Mellon might be willing to be bought by us but both he and I had the impression at that meeting Frank Cahoet expected the reverse. On October 8, 1997 Mellon Bank made a $17.7 billion unannounced and unsolicited offer to acquire Corestates.

Corestates' board met the next day, although I was unaware of the meeting or how long it took. The board apparently rejected the offer and asked Mellon bank to withdraw the offer, which they did. It could have ended right there, but on Friday an article appeared in the Wall Street Journal describing the offer and that unanimous rejection by CoreStates. Someone was talking. We were now in play.

In my opinion, at that point we were finished as an independent entity. Had the price offered by Mellon been low ball, we might have survived. But it wasn't. Had we had a unanimous board fully committed to our independence, we might have survived. But we didn't. Had Bank Analysts agreed that there would be greater long-term value as an independent bank, we could have survived for a while. But they didn't. Most of them ridiculed the idea of Corestates remaining independent given the high price of almost six times book value offered by Mellon.

I was not privy to what happened next. However, on October 22 an unsigned clip in the Pittsburgh business journal reported that Corestates had confirmed its previous rejection of Mellon's offer. There was nothing in the local papers or in the Wall Street Journal, which had covered the story the previous week. Someone was talking to the press to keep the deal alive, and it had to have been one or more of our board members.

Five days later, Peg Brickley of the Philadelphia Business Journal wrote a longer piece. She reported that on October 21 there was a six hour meeting of the Corestates board. She noted that while previously CoreStates had described its rejection as unanimous, this time they did not. She reported that no longer was the word "independent" used to describe our strategy. She reported that there was a split within Corestates' board and that previous directors of Meridian Bank were pushing for a sale, meaning George Strawbridge for one. She suggested that unnamed merger experts expected Mellon would go higher than the $88 per share of the original offer. Simply put, Peg had a direct pipeline into CoreStates' board. With that, I absolutely knew it was over.

I really don't know very much about what happened next. For the most part, Terry was incommunicado. Periodically he would ask me about one or another bank, and I understood he was looking for alternatives to Mellon. We talked about Fleet, PNC again and even Mellon. First Union came up several times but I knew he still had an aversion to the South.

In mid-November he told me that Ed Crutchfield of First Union wanted to talk about a merger and was intending to bring his entire senior leadership up to meet ours. It was an uncomfortable meeting to say the least. Just before that meeting Crutchfield, Ken Thompson, Larsen, and I were together in Terry's office. Crutchfield introduced Ken as my counterpart at First Union and, committing us to secrecy, indicated Ken would be his successor as CEO of First Union. He told Terry that he was buying CoreStates for its powerful wholesale business model, which was something Terry must have previously discussed with him. Ed said that should the merger go through Ken would report to me. I did not take his comment to mean anything more than that Ken would take over after learning our business model from me. It did seem to make sense. Why else would Crutchfield be willing to pay such a high premium? He wasn't adding much geography because they bought Fidelity Bank two years before. Yes, there would be some additional economies but nothing to justify five and a half times book. The only thing that made sense was they must really value our wholesale business strategy.

The acquisition was made official on the morning of November 19, 1997. The price was 16.6 billion. Ed Crutchfield remained CEO and there were no promises that Larsen would replace him. Headquarters would be in Charlotte, although Philadelphia was described as the headquarters of corporate banking which Larsen, as ostensibly number three in the bank, would manage. First Union's board would now have 34 members, of which six would be from Corestates. In other words, all of the social issues belonged for First Union. This was no merger; it was an acquisition.

Analysts were mostly in favor. They pointed out that First Union could bring a modern retail delivery model which had been a drag on Corestates earnings for some time. First Union had already made investments in new operations technology Corestates was still to make. Other than a great Trust business, Mellon had not offered much to the equation. Analyst praise, however, was not what the average Corestates employee wanted to hear!

Fear and anger were the two most common reactions from CoreStates people on the day the deal was announced. Fear was understandable. Press articles talked about at least 3000 jobs disappearing from the Philadelphia region, most of which would come from Corestates. The Fidelity people had had two years to become well entrenched and would be hard to displace.

Anger was widespread and mostly directed towards those of us at the top, especially Larsen. For years we had been talking openly about following an independent course. And now this! One quote from announcement day by one CoreStates employee sums it up pretty well. She said she felt betrayed by Larsen. "He kind of told us we'd be OK. He made a strong point that he wanted to stand by Philadelphia. He's in it for himself. We thought he cared. Maybe he doesn't care after all". Another article noted that the Mellon offer was higher than the deal finally accepted, pointing out that Mellon did not offer a job to Larsen but First Union did, inferring that might have been the reason he took the lower price.

The belief in Philadelphia's business community then, and in particular among former Corestates employees, is that Larsen sold out for his own personal benefit. That opinion persists today. At an employee reunion three years ago the kindest thing I heard someone say about Terry Larsen is "…..Sure he did it for his own benefit but so what. That's what I would have done too". I am one of the few with the opinion that Terry Larsen did not sell for personal gain but I am the only person who knows that for certain.

I will present my evidence, starting with the price issue, namely that Larsen took a lower price from First Union in exchange for having a job in the three person office of the chairman running corporate banking. First, Terry Larson did not trust Ed Crutchfield. Right from the beginning he made his rule never to meet with him one on one. At most private meetings the two had Terry asked me to be present and I was. Early on, after one of those meetings, Terry asked me to commit that I would stay at First Union for at least one year after he left in order to protect CoreStates people as best I could. My natural question was how long he expected to stay. He said "probably no longer than one year". In other words he never intended to stay. In fact, he left after only three months and I followed 12 months later, as promised. A years salary was meaningless in the context

And was Mellon's the better price? I don't think so. I believe Mellon, desperate to do a deal to save them selves, significantly overstated the savings they could generate from the transaction. Their Philadelphia footprint was substantially smaller than that of First Union which was still consolidating Fidelity. As a result, dilution to their stock would be far greater than might occur with First Union as was shown in the days following the announcement.

First Union's "price" also included three things for which Terry negotiated extremely hard. I witnessed some of those negotiations. First Union agreed to fund a $100 million foundation to be used in the Philadelphia market and directed by CoreStates directors **selected by Larsen.** (As I said before, Larsen didn't trust Ed Crutchfield).

As most Corestates employees know, we were the largest single charitable contributor in the city, dispersing $17 million a year to charitable organizations, more than double the second largest corporate. donor. While a $100 million foundation would only generate $5 million of contributions in the beginning, it was at least a start. Second, he also pushed for a pool of money to be set up side for retraining Corestates employees displaced by the merger. Originally seeking $25 million, he settled for $16 million after Crutchfield balked at the higher number. Finally, and this was the most important factor, Crutchfield promised to move 3000 jobs from Charlotte to Philadelphia to help offset the loss expected from consolidation. I don't know if anyone has kept track, and I doubt even if they had that it would be accurate. Certainly some jobs did move north but certainly not the full 3000. Nevertheless, that promise was an important consideration to Larsen.

Larsen critics often simply just point to the buyout package First Union gave him. It was certainly substantial, but nothing out of the ordinary from previous acquisitions in the banking industry. He received just under $10 million in restricted stock. The first offer from Mellon bank gave Larson $10 million, but there was no reference to a position in the company. However, First Union offered him a five-year employment contract guaranteeing $1 million in salary and $2 1/2 million in bonus each year. That is certainly substantial but, as noted above, Terry told me he would leave after a year **at the latest,** and gave all of that up anyway by leaving almost immediately. In short, his actions suggest a motive different than money.

Furthermore, I am virtually certain Terry had no idea what his package was actually going to be before the deal was announced. I was with Terry and Ed when Ed handed him his "package". It was sealed. Ed was excited and wanted Terry to open it then and there, in front of me no less. Larsen demurred, which caused Ed to say, "I think you're going to like it". Ed's comment tells me Terry had no idea what his package was. He did not open the envelope but put it on his desk, which, as those of you who know Larsen well, was a mess. At the next meeting a week later Crutchfield, right at the outset, said he needed to talk about Terry's package because they were preparing the prospectus and wanted to make sure Terry had no objections to it. Terry then rummaged through his desk, found it, broke the sealed envelope and opened it for the first time, read it and then just said, "that's OK."

Terry Larsen was simply not of the mindset to negotiate on his own behalf. For that matter he was not of the mindset to negotiate on behalf of his management team either. I was the only individual who received something more than what had originally been set up for us a few years earlier in the event of a sale. And I only got that because I asked for it directly in exchange for agreeing to stay a year longer than Terry did. I knew that by staying an extra year my market value would have dropped. All of the second tier of management in previous large bank mergers did a lot better than those of us at Corestates. I know because I looked at the comparative numbers at the time.

Holidays ensued, followed by a winter of discontent in Philadelphia and mostly silence from Charlotte. Much of our time was spent reassuring customers that little would change under First Union. Most customers were complacent at worst, positive at best. Our story made sense to customers. First Union did not have corporate or international cash management products so most accepted that Corestates would dominate in this arena.

My first trip to Charlotte was to get a sense of their International Division, people and loan portfolio. I found weak castoffs from other banks, little ability to evaluate country risk and zero product knowledge. When we were running our loans in Asia down, they were piling on, at thin spreads for 'clean advances'. I took personal control of that part of the business without objection. I begged Mike Heavener to find room for as many of their international people he could. That trip went well; it was the last one that did.

A few weeks later Ken Thompson asked me to come down to meet some of his best people. Few were home-grown. Most were from various New York banks, heavily deal oriented without any product knowledge. There was a product sales team but they had almost no contact with line groups. Line groups also rarely had contact with operations. Their verbiage was strictly about deals they had done, almost always as a participant, rarely as lead. Most corporate banking was done in the geographical territories not in Ken's unit. The idea of relationship banking might exist there but it most certainly did not in what I was seeing. The only positive thing about the people I spoke to was that most were bright if also unjustifiably arrogant.

Although on paper I was Ken's boss, I knew very well that I was more the supplicant when in Charlotte. Still I did not expect to be treated the way I was by the people I was interviewing, which I would describe as a range between disrespectful and insulting. At first I was angry but on reflection their attitude was to be expected. They came from New York; they knew best, How could a banker from minor league Philadelphia.have anything to teach them. For that matter, they also did not give Ken all that much respect either. Perhaps I am excessively harsh here because there were exceptions, but not many.

On that same trip, I attended my first merger integration meeting led by Ed's right hand man, John Georgius. His introductory speech was instructive. He addressed both CoreStates people and his own with the same message: First Union has integrated many banks, we know how to do it, our formula is tested and this one is only just a little bigger than all the others. I kept silent but remember thinking at the time that he is going to have a rude awakening. They had integrated many banks as he said, but never integrated one with the highest return on equity of the top 25 banks in the country. I naively believed that they would inevitably have to adjust their process as a result. They didn't, and ultimately paid a huge price. Unfortunately that price was also paid by far too many CoreStates employees.

My ride back north was depressing. CoreStates corporate business was a highly successful relationship banking approach. Ken Thompson's capital markets group with which I was supposed to work was a deal-driven mixture of widely diverse cultures without a central core strategy that I could see. Furthermore, as Ken described his experience as Florida bank president, I got the impression that there he had virtually no direction but could run his region as he chose. In First Union, each region seemed to have its own corporate culture and strategy. That assessment was consistent with comments I had heard Roland Bullard make in his early days under a First Union banner. The only way I could see myself succeeding would be if First Union had truly acquired Corestates for the reasons they gave originally. But nothing I saw on my first two trips to Charlotte supported that hope.

If we had been acquired for our successful wholesale banking level, my assumption was that they would be asking about how we did things. So far that had not happened with me. My hope was if I brought a couple of my direct reports down to Charlotte, the results might be different. Paul Geraghty and Dan Aboyan joined me on the next visit. They were the two key players to explain our relationship banking strategy. Paul was fully knowledgeable and even an architect of much of our cash management approach with the large corporate market and Dan had integrated investment banking into our corporate and specialized lending relationships.

I chose not to let either of them know how concerned I was about the merger. My thought was I would learn a lot more when I debriefed them about their interviews. In retrospect that was probably another mistake, because neither was prepared for what they found. Both had the same round of interviews I did, with the same attitudes. I spoke with Ken at the end of the day. It was obvious he had been briefed by his people. Ken did not like Paul Geraghty and said the investment bank would have no use for him. He was more positive on Aboyan, but noted both had not treated their meetings with him as the job interview it was. That's when I knew that everything that Ed Crutchfield had said to us was nothing more than salesmanship. There was no truth in it. At that point all I could do was to tell my directs they should negotiate as best they could for themselves, and there was very little more I could do. It was a horrible feeling.

I liked Ken Thompson. Despite it all. Yes, he knew he reported to me only on paper. Yes, he looked elsewhere for any direction and guidance. Yes, he listened only to his own people, and did not take what Corestates people did very seriously. But he was only following the normal process First Union took with every acquisition. He could have ignored me completely but he didn't. He did ask questions and accepted some answers, so long as they did not conflict with what Ed Crutchfield or John Georgius believed. He knew he was the anointed one and was not going to risk that for anything. I could understand that.

Getting time with him, however, was never easy. Every couple of weeks I would go down to Charlotte and drop in his office around 7 AM. Then we would have an hour to talk. He did ask questions. He did listen. On Wednesday, March 4 he was very pleased to see me, and quite excited. He told me that in an hour Crutchfield was going to announce a major acquisition. Ken not see the irony that he was telling me this, someone that he supposedly reported to. First Union was buying The Money Store. I think my response was something like, "Oh God no".

I told him how CoreStates, when I was CCO, had thrown that company out of the bank when we purchased First Pennsylvania. I told him about the credit and accounting issues we had uncovered. He was both concerned and a little skeptical, noting that that was five years ago and the company was still operating successfully. The fact that due diligence had been done over the previous three weeks and no one had bothered to ask anyone at CoreStates what they might think was enlightening. Someone at the Money Store had to have had concerns CoreStates people were part of the buyer, and told First Union a little of the history. And First Union still didn't bother to check? Ken and I agreed to disagree. A little over two years later, as one of Ken's first decisions as CEO First Union wrote off the entire $2.1 billion they paid, but that was not the extent of their losses. I do not know the total, but if they didn't write off at least another $2 billion I would be surprised.

The merger integration teams had been working around the clock in order to consolidate the operating systems as fast as possible. Doing so would get a lot of the promised cost savings out. I attended many of them, but merely as an observer. Over the years I had developed some pretty good relationships with various levels of both CoreStates operations group and technology teams. One day there was a meeting with two VPs, one from each group, scheduled by my secretary Debby without my knowledge. What they told me was disturbing. They said that the integration teams from First Union had no understanding about the systems that ran our clearing business in New York City and the balance reporting that came from it. They also told me First Union people were not listening to the Corestates people who did understand it. When they described how the meetings were run, I recognized that our people were behaving in a classic subordinate role as taught to us during diversity training. We agreed they needed to be more forceful. I also asked them to talk to others to see whether this was common. It was. I started to raise the alarm, but no one paid any attention.

Customers were concerned as well, but I did what I could to reassure them. Most accepted our explanation but our largest cash management customer, Vanguard, demanded a private meeting with top management. After all, their entire customer communication system was based on our transaction processing and balance reporting. They were unwilling to accept me as a representative. They asked for Ed Crutchfield. They got John Georgius. After all, he was Ed's right hand man and responsible for the integration of acquired banks. They had a group of eight people, including their COO. We had about six. John was peppered with questions that he deferred to his experts. Vanguard was assured that nothing would go wrong. The meeting made me feel a bit more comfortable as well.

On April 13, 1998 the Federal Reserve finally approved the merger. The transaction officially closed on April 30. A few weeks later Terry Larsen called me into his office and informed me that he would be leaving the bank on July 1. He quietly reminded me of my commitment to him to stay on for a further 12 months from that date. I promised him I would. A few days later it was officially announced by First Union and I was named to fill his place with no change in title as several newspapers pointed out. Some inferred this was a clear message to Corestates people.

Consolidation of operations and systems are usually planned for over a three day weekend. My memory is a bit hazy but I assume it must have been the Memorial Day weekend. I do remember calling several times and being assured everything was going smoothly. Tuesday seemed like a pretty normal day from what I could see. The problem was what I couldn't see. The back office was in chaos.

About 3 AM on Wednesday morning I received a call from our Philippines representative, Chit Suria, who I'd known well for years. After apologizing for the early hour and calling me directly outside the chain of command, she reported she had been on the phone with Philadelphia for over four hours. There was absolutely no reporting whatsoever on transactions of the previous day. We were the clearing bank for the Central Bank of the Philippines, which moved between $100 and $200 million every day. They wanted to know what what's going on in their account. No one in Philadelphia could tell them. Neither could anyone in Charlotte.

That phone call was the beginning of the worst 10 day period of my banking career. At the time of the merger, Corestates was probably the 10th largest cash management bank in the United States. We were the sole provider to the biggest insurance companies in the country, just to name one industry. We processed for mutual funds also. Vanguard was our biggest example but SEI investments was another major player. None of those companies received any balance reporting or transaction detail on Tuesday evening when they expected it. Nothing.

That was bad enough, but Corestates was also the fifth largest dollar clearing bank in New York and we moved over $1 billion a day from over 3000 transactions per day. Our customers were large banks and medium size banks world-wide from London, Luxembourg, Singapore, etc. branches of the largest banks in the world. We could tell them nothing about what payments we had made for them, received for them or a current balance.

Michael Heavener, our international head, was an absolute champion. He fielded so many calls from all over the world and somehow managed to keep all our foreign representatives sane in the midst of a marketing disaster. What concerned most of our clearing customers was that payments they needed to make got made. Sometimes incoming funds never showed up putting the account in overdraft. Would we honor their credit and make the payments anyway? I reassured them we would. Michael looked at me with a quizzical eye the first time I made that promise. Would First Union's credit people understand and allow us to do so? I was glad Michael did not witness the shouting match between me and the chief credit officer but in the end, by going to Crutchfield, he supported us. He accepted my declaration that failure to do so would permanently damage his bank's reputation worldwide.

As I said, the next 10 days were the worst in my banking career. We took thousands of telephone calls from irate customers making promises we could not keep because we simply had absolutely no information from the merger integration team. Vanguard demanded and received daily meetings with the integration team. They asked John Georgius to attend which he did only once. The good news was that after a few days First Union people started talking with Corestates systems people.

After three or four days some of the simpler transactions for the corporate client started to appear on statements. A couple of days later we started to see progress for the larger domestic clients. Nothing for international clients. We now had quite a few significant overdrafts from that customer base. It is possible word had gotten out about our integration problems, and some banks which were supposed to pay us decided not to. On the other hand, some of our customers might have decided to take advantage of the situation and have us fund them at no cost by, not sending us funds. The ultimate financial cost had to be enormous.

Some international customers had already moved their clearing business to other banks; most promised to return when we had our problems fixed, but none of us held our breath. All day long we fielded complaints, and for the much of the night we did the same thing. Every day Michael and I spoke to all of the Asian representative officers at about midnight our time. There wasn't too much we could do other than give them various excuses that seemed to have worked elsewhere. There were many tears. Our job was simply to listen.

On the fifth day, I got my first call from a bank analyst. He was a bit circumspect, but I could tell he knew a lot more than we wanted him to. I decided to acknowledge there were problems, but said we did expect to resolve them shortly. Over the next couple days three or four other analysts called about the same subject. So the word was out. This was particularly problematic, because on June 12 First Union was holding their annual analyst meeting with over 200 expected. I called Ed Crutchfield's office. He did not take the call so I left a message. His secretary then asked me to come to Charlotte to meet with Ed and I reminded her I had been in Charlotte since the problems surfaced.

We met in his office. He displayed his sales voice, and his sales face. He was very empathetic about what we had gone through and thanked me and our team for what we were doing. He then asked me to do something I simply could not do. He said that he expected tough questions on the subject at the analyst meeting that coming Monday. He said he expected me to answer that there had been a few hiccups but that everything was now working fine.

I told Ed I had been promised, once again, the issues would be resolved over the coming weekend. I told him I certainly hoped that would be the case, and if so, I would be entirely supportive. However, if the situation had not changed, I was not prepared to do anything but tell analysts the truth. I reminded him that I had been working with bank analysts since the LDC debt crisis in 1982, and again during the real estate crisis. I would not destroy my reputation built up over so many years. I do not think he expected that answer, and he was not happy.

I don't remember the exact details but the first time I called the Philippines on the Tuesday morning, hoping to hear that they had transaction information for all the customers, they told me no. My heart sank. I called down to systems and was told that they hadn't yet sent information. A couple of hours later we were told that for the first time the previous day's transactions were fully visible on the account statements. It was done. At the analyst meeting, I was given no role but answered questions individually.

Not being given any role at all at a meeting with people I knew well, and who respected me, was frustrating. It was just stupid, exemplifying everything First Union was doing wrong. It reinforced my role; I had none. All I could do was try to protect Corestates people as much as possible (which Terry committed me to do), push our broad cash management strategy and try to get First Union to understand what they had in their new international division.

The acquisition by First Union was going to be very good for the Corestates international business and strategy. In many ways, Corestates had come to the limit of what we could accomplish internationally. Our products were great. Our execution in New York superb. Our people focused and committed. We were performing in transaction processing far above our weight class. Simply put, however, Corestates was too small to grow much further. First Union changed that. One simple example: Steve Nichols had been pushing hard for several years to get one of the top Australian banks to use our Hong Kong operation. He had not been successful. However, in mid July 1998, shortly after the formal merger, the Australia and New Zealand banking group, the largest international trade bank in the country, signed with us. Shortly thereafter came one of the top South African banks. Now we had the size and scale we needed to get the attention of the biggest banks in the world. In Latin America, always in need of credit lines, we were able to double our lines of credit to compete with Chase and Citibank. Everyone at First Union now understood Corestates people would run international and Michael Heavener was the right man to do so.

What could my role be? Michael was a bit further down on the First Union organization chart then he had been at Corestates. If we were going to now go head to head with Chase, Citibank, Morgan Guaranty and UBS we had to get our case in front of the top people at our prospective customer base. My previous tactics of working at the lower levels no longer applied. I could play the senior statesman role so long as I was reporting directly to Ed Crutchfield and had the appropriate title. I shared these thoughts with Ken Thompson and shortly thereafter met with Ed to outline my thinking. On October 20, 1998 I was promoted to my previous title of Vice Chairman. Simultaneously John Georgius was named chief operating officer and Ken Thompson was also promoted to Vice Chairman. He no longer reported to me on paper.

So I played the role of international senior statesman, much like Fred Heldring had done years before. I certainly did not have anything like the stature Fred did in his day. I traveled a lot and Michael Heavener used me well. Once I flew out to Hong Kong, made a speech for Steve Nichols, and then flew back the next day. I only did it because I was allowed to travel first class.

Appalachian State, where my son Clayton graduated, had developed a brother/ sister relationship with Fudan University in Shanghai. The relationship was extremely important to Appalachian State because Fudan was one of the most prestigious universities in China. The Chinese banking system was under a lot of pressure and Fudan wanted to host a three day seminar on banking. Accordingly, Appalachian

State pulled out all the stops to get top bankers from North Carolina to speak. I was selected from First Union. Wachovia Bank's CEO, Bud Baker, attended and spoke. There were senior officials from both the OCC and Federal Reserve. It was a pretty impressive event.

I decided to say what I really thought about Chinese banks. The objective of the conference was to study how the system needed to change. Most speakers talked about the banks themselves. I said that China could never have a stable banking system unless they fixed their accounting system and standards, as well as their legal system. Without the ability to have an effective bankruptcy process and be able to foreclose readily, there was simply no chance to reform banking itself. Poor accounting and false reporting needed to be prosecuted. It was not a message that was well received, and from I hear today the problem still exists.

The most interesting part of the three days for me was a sidebar I had with Bud Baker. At the various receptions, I got the impression he was not a great fan of Ed Crutchfield. But what did surprise me was his interest in Ken Thompson. He asked a lot of questions about Ken and I was quite positive in my replies. I said the Ken appeared to be the heir apparent, but that he was quite a different person than Ed Crutchfield. I said Ken listened and did not presume to have all the answers. My impression then was that Ed had been talking to Bud about acquiring Wachovia.

Over the years I've always had an extremely high opinion of Wachovia, especially John Medlin and the credit culture he built. It never occurred to me Wachovia might seriously accept First Union. What I did not know, however, was that the credit culture built by Medlin had been destroyed under Bud Baker's leadership, loan losses inevitably following. On September 1, 2001, First Union acquired Wachovia, replaced the sullied First Union name with well respected Wachovia, but kept none of their senior people. Even after blowing the Corestates acquisition, First Union still had learned nothing.

All in all, I lived a pretty meaningless existence for the rest of my time at First Union. There was one major battle to go which, had I won it, would have led me to stay a lot longer, but unfortunately that did not happen. The battle began when First Union product management decided to limit product offerings to the largest Corestates corporate clients to electronic payments, and end handling paper products.

First Union had long before decided that electronics was the future of transaction processing. In this, they were right of course. But their approach and solution was indicative of the deal mentality existing all through the organization, which was quite in conflict with the relationship approach of Corestates. Their ideal customer would be one which gave them all the electronic business, with other banks doing the paper transactions. CoreStates wanted to totally dominate a customers transaction business knowing most major companies, while moving to electronics, had a lot of legacy systems dependent on paper processing.

Early in 1999, First Union established a wholesale customer service project team. Its primary purpose was to evaluate the CoreStates corporate business they had acquired. A man who I had never met, Jack Mitchell, was put in charge. Over the next couple of weeks there were several product meetings where Mitchell argued for transition to their original, electronics-only, strategy. I actually thought I had won the day when I pointed out that changing our product mix in this way would result in losing almost all of CoreStates' cash management customer base. I brought out old numbers I had, showing the correlation between significantly increasing volume of these transactions and our commercial business increasing profitability in the previous two years. I warned that their approach would ultimately lead to the loss of much of the core revenue stream which had made us so profitable at Corestates. On February 5, 1999 I wrote a memo to the team summarizing my verbal comments. Unfortunately, I did not keep a copy of that memo. I got no formal response.

The next argument came over exception processing. The more standardized a product, the easier it is to automate and lower costs of processing items, hence greater profitability. Each time exception processing is offered it makes things a lot tougher for operations. Corestates had a lot of exception processing. However, CoreStates used exception processing to tie corporate clients systems to our own, making it very difficult for them to move should a competitor seek to win pieces of their business, like lowballing pricing on electronics as First Union was prone to do. I understood this. I had had regular battles on the subject at CoreStates with our cash management people as they battled with our operations groups. It was hard to argue with several of their points and I knew I was on the defensive, so I suggested a compromise where we would evaluate each customer and decide where we could increase prices but also we would still keep exception processing in the short term. This time I was virtually certain I had won the argument. But I hadn't.

On February 17, Jack Mitchell wrote a memo he believed addressed my concerns. They did not. His language was very general, talked about cost cutting and simultaneously improving services across the entire corporate customer base. He was looking for the team recommendations by June. But nothing in the memo suggested any change in their approach. Unfortunately I also don't have a copy of that memo. However, I do have a hand written copy of a memo I subsequently wrote to Ed Crutchfield where I described Mitchell's memo as a "solving world hunger answer which will not cut it". I also said that the overall goals are good but CoreStates' key customers and revenue streams won't be around to enjoy the benefits. I heard nothing from Ed so thought I might have won the argument, but such was not the case.

One of the team members was Ben Maffitt. He had taken over Questpoint with the merger and was now in charge of all remittance processing. I had met with him a number of times over the previous months and we clearly understood each other. Jack Mitchell's next presentation to the product group attacked remittance processing, claiming that the business is fundamentally unprofitable and containing a list of clients that should be eliminated. Most of those on the list were CoreStates's largest processing customers. I don't have a copy of that memo either but I do have my March 10 four page reply sent to Ben summarizing my comments of that meeting.

My first paragraph acknowledged the value of periodically reviewing product profitability and pricing. I agreed there might be some cases where we can increase penny pricing because of the pricing leverage we had with First Union now being the largest retail lockbox bank in the country. I also wrote there may be some places we can increase prices where we have exception processing built-in. That was my sales pitch. The next 11 paragraphs was a blistering attack on virtually everything Mitchell had written.

Paragraph two started as follows: " That said, however, I do not agree with most of the study's conclusions. In my opinion the analysis is fundamentally flawed. The starting assumptions are invalid and, because of that, the subsequent outcomes are as well. Furthermore...... If (the analysis of) each product set has similar flaws then there is a multiple (sic) effect.".

Cost accounting is an art. It can be used to show reality. It can also be used to show a reality that someone wants others to reach. Mitchell's memo was a good example of the second type in the analysis of the retail lockbox business. For readers unfamiliar with the product, companies set up post office boxes under control of their banks so their customers could send payments. The bank opens each post office box, collects the letters containing checks, process the checks and deposit proceeds into the customers bank account. High-volume customers tend to be very clean work, such as monthly cable bills, utility bills etc. Processing for them is very standardized and very fast. Small companies, however, have more complex work; more inquiries, equal set-up times to high volume customers, more errors to be fixed, etc.

First Union's cost accounting process was simplistic. First Union used the number of units (checks sent in) as the basis to assigning all costs and overhead. It penalized the biggest high-volume users and made the small lock box customers resident in the state banking units appear far more profitable than they really were.

All this is pretty complex for the layman to understand. Let me give one example. Corestates and First Union's combined cash management sales groups had expenses of approximately $30 million. How do those expenses get allocated? A nice and simple way is to do it by the number of checks collected, as per First Union. Just for the sake of argument, let's assume the combined volume of checks collected each year was 2 billion. One middle-market client in the Florida bank sets up a lockbox with First Union in four geographic locations with an annual check collection volume of say 25,000 items. A cable company has a retail lockbox at Corestates which processes 8 million checks a year. The small company is charged sales expense each year of $375 and Comcast is charged $125,000, back then more than one person's salary. Admittedly, these are not actual numbers, with the exception of the $30 million, but how does this make any sense? Furthermore they use the same technique for $65.4 million of additional overhead bringing the cost for the mythical small company up to $1175 and the utility to $386,600 a year.

The fundamental point I kept hammering home at the meeting was that, in our experience, the largest customers carried the product development costs and technology investments that every bank needs. What would happen if we no longer had these large volume customers? In addition, if we kicked these customers out of the bank as was being proposed, what actual costs would go away. Certainly not $386,000 from one utility user!!

Every large bank has internal politics that sways decisions. We had ours. They had theirs. For First Union, power rested in each state banking unit, whether it be North Carolina, Georgia, Virginia or Florida. Only people who had run a state wide operation could move to the top at First Union. Cash management was treated as a sideline, as a cost center not a revenue producer. The state presidents had no interest in seeing anything change around cost allocations for their middle-market customer base. Credit was the driver of the relationship in the states' organizations. Credit was important at Corestates as well but the most valuable and rewarded source of revenue across the corporation was non-credit income. At virtually every Corestates credit discussion the question was asked "what non-credit income do we get from them?"

If I was comfortable addressing the cost side of their argument, I was even more so in addressing the revenue side. Mitchell focused entirely on penny price per item, noting that our number was very low compared to theirs. They were correct, but that was all they focused on. In fact, there are three sources of revenue in a lockbox product, penny price, float and earnings credit. Penny price is visible to everyone and is what everyone, including the customer, tends to focus on. Earnings credit income and float skim are far more subtle and less visible. CoreStates' pricing models always lowballed the penny price and maximized the other two. First Union's analysis totally ignored the other two sources of revenue, most probably because they did not understand them and never used them as a way to enhance income.

Float skim is the time difference between when a bank gives credit to a customer for deposits and when it actually is able to collect the funds from the bank on which checks are drawn. For example, if we give credit to the customer at an average of 1.7 days but actually are able to collect those checks from the paying bank in 1.2 days that gives us a half day benefit, invisible to the customer. For smaller customers that number is meaningless but for large customers, such as those Corestates had, the dollar value of float skim was significant, especially since we focused major efforts in maximizing collection times with many direct send (direct couriers to paying banks) programs.

Earnings credit income derives from the difference in the earnings credit for demand balances given to the customer, and the benefit accruing to the bank from placing funds in the market. Again, high volume customers tend to keep larger balances, and even a 30 basis point difference between the two rates can bring substantial revenue.

First Union ignored both of these income sources. I had obtained a copy of a large deal profitability analysis they had done for Kemper insurance, one of Corestates' high volume remittance processing customers. Their analysis showed it was a loss account recommended for elimination with only a gross margin of 28%, insufficient to cover those very high and unrealistic allocated costs described previously. I countered their work with a 1995 CoreStates analysis of that same account, but this time including both float skim and earnings credit differential. Ours showed a return on expense of 98%, and a highly profitable account.

The final point I made in the last paragraph was, in my opinion, the most important and one both John Georgius and Ed Crutchfield should have taken to heart. I said that in banking, high reward generally requires taking higher risk. But it doesn't always need to be that way. I ended with the following: " The higher the level of annuity streams of processing profits puts less pressure on line units to take greater credit risk to meet profit goals".

I had addressed my reply to Ben Maffitt, who I knew was both an ally of mine and close to Ed Crutchfield. First Union's top two cash management people, Nina Archer and Michael Daley were also supporters so they were also copied. Ken Thompson was on the memo, but he had made it clear to me he would stay neutral; it would be a John Georgius decision with input from Beth McCague from Finance.

I wrote my memo on a Wednesday, which should have been delivered sometime Friday. I heard nothing the following week. On March 22 I flew to Charlotte and met with Ben Maffitt and asked him what had happened. Ben was depressed, and even upset. He said he tried as best he could, even to the point of writing directly to Ed Crutchfield pleading my case. He did not show me his entire memo but he did show me one page where he gave his opinion of me. That one page is probably the most complimentary thing that anyone has ever said about me in my life. I treasure it, but do not think I ever thanked Ben as much as I should have because, after leaving Ben's office, I asked to meet with Crutchfield where I resigned, effective June 30.

Had I won the argument there was a little doubt I would have stayed. If I did win, it would have meant that First Union senior management were prepared to let me lead the strategy of bringing noncredit products to the forefront of relationship building with their customers. A lot more of our people, especially those led by Ana Southern, would have stayed as well. However, that was not to be. I simply had no credibility with Crutchfield and Georgius.

Although I stayed the 12 months Terry Larsen had required of me, I suspect he was disappointed that so little was accomplished. I certainly was. The only parts of Corestates that survived were International, now better than it would have been under us, and Congress Financial, our national asset based commercial finance subsidiary. Everything else was just absorbed into whatever structures suited First Union. I was able to give support to some of our senior women when asked whether they had been promoted because they were women, and I assured the questioner that was not the case. But that was about all.

Before I actually left, First Union began to implement their new strategy with our large cash management clients. A few of them were able to leave quickly but the largest ones had to do so gradually did so gradually because it was extremely difficult for them to separate their operations from Corestates. That, of course, was our original strategy with the biggest customers. I was told it took Vanguard almost a year and a half before they were able to finally extricate themselves from First Union, although I don't know that for certain.

Over the next nine months First Union consistently disappointed analysts with earnings. Most blamed the Money Store debacle (which should never have happened had anyone at First Union talked to anyone from Corestates before committing) and the failure to properly integrate CoreStates. One report I saw said that they had lost 15% of Corestates retail accounts and 25% of wholesale banking's revenue stream. I could not find many specifics in press reports and since I was not there I don't know for sure where all the problems arose.

Certainly the botched integration of our systems resulted in thousands of account reconciliation problems and substantial write offs. Other than that, First Union was very experienced with integrating banks, especially retail operations. I doubt if our middle market segment missed a beat with Charlie Connolly running that business. Since international earnings would have been up that leaves the majority of the problems being the demise of Corestates' cash management customer base. And, as my old team members expected, kicking out high volume customers didn't result in any expenses actually leaving.

Only 30 days after I physically left the bank, on July 30, 1999, John Georgius took early retirement. He was only 54 years old and had been Crutchfield's right hand man. Was he forced out? If so, why? Unfortunately it was already too late to stop the outflow of Corestates' largest customers that started with the bungled systems consolidation and continued as part of his plan described above. One option is that he fell on his sword as a good Lieutenant does. The chickens had come home to roost, and First Union was paying the price of two failed acquisitions, the Money Store and Corestates Financial Corporation. Neither disaster needed to happen.

On March 13, 2000 Ed Crutchfield resigned as CEO of First Union and the board named Ken Thompson to replace him. It was also announced that Crutchfield would seek treatment for lymphoma which he described as "a highly curable form of cancer". The question arises, was that voluntary or was he forced out? I believe it was the latter. Disappointing bank analysts by substantial margins three times in one year has its consequences. In my opinion, it need not have happened but there is a cost to uncontrollable hubris.

My resignation was announced on March 24, 1999 effective June 30. I met with a lot of people over my remaining time from all parts of the bank. Most were sympathetic but some were angry. International was in great shape under Michael Heavener's leadership. Charlie Connolly kept most of his group intact and while First Union shrunk his territory a little bit by creating separate units in New Jersey for middle-market lending, he and his people seemed to be doing well in the new environment.

My former dominion, with the exception of international, were having the worst of it under First Union, despite year to year earnings growth in 1998 of over 15% As described , the specialized lending people in First Union were all fairly recent hires from major New York banks, none of whom had any respect for Corestates people. Even though Corestates was far more experienced in telecommunications lending than was anyone in First Union, our people were shut out. First Union did not have a Transportation and Equipment specialty and paid no attention to ours. Again, with the exception of international and some use of our superior cash management sales professionals, the best parts of Corestates' wholesale business found no home in the combined company. When I had announced my intention to resign effective June 30, I knew that something had to be done about my old team quickly. Doing so would also help honor my commitment to Terry Larsen to protect as many of our people as possible.

Chapter 16

NATIONAL CITY AND REGULATORY OVERREACH

IN EARLY APRIL I started conversations with the four people most capable of leading a team of Corestates employees leaving First Union to start new careers elsewhere. They were: Paul Geraghty, EVP and the architect of our large corporate cash management business, Dan Aboyan, EVP the builder of our investment banking, Jim Brooks, SVP, the best credit man in the bank and an expert in telecommunications, and Ed O'Donnell, SVP head of transportation and equipment.

I was candid with this group, characterizing their responses as "willing to listen". None were happy and it showed. Knowing any bank prepared to hire an independent team would want that team at headquarters, I asked whether they would consider moving from Philadelphia. The answer to that was more direct. Absolutely no way! So I set out to find a bank willing to hire a 40+ person team based in a different city without tight headquarter monitoring. Any independent Philadelphia operation would require significant lending authority. That would be the sticking point for any potential partner.

A partner would have to be big enough to have sufficient lending capacity to build meaningful portfolios, but it couldn't be so big that our contribution would not be meaningful. It would have to have broad commercial lending experience but not have national specialized lending portfolios, or be known as a lead commercial bank. Our skill sets had to provide immediate value. It would have to have a conservative credit culture and historically low non-performing asset ratios. It would have to have a relationship banking approach like Corestates, not a product driven First Union. Ideally it should have some small activities in the Philadelphia region but if not, it had to be geographically close enough that operating in Philadelphia made strategic sense. Finally, it's CEO had to be someone who knew and respected me, and who I also respected.

The obvious first choice was Mellon. They had already made it clear they wanted to move more heavily into the Philadelphia market when they tried to acquire Corestates. They had existing branch operations in Philadelphia and strong middle market presence west and north. Frank Cahouet had just retired, and thought I could work with Marty McGuinn. A sticking point was how Mellon felt about me after having fought them so hard in the previous year or two. In the end, I decided not to approach them for two reasons.

First, I wasn't sure how our strong middle market group would fare in the First Union consolidation that seemingly was under the control of ex-Fidelity Bank people. If that didn't go well, then our new venture could also be a place for our middle-market people, not of interest to Mellon. In hindsight, I should have known that Charlie Connolly would win out.

Second, shortly after CoreStates was acquired, a Wall Street Journal article suggested, as a result of the failure to acquire Corestates, Mellon was now vulnerable and would be acquired in the next year or two.

That would not bode well for any independent lending group operating in Philadelphia. I spoke with a couple of Bank analysts I knew well and they shared that opinion. I did not anticipate that Marty McGuinn would hold off being acquired until 2006 by some brilliant strategic moves selling four non-core businesses and using the proceeds to buy back their own stock. In hindsight once again, the combination of Bank of New York/Mellon would probably have been better for my old team than what I finally did.

The second option was National City Bank of Cleveland. I had met President and CEO David Daberko many times at the semi-annual bankers roundtable meetings. He would often ask me questions about Corestates' wholesale banking and international businesses, which he knew I ran. His bank fit most of my criteria. They were known as a very conservative lender, with non-performing loan ratios equal or less than .4%, about half of Corestates. Return on assets was comparable to ours and return on equity in the middle of the super regional banks at over 18%. It was a big bank, the 10th largest in the United States but built from several medium size acquisitions so that there was very little concentration in their loan portfolio. There would be plenty of room for us to grow with our old specialized customers. They had no specialized industry expertise. They seemed like the perfect fit.

My last day at First Union was June 30, 1999. On the 29th, I called Dave Daberko's office and made an appointment for noon on July 1. He was well prepared. He had an EVP of wholesale banking, Bill MacDonald, and his chief credit officer, Bob Undersick, in attendance. I talked about the impact of the acquisition by First Union on a highly successful and profitable commercial lending group of Corestates. He knew a lot of the story already. I told Dave that I wanted to bring a team of wholesale bankers to National City but based in Philadelphia. I promised him that they would be my top people. I then described the backgrounds of the other four senior executives I expected to join me and suggested that we would eventually recruit at least 40 officers to join us.

The most important thing, I said, was that we needed to have a minimum level of $10 million lending authority out of our office without getting approval from Cleveland. As I recall, the answer from Dave was "…that shouldn't be much of a problem". I should have known better because it later became a problem. After lunch, Dave left and the rest of the afternoon was about my compensation package and those of the other four individuals, still unnamed. My package was based upon successful recruitment of people and growth in assets. My contract would only be for three years, with a mutual option to extend for an additional year. Their reasoning was sound. So long as I was there, the Philadelphia team would never be completely theirs. For that to happen, I needed to leave. That was fine with me. My primary objective was to find a good place for some really good people.

The details were worked out over the next two months, such as finding and contracting space (for me, the only possible location was the old PNB tower right next to City Hall because of the message it would send to the Philadelphia business community), finalizing the top executive contracts, preparation of one year and three year plans. National City waited until all the contracts were signed before they delivered a shock. Our number one priority, on which we believed we had a commitment from them, was withdrawn. There would be no local lending authority and everything would have to go to loan committee in Cleveland. This message was delivered jointly by the head of wholesale banking and the chief credit officer. Dave Daberko was nowhere to be found.

For almost 3 weeks we were at an impasse and I threatened to withdraw the proposal. But there was little we could do. We had no choice and they knew it. So we pushed for a compromise and eventually the chief credit officer agreed to have his number two, Bruce Muddell, spend three days a week in Philadelphia. In the end, Bruce learned to trust the credit skills of our people, who were certainly stronger than he was. He was able to approve up to $5 million alone and anything over that went to loan committee.

This one decision on their part slowed our growth significantly, perhaps by as much as 100% over the next three years. On the other hand, it also reinforced to us how generally conservative they were as lenders which was one of our criteria for selecting them in the first place. I did not pay any attention when, in mid August, Nat City agreed to acquire First Franklin Financial, a high risk mortgage lender and distributor based in San Diego, California. I should have.

Until our public announcement all of us were quietly talking to other people we felt might be willing to join. No one we talked to before our formal announcement broke our confidence, including the one person I wanted to join our top management group running the middle-market and asset-based lending business, Dave Swoyer. Dave had actually agreed to join Nat City but after the announcement changed his mind which was quite disappointing. He was, however, extremely close to Charlie Connolly who obviously convinced him to stay with him.

On September 3, 1999 the lead article on the Philadelphia Inquirer business page reported what we were doing, with the secondary headline pointing out that we would locate in "PNB's old headquarters". Lead finance writer Joseph DiStefano was already calling Corestates First Union a "…troubled takeover…"

I had not started a de novo operation since opening a representative office in Australia in 1972 and had forgotten how complex it could be. Furthermore, I had become increasingly dependent on others for administrative support. Fortunately we had super star Tina Zane join us early who was able to work miracles. The office was done on the cheap, used desk and filing cabinets the norm. Jim Brooks was able to quickly get two top communications/media lenders, Mike Grimes and Jon Peterson, to join us. O'Donnell brought over Mike Labrum, Cliff Cooley and Chris Chrystidis. Paul Geraghty recruited Chuck Stanback, Melissa Landay, Lyle Cunningham and Tara Handforth. We were on our way.

Within a few weeks we had already outgrown our 2000 square foot office space. Out of necessity, we pioneered an open floor plan, with our 17 people sharing desks, telephones, and filing cabinets. I wanted a small office for myself because I didn't want the team hearing my frequent arguments with people at Nat City headquarters but very quickly that office became our only conference room and I would often be on the phone outside in the halls. Fortunately Tina was able to get more space in the building before the end of the year.

With the influx of additional people once year-end bonuses were distributed at First Union, there was even more pressure on our infrastructure. One weakness continued. We were never able to attract a top middle-market banker to join us after Dave Swoyer reversed his original decision. I attribute that to the confidence most Corestates middle-market bankers had in Charlie Connolly. We also weren't successful in attracting good real estate lenders which surprised me. Nevertheless, by May 2000 our staff had reached 32 people and we had more than 350 million in loans on the books. We also finalized our permanent space on the entire 13th floor of the PNB building vacated by the law firm, Drinker Biddle.

Most of my time at Nat City was devoted to recruitment, some customer contact but mostly interfacing with executive leadership on the 35th floor of the National City headquarters building in Cleveland. Paul Geraghty had the least defined role in Nat City, but he was also the person who could be a the greatest value to Cleveland. My job was to make sure he got plenty of face time with National City senior management and eventually he was able to take over their insurance and retailer portfolios.

Ed O'Donnell's team hit the ground running and did not need any help from me. Jim Brooks was one of those rare individuals who could run a unit like communications and media while still being our chief credit officer. However, Cleveland would never accept that, so we needed to make sure that Jim remained a senior credit officer; his hires, Jon Peterson and Mike Grimes, would take his direction anyway. By the time I left in early 2004, our assets approached 2 billion and we had more than 55 employees but most importantly we provided a good home for very talented Corestates people, which continued operating until National City was also forced to sell to PNC. After that, Jim Brooks assumed, the role of making sure our people found good jobs in PNC or he helped them move elsewhere. Paul Geraghty had already left to become CEO of a troubled smaller bank in the Philadelphia region.

During the little over three years I worked for National City, I spent a fair amount of time on their 35th floor to help establish credibility for Corestates' people among executive leadership. I began to notice strains between Dave Daberko and Bob Undersick, the Chief Credit Officer. The tension did not revolve around the corporate lending Philadelphia was doing, so it had to be something else. I never really got to the bottom of it before I left, but it was a concern. Only after a few years did it become apparent that National City was experiencing a classic breakdown in credit culture caused by actions of their CEO.

In earlier parts of this book, I often refer to credit culture and its contribution to the success we had at Corestates. When I am asked by non-bankers what that means, I answered that it means you can ask the same question to people in all parts of the commercial bank and at all levels but still get the exact same answer. This presumes the majority of employees are homegrown and home trained. Mergers dilute the culture, and so the first year after an acquisition much work must be done to ensure culture is communicated to the new employees. Building a credit culture is hard work.

In my banking lifetime, significant progress has been made in how banks approve loans. When I first joined PNB, and for the next 10 years, loans were approved by a loan committee. I described committee flaws earlier, how in most committees heads tended to turn toward the person with the highest rank and start nodding whenever they say something. Lending was even more problematic in smaller banks where approvals were often made by bank directors who simply had no time to spend analyzing the credit.

Eventually the industry learned to divide responsibilities between marketing and credit approval. At Corestates, we followed the design originated by Henry Mueller and George Moore of Citibank, granting primary credit approval to professional credit officers supporting line management. Officer titles continue to have some credit authority, but now the chief credit officer granted authority based on perceived credit skills, not rank. In addition, relationship officers were required to have a credit officer sign with them. The final step we took at Corestates was take all lending authority away from the relationship officers, division heads and group heads, placing it entirely within the credit officer structure.

This did not mean relationship officers and managers were not involved in the credit process. Far from it. They were an integral part of making loans, preparing the write up on the company, analyzing the balance sheet, visiting the company and assessing operations and management. In short, relationship officers, supported by his or her manager, did the work. At any point along the process, the relationship officer or manager could decide not to proceed if they felt there was excessive risk.

A good credit culture requires a constant push and pull between judgments of both credit officers and line (relationship officers, managers). Both sides need to visit the business and talk with management. Both sides also use the same analytic tools, but each looks at a judgment from a slightly different perspective, one focusing more on what 'might be' and the other on what 'could happen'. Negotiation and compromise follows, until a structure results with which neither is fully happy but both can live with. The key ingredient is human judgment.

At CoreStates, we believed it imperative credit officers and line be in close proximity with each other. In this way, ideas and perspectives are shared and mutual respect is built between the two sides. We believed isolation would breed contempt. Mutual respect is vital to effective credit culture. Furthermore, having credit officers imbedded in line units improves efficiency. For example, before visiting a client or prospect, a relationship officer can share numbers with the credit officer, get a quick reaction or even some specific questions which should be asked. In addition, when the two are located together much more dialogue takes place on credit subjects, which keeps the line focused on what is vital to any bank, credit quality. When something of an urgent nature comes up and the relationship manager needs to visit the client quickly, it is easy to arrange for the credit officer to join.

Our credit officers reported on a solid line to the group heads so they were seen by the line as being a part of "them", and not some separate group. It also allowed them to be part of the planning process of each unit, including the financial plan. While some banks found this awkward, and feared credit officers would lose their independence, CoreStates did not. The credit officers reported to the chief credit officer on a dotted line, which in practice was sometimes stronger than a solid line. The chief credit officer protects the credit officers from excessive pressure from group heads. The point was that line and credit each knew their function, but also understood the other function. Officers who are both good relationship people and good credit individuals are few and far between. Nevertheless, wherever possible management would move the best of the best, back-and-forth between credit and line. That is how a bank maintains a strong credit culture.

Building and maintaining a strong credit culture, in my judgment, should be the the most important single function of management. Without it no Bank can succeed or make money for shareholders; ultimately, the bank will fail. Unfortunately, few banks have understood this over the last two generations and neither have regulators made examination and evaluation of bank credit cultures a high priority.

Unfortunately, even the strongest Credit culture can be killed in a very short time but, fortunately, only a bank CEO that can do that. The CEO must be the keeper and protector of the credit culture, never doing anything that suggests he wishes to do something that his credit people do not. Interfering once or twice, or pushing earnings too hard ahead of credit quality, will be sufficient to destroy culture. Just as the CEO is the keeper and protector of that culture, so it is the board's responsibility to make sure that he or she never deviates from that responsibility.

Bank of New England got into trouble when their CEO decided he could make loans in real estate on his own. PNC almost failed when, needing higher spread assets as profitability declined, the CEO directed the bank to take excessive risk in telecommunication loans. I always believed Wachovia had one of the top credit cultures in the country under John Medlin but, with a new CEO, in just a few years had generated so many bad loans the bank ultimately had to sell. Had

Terry Larsen stopped me from throwing out the Money Store after our acquisition of First Pennsylvania, I might have started down that slippery slope myself. I don't think anyone at First Union was able to tell Ed Crutchfield not to buy the Money Store. The list goes on and on.

Did the regulatory authorities have alternatives to completely separating the credit and line sides of a bank in order to protect banks from self-destruction? Yes, I think they did. But that alternative approach would have required significant intestinal fortitude by regulators, because it would have meant going up against bank boards of directors, with all the influence and political power those individuals had.

Every example that I have shared of a bank failure has been caused by a CEO, either making loan decisions themselves without the use of their top credit people, pushing for loan growth and spread income at the expense of credit quality or a clear rejection of advice from the people responsible for the quality of the loan portfolio. The CEO must never be permitted to interfere with the loan approval process within a bank or the independent assessment of the quality and trends within that loan portfolio. In other words, if the issue is the CEO, the CEO has to be controlled and the only way the CEO can be controlled is by the Board of Directors.

I believe the regulators had all the tools they needed to control CEOs through the Board of Directors, with one possible exception. Regulators conducted regular examinations of their banks. They examined individual loans and stress tested portfolios. They evaluated how well banks rated their own loans and corrected them them when necessary. They met with individuals, both credit people and line officers. They tested how well all groups within the bank understood the rules. In short, the regulators were good at their jobs, knew what they had to do and generally did it well.

At the end of the examination they would hold meetings at all levels of the bank, especially with the top credit people and business line managers. Finally they met with the CEO, if necessary, delivering a message to him or her of what needed to change. The final meeting was with the Board of Directors.

Regulators had the power to ask for the board meeting without the presence of the CEO, if they needed to communicate significant issues. Had there been a bank Credit committee similar to bank Audit committee, this aspect of the regulator's function would have been easier. Prior to meeting with the full board they would have had several conversations with the independent directors running the Credit committee to relay their concerns. In turn, those directors had a fiduciary responsibility to re-convey those opinions to the full board.

Even without an independent bank Credit sub-committee, regulators had all the tools they needed. There was one exception. Bank directors who failed to follow bank regulations and rules were subject to significant cash penalties. That was fine as far as it went. But what could regulators do if boards, despite being warned about actions of the CEO, still do nothing? Many directors are wealthy in their own right and could easily afford the low fines imposed by bank regulations. In such circumstances, many directors might instead side with an aggressive and charismatic CEO.

But what if consistently ignoring regulator guidance were a felony offense? That is something no Director would be willing to risk. Some believe, however, that a penalty like that might also make too risky for competent people to serve as bank directors. That is a risk but I think the language could have been written so that failure to take action would be egregious enough to justify such a penalty.

There was one challenge which regulators faced for which I have no solution. Bank directors are among the most powerful people in American industry. Their reputations often extend far beyond their bank's. How easy is it for an upper middle bureaucrat (bank examiner) to admonish said director for his or her possibly unjustified confidence in a powerful banker? I was never in a room where this confrontation had to occur, but of course at CoreStates it was never necessary. It wasn't just reputations regulators had to fear but also a director's political power, at least within the largest banks. Most examiners were well protected by Civil Service rules but their bosses' bosses were likely political appointees.

I know of one relatively small mid-Atlantic bank that was taken over by the FDIC as a result of bad loans, and some improper dealings between the bank and some directors. The FDIC sued the Directors for malfeasance. Correction: They sued **some** directors and left others alone. One of the sued directors was a friend of mine who never served on either board loan committees or the bank audit committee but was simply on a marketing committee. He never had any business transactions with the bank and had actually left the board before the bank was seriously in trouble. Nevertheless he was sued. Several directors without any connections eventually declared bankruptcy. The treasurer of a major corporation was not sued. The wife of a United States senator was not sued. Selective enforcement and bowing to political pressure happens all too often.

My criticism of the regulatory system built up over the last 25 years is based on my own personal experiences with various credit crises: REITs, LDCs, Real Estate, HLTs, ect.. it was also based on working and operating in a successful system using both an independent credit staff and an experienced line group. Both teams analyzed the numbers, the industry, the management, the competition, and prospects. While one team might tend to speak more for the customer at times that rarely resulted in weak loan structures. It did result in transactions good for the borrower (read: economy, jobs, ect.) while still keeping the bank protected.

Clearly as banks grew bigger and assumed more risk, regulators had to change their approach. Requiring higher levels of capital and assigning higher levels of capital for higher risk was good. It was their reducing lending approvals to small back office number crunchers which I object to. Banks are supposed to provide capital to the small, the innovative, the men and women with that new idea. Today the American banker is not listening to those stories; Shark Tank is and taking a heftier share of the equity than they might have had banks still been in the business. My fear is that banks have lost the skill of how to extend credit. Regulators have also, now depending on ratios, numbers and formulas instead of credit analysis requiring human judgement.

Let's look at two industries that grew up over the last 50 years, predominantly financed by banks but would not be today: Cable Television and Wireless Technology. Say I am a small home builder and I hear about this new technology that allows me to carry television signals across a cable. That interests me because my television reception in my medium-size town 80+ miles from a much bigger city is very poor. So I go into my bank and say I have about $300,000 which I'm willing to invest. My business plan calls for construction of cable lines from the city to a hub I will build and then I will build out 400 miles of cable along the streets in my town and it's suburbs. I am sure that most of my neighbors will jump at the opportunity to improve their reception. I'm sure that my town will give me an exclusive for 25 years or so and my customers will sign up for 25 years also. All I need is $40 million to get started.

In today's banking world, what do you suppose the reaction of a credit person would be to that? Right! Not a chance!! But it was conversations like that all over the country which built an entire industry and improved the lives of millions of Americans. I'm sure that there were many negotiations requiring further equity and subordinated debt but you get the point. Many of these early pioneers were trusted individuals in small towns with close personal relationships on the line side of a local bank who was also able to gain the trust of the credit side as well. In the 70s, Philadelphia National Bank and later CoreStates was a early lender to that industry, and not only because Ralph Roberts and Comcast was a trusted existing customer.

Now the entire country is interlaced with cable lines. Customers are happy. In the 80s and early 90s, the industry is consolidating at enormous prices which banks are financing with ever increasing leverage. Now another guy comes along and says, " Why use cables? All we need to do is transmit those signals over the air. But this time it can't be done in small towns but rather an entire region. This time all we need to do is build towers that can see each other without interference. And if we can steal customers from the cable industry we can do the same thing from the telephone company. Portable telephones are very popular but big and cumbersome so we will produce a smaller and much more efficient phone at a great price as long as 10 to 20,000,000 people will want to carry one in their purse. And I'm sure they will. Don't you remember the Dick Tracy watch?

Yes, of course I am being simplistic, but the point remains; this would not be something a bank would do today, but they did 25 years ago. I'm not saying the wireless industry would not eventually develop using private investors with the help of investment bankers. Of course it would, but nowhere near as quickly. Many other smaller innovative ideas from imaginative people without access to hedge funds and investment bankers are probably unable to get their idea turned into a thriving business today. That is a loss to innovation, communities and ultimately economic growth. As I said before, many of them will just try to get on Shark Tank for a hearing. Their local banker could not listen.

Taking risk is not a bad thing. Taking risk is what built America. It is what banks have done throughout history. I fear what we have done has taken away banks' ability to evaluate risk and regulators ability to evaluate bank credit processes and cultures, to the detriment of those innovative imaginations who create new industries. Yes, we can look at the Amazons and Teslas and be proud. But neither of these were funded by traditional banks and so I wonder how many things are not getting done that should be done, because so many creative minds have no access to investment banks or venture funds.

I remember one bank examination at CoreStates while I was chief credit officer. The final report said that Corestates' loan portfolio had a risk level "well above average". When I first read that, I got angry: How could they say that? Upon reflection, I realize it was actually a compliment. CoreStates' loan portfolio was higher risk than most banks but our loan losses and nonperforming assets were lower than most of banks. That means our credit process could take higher risk and manage it well. I attribute that to a strong credit culture, in which line and credit complement each other and reach decisions best for corporate clients. That is what banks should be doing; today, I believe, they are not.

Where are we today? For regulators, evaluating a bank loan portfolio is purely a numerical exercise, using formula and ratio analysis. I doubt there is much need for credit skill and judgment for examiners today. Bank examiners used to be pretty good evaluators of credit, albeit naturally very conservative. Today most of the higher risk transactions created by the largest banks are distributed elsewhere, mostly to non-bank investors or hedge funds. The largest banks have significantly higher levels of capital than historically. Most observers, and even some bankers, believe that this is all to the good. Certainly Congress and Senator Warren are pleased. But I think about all the deals that won't be done by banks that should be done.

I have always felt badly about bringing my old team to a bank that failed, or at least was forced to sell. Did that have to happen? It really didn't. It was, however, a fairly common story of a bank making inadequate returns, not meeting expectations of bank analysts, and the bank CEO thinking his only way to get them was to put high-yield consumer mortgage loans into his investment portfolio, ones that subsequently became toxic. When CEO David Daberko originally made the acquisition of First Franklin, he was asked by a bank analyst if it meant a change of corporate strategy. Historically, Nat City was a commercial lender, not a retail credit bank. He answered that it wasn't and I am sure he meant it at the time.

The impression those of us from Corestates had of Nat City was that there was no central wholesale corporate strategy. Essentially, Nat City continued to run each acquisition as a separate geographic unit, after consolidating operational and support staff at headquarters. Accordingly, while acquisitions could bring initial positive growth, very quickly thereafter growth rates would revert to what was normal in each geographic location. That growth rate was certainly not sufficient to compete with other super regional banks which put significant pressure on Daberko to increase yield using the subprime portfolios.

None of that was visible to me when I left Nat City in 2003. What was visible was the increasing tension between Bob Undersick, CCO and Daberko. Undersick was still making it very difficult for Philadelphia to grow and Daberko was staying out of the fray, so there had to be some other reason for the tension. It is certainly no stretch to suggest growth of the high risk mortgage portfolio was the reason. Eventually, Bob Undersick retired, and the last restraining influence on the CEO was gone.

Over the next couple of years, the composition of Nat City's loan portfolio began to shift away from the heavy concentration in commercial loans across all of the geographic markets in which they operated.

Increasingly, instead of selling the subprime mortgage loans originated from First Franklin as had been done previously, they began to hold more of the loans on their own balance sheet, thereby increasing yields substantially. Within three years this was their primary source of income growth. Nat City and Dave Daberko needed to satisfy bank analyst demands. I do know he had some very close relationships with some analysts, perhaps too close.

How could National City have been saved, and by whom. The credit structure imposed by regulators separating credit people from line officers would not have helped; the decision to retain greater amounts of assets generated by the second mortgage subsidiary would not have been made by credit officers. At best, the decision would have been made by the CCO alone, at the CEO's request. At worst, the assets might have been categorized as investments, approved by the CFO and CEO. The fundamental issue is always board control over both risk assumed and CEO behavior.

In Nat City's case there were plenty of warnings. Had there been an effective bank board control system in place the accretion of toxic mortgage assets would have ended much earlier. Bob Undersick had already expressed his concerns and retired. Later, I was told by a Nat City EVP, that the numbers two and three executives at the bank, rivals for the CEO slot, jointly penned a memo to Daberko warning of the bank's growing over-exposure to the mortgage industry. For rivals to jointly write such a memo, their concern had to be very high. The CEO was free to disagree, but the key point here is that, as far as I know, the board never knew of the concerns.

The board should have known. If, instead of separating line and credit at the operating level, bank regulators had instead made it totally clear to the board that their primary function was to control the level of risk being assumed by the bank just as regulators made sure bank

Audit committees had independent lines of communication to protect against financial manipulation, so should regulators set up board Credit committees with similar powers. In addition to monitoring credit culture and adherence to credit policies the board Credit committee would also be responsible for ensuring that the CEO was not unduly influencing credit decisions. Had such a system been in place following the 1989 - 1992 real estate debacle, I do not believe 2008 would have happened.

Facing mounting losses from their subprime mortgage portfolios, and despite otherwise having quite healthy loan portfolios, the bank put itself up for sale in March 2008 in the midst of failures or impending failures across the industry. There were no takers at first but finally after the failure of Washington Mutual and the forced sale of Wachovia (former First Union) to Wells Fargo, PNC Bank stepped forward in October to acquire National City. That was ironic.

PNC got into trouble well before anyone else, even when the industry as a whole was quite healthy. Consequently the regulators were able to impose their system while the bank was under a regulatory memorandum of understanding. So when they acquired Nat City, PNC's regulatory-imposed, credit structure immediately started to downgrade their loans. By this time, our old Corestates team had built a portfolio in Philadelphia of over $10 billion, the majority of which were from the two specialized industry groups. . Certainly these loans were in the higher risk category, but the people from Corestates now managing them were among the most experienced people lending to those industries in the country,, and some of the best lenders I ever knew.

But that made no difference to PNC. Across the board downgrades forced withdrawals from relationships built over years. There were also forced sales of loans that cost PNC dearly. Less well understood was the long-term effect of forced repayments by borrowers at the worst possible moment. Most of Nat City's borrowers survived. but what about their smaller customers now forced to repay when there was no alternative source of funds?

The question is, was it necessary? At the time, only one loan in the the Philadelphia portfolio of those two industries was having difficulty. All were current. Three years later, none of the loans had gone bad, and the big winners were the companies that had bought up the loans at substantial discounts.

Looking back on what happened between 2007 and 2009 in the financial world, and especially after reading The Big Short, I often wonder why it was not me, instead of the authors of that book, collecting dividends and interest from proceeds of my own 'big short'. If there was anyone who should have foreseen what was going to happen, it was me.

My entire career prepared me for this moment, and I simply ignored all the signs. The first part of my career was lending to banks, witnessing bank failures and runs on banks in country after country. I understood credit risk, and how concentrations were a ticking time bomb. I saw what what would happen when regulators began to focus on a problem situation very aggressively. I had been through it all, even making the right call on the first failure of a high risk mortgage lender, the Money Store, caused by toxic 'tails' similar to the assets carried in investment portfolios by so many banks all over the world in 2008. I should have seen it coming, but I didn't.

The final trip on my banker's journey was short, and not a successful one. By early 2009 the US financial system was in meltdown crisis mode. Having seen that before, I knew the bankers would be doing everything possible to shrink problematic assets, even some that weren't so bad but regulators might think were. Bulk asset sales was in the cards.

Conversations with my old team now under PNC rule just confirmed that. Why not set up a new bank to buy these assets are at huge discounts when most of them, especially in our old specialized lending businesses, would be fully paid eventually? I contacted Jim Brooks to see what he thought. He said we would easily be able to put a team together to pick out the best opportunities. We both realized that the only problem was that the capital base had to be large enough to support a substantial lending limit, under regulatory requirements, 10% of capital. To get that done we needed help.

A fellow member of the Society of the Cincinnati knew top people at the Carlyle group. I arranged an appointment with their head of banking and met them with a copy of my strategic plan. Even though I used discounts on these loans of well above what I actually thought we might have to pay, after five years was an annual rate of return of 36%, on a pretty high capital base. My plan called for selling the entity after five years at a modest premium, which would even add to the overall return. And virtually all of the support functions of the entity would be outsourced, as was now becoming increasingly common. It seemed like a pretty good proposal to me.

Carlyle's head of banking was the son of a well-known French politician. He was very smart, but he knew nothing about lending and our whole proposal was based on good people knowing good loans from bad. He was a classic New York investment banker to whom banking was originate, distribute the risk and then move on. Keeping risk and being paid for it was simply not in his vocabulary. He politely turned me down.

In retrospect, the structure should never have been a bank. Too many regulators and too many rules. There was a formula left over from the last real estate crisis. When banks are forced to sell at huge losses to reduce non-performing loans, the only people who do well are the special purpose companies, which buy distressed assets at a good price and then sell them back into the market when things improve. We could have done the same had I thought of it, and perhaps talked to some of those who did that with real estate, even LDC a debt. years before.

While this ended my banker's journey, withdrawal wasn't so easy. 2008 to 2010 impacted so many people who found themselves in trouble with their banks. Some reached out to me to see if I could help and it was too tempting not to try, charging one dollar a year. What made it fun was this time I was on the other side of the table, working for the borrower against the credit people at a bank.

For the past seven years I have enjoyed life in Palm Beach Florida and also just outside Annapolis Maryland. Banking has been the furthest thing from my mind. However, just prior to Covid, I attended a reunion of Corestates employees along the Philadelphia waterfront. It was a wonderful experience, sharing so many stories and experiences with people I respected so very much.

What did strike me, however, was how little the Corestates people knew about both the final days of the bank, and also the disaster that was First Union. They also expressed some opinions I knew were simply not true. Years before I had started writing about my life for my grandchildren to read at some point when I am gone. But for six or seven years I was too busy enjoying life, and had let it lapse. The Corestates reunion got me going again, but this time I wanted to create a document which would also be for CoreStates people and old bankers everywhere, not just my family. And so *A Banker's Journey* was born.

CPSIA information can be obtained
at www.ICGtesting.com
Printed in the USA
LVHW041528200123
737530LV00035B/864